SUBCONSCIOUS PHENOMENA • PIERRE JANE
JASTROW AND BERNARD HART AND MORTON PRINCE

Publisher's Note

The book descriptions we ask booksellers to display prominently warn that this is an historic book with numerous typos, missing text or index and is not illustrated.

We scanned this book using character recognition software that includes an automated spell check. Our software is 99 percent accurate if the book is in good condition. However, we do understand that even less than one percent can be a very annoying number of typos! And sometimes all or part of a page is missing from our copy of a book. Or the paper may be so discolored from age that you can no longer read the type. Please accept our sincere apologies.

After we re-typeset and design a book, the page numbers change so the old index and table of contents no longer work. Therefore, we usually remove them.

Our books sell so few copies that you would have to pay hundreds of dollars to cover the cost of proof reading and fixing the typos, missing text and index. Therefore, whenever possible, we let our customers download a free copy of the original typo-free scanned book. Simply enter the barcode number from the back cover of the paperback in the Free Book form at www.general-books. net. You may also qualify for a free trial membership in our book club to download up to four books for free. Simply enter the barcode number from the back cover onto the membership form on the same page. The book club entitles you to select from more than a million books at no additional charge. Simply enter the title or subject onto the search form to find the books.

If you have any questions, could you please be so kind as to consult our Frequently Asked Questions page at www. general-books.net/faqs.cfm? You are also welcome to contact us there.

General Books LLC™, Memphis, USA, 2012. ISBN: 9780217059688.

⚹⚹ ⚹⚹ ⚹⚹ ⚹⚹ ⚹⚹ ⚹⚹ ⚹⚹ ⚹⚹

transcends all facts which one can possibly observe in others or introspect in himself. It is more specifically described as the "subliminal," which is used as a synonym for subconscious. The subconscious ideas, instead of being mental states dissociated from the main personality, now become the main reservoir of consciousness and the personal consciousness becomes a subordinate stream flowing out of this great storage basis of "subliminal" ideas as they are called. We have within us a great tank of consciousness but we are conscious of only a small portion of its contents. In other words, of the sum total of conscious states within us only a small portion forms the personal consciousness. The personal self becomes even an inferior consciousness emerging out of a superior subliminal consciousness sometimes conceived as part of a transcendental world, and this subliminal consciousness is made the source of flights of genius on the one hand, while it controls the physical processes of the body on the other.

The sixth meaning (Professor Miinsterberg's third type) of the term is an interpretation on pure physiological principles of the phenomena customarily attributed to the activity of dissociated ideas. Some psychologists believe that phenomena like automatic writing and speech, the so-called subconscious solution of arithmetical problems, hysterical outbursts, etc., can be best explained as pure neural processes unaccompanied by any mentation whatsoever. These phenomena become therefore pure physiological organic processes of the body. The term subconscious thus becomes equivalent to the old theory of Carpenter's "unconscious cerebration.

CHAPTER ONE BY HUGO MUNSTERBERG
Professor of Psychology, Harvard

THE few pages which a symposium allows do not give opportunity to sift the material which has led to the doctrine of the subliminal consciousness. My practical studies in hypnotism, hysteria, automatic writing and similar abnormalities suggest to me decided hesitation in accepting the whole of the usual evidence without cross-examination. And yet, to find a common basis for a theoretical inquiry, it certainly seems wiser not to quarrel about the experiences but rather to accept the facts as the most sanguine observer might present them.

Yet, even if we welcome the observed facts in their widest limits, there can be no doubt that the subconscious itself is never among them. The facts which we find must be either conscious psychical facts from which we draw inferences as to subconscious psychical states, or physical expressions which cannot be explained by conscious ideas, emotions, volitions, and which thus demand not-conscious factors for their explanation. The conscious experience of crystal-vision or of remembering the tactual experiences of an anaesthetic hand or the sudden solution of a problem which had slipped from consciousness, or, if you will, every act of genius may point to such hypothetical subconscious processes, but certainly the conscious seeing and remembering and solving is given, while the subconscious is constructed for purposes of explanation. In the same way the physical processes of automatic writing or of hysteric action are observable; the subconscious agencies are super-added elaborations.

To acknowledge that the subconscious is found only through constructions in the service of explanation does not detract from its scientific reality; the fluid core of the earth is of the same logical type. But such acknowledgment does imply that the only correct question is this: which of the many constructions of the not-conscious causes is most useful for the explanation of the observed facts? It is evident, however, that the preference for one construction or another may and must be influenced by various sidefactors. When, for instance, the physician approaches those facts, his interest tends naturally to their practical treatment. He thus shapes his constructions in a way which brings the differences from normal mental life to the clearest relief and which offers a simple working description, definite enough to determine beforehand the events to be expected in the behavior of the patient. When on the other hand the layman comes to the same facts, he is struck bytheir surprising character and this wonder awakes the feeling of the general mysteriousness of the world; he thus tends to prefer a construction which explains the observed facts in a way that leads at the same time to the satisfaction of higher desires, perhaps even of religious emotions. When, finally, the theoretical psychologist approaches the same facts, he has in mind no therapeutical treatment or emotional demand, and yet he too looks out far beyond the curious facts themselves; his interest is turned toward the remainder of mental life, and he thus prefers explanations which bring the abnormal facts in closest relation to the normal processes and cover both by the same formulae. normal facts is the same that underlies the ordinary processes of memory, attention, etc.: it is not psychical at all but a physiological brain process.

We therefore find three types of theories, the first backed mostly by laymen, the second by physicians, the third by psychologists. Yet the lines are not to be drawn sharply. That first group says: the subconsciousness is the psychical system of a full real personality below the conscious person; that subconscious self remembers, thinks, feels, wills on its own accord, influences our conscious life, helps it out, shines through it and causes the abnormal facts. The popular mind clings to such a convenient method of explanation the more closely as it is on this basis easy to bring the subconscious selves into telepathic connection or to link them with mystical agencies. The second group says: the subconscious is psychical but

not a system, it is made up of ideas, but they do not at first form a personality; it is dissociated split off mental material which only in a secondary way may flow together into a new detached self. The subconscious is then not at all a regular psychical foundation but something either pathological or at least artificial. The third group, finally, says: the subconscious that underlies the ab

The emotional demands of the mystic, the practical demands of the physician, and the theoretical demands of the psychologist are well fulfilled by these three types of theories, and to a certain extent they can be helpful side by side; the purpose which we have before us determines each time which of the three modes of construction is most useful for our special end. At least the second theory finds points of contact with each of the others. With the first it shares the belief that the subconscious is psychical, while the one conceives it as systematized, the other as dissociated. With the third it shares the conviction that there is no independent self below the consciousness, while the one calls the underlying processes psychical, the other physiological. This latter difference does not deter the friends of the second theory from admitting also a physiological basis for the subconscious ideas, nor the adherents of the third theory from using psychological terms like idea, emotion, volition, for the short description of those complex physiological events as if they were accompanied by psychical phenomena. Yet, the difference of principle remains, and if I have to choose, I feel inclined to take the place with the psychologists in the third group; the subconscious is not psychical at all.

I point here only to the most general reasons which determine my decision. The explanations which every theory of the subconscious offers are twofold. There is firstly a reservoir which keeps the subconscious ideas, and secondly a mental workshop which manufactures the products of thought as far as they are not elaborated consciously. The reservoir, full of dissociated ideas, has to explain the occurrence of strange con-

scious ideas and of otherwise surprising behavior. The workshop has to explain the conscious results of the evidently synthetic labor which goes on independently of our conscious control. What is that reservoir? Of course, if we call it a reservoir of ideas we have yielded the whole point; ideas are of mental stuff. Students of abnormal psychology here indulge in the same type of circular conclusion which is frequent with animal psychologists. The latter reason that animals of a certain development must have consciousness because they have memory. Memory is of course a psychological expression, and the question is just whether the behavior of those animals has to be explained psychologically by memory or physiologically by an aftereffect of earlier stimulations. The decision whether the onemode of explanation or other is to be applied cannot itself be deduced from the observed facts, but must precede the study of the facts; with other words: the question whether animals have consciousness or not cannot be answered by observation but belongs to epistemological arguments. In the same way here; no fact of abnormal experience can by itself prove that a psychological and not a physiological explanation is needed; it is a philosophical problem which must be settled by principle before the explanation of the special facts begins.

To make the explanation dependent on the special abnormal facts is the more unjustified as the situation is in no way different from that of ordinary memory. If I reproduce by association a name or a landscape seen ten years ago I can postulate too that all this was lying in me as a subconscious idea or at least as a mental disposition and that it could not be reproduced if something on the psychical side were not lasting through those ten years outside of my consciousness. But those who insist that the memory idea presupposes a lasting mental disposition and cannot be explained by physiological after-effect, only forget that the same logic would demand a special mental disposition also for each new perception. The whole "mystery" of an idea entering into consciousness presents itself perfectly every time when we use our eyes or ears, and it is astonishing how easily psychologists overlook the parallelism of the problems in regular perception, in ordinary memory and in the abnormal awakening of dissociated ideas. To say that the perceptive idea too finds a special psychical disposition would be absurd, as we should then need such subconscious mental agency for every possible impression, and if every possible impression is equally prepared in the subconscious the appearance of no one would really find its explanation as every other would have the same chance. In the case of the perception we are thus obliged to rest in the explanation of a psychical idea by a physical brain process only. But if the fresh idea is dependent only on the fresh excitement in the brain, there is not the slightest additional difficulty in interpreting by the same principle the recurrent idea of memory by the recurrent brain process without any reference to a lasting psychical trace. And if the normal memory can work without subconscious mental help, there is no reason suddenly to presuppose it for the abnormal awaking of apparently unaccountable ideas as in crystal vision and a hundred similar phenomena. The illusions of the ordinary memory easily lead over from the normal reproduction to the pathological. Brain processes without subconscious psychical forerunners furnish all that we need in the abnormal cases for the same kind of understanding which science has for seeing and hearing.

But if we have no reservoir with stored-up subconscious ideas, we cannot have a workshop either to prepare therein subconsciously combinations of subliminal material. It is again the physiological action which is entirely sufficient to explain just as much as the mental mechanism could explain. Of course popular science turns naturally to psychical conceptions first, because those hidden processes which we must presuppose to explain the conscious results are thoroughly purposive and selective. But have we really a right to insist that purpose and selection refer necessarily

to psychical factors and are incomparable with physiological processes? On the contrary, whenever purpose means as it does mean in this case a certain adaptation to the ends of the individual we must acknowledge that every organism shows such purposiveness. When the body digests a meal a hundred thousand cells are performing the most complex acts for the purposes of the organism, and they select the right chemical processes more safely than any chemist would be able to do; yet nobody presupposes that there is a mental interplay in the intestines. In the same way all the other tissues are performing adjusted acts by physiological causes: have we any reason to expect less from the tissues of the central nervous system? Why cannot they too produce physiological processes that lead to well-adjusted results and that means to apparently purposive sensorial excitements and motor impulses. But we must go much further still. Not only that the physiological cerebration is well able to produce the "intellectual" result, but the physiological side alone is fit for it, the psychological is utterly unfit. To the popular mind that statement seems of course absurd, and indeed it needs some philosophical insight into the logic of sciences to appreciate the situation. To bring it to short formulation, of course without full argument, we might characterize it as follows. Our inner life is a system of attitudes, of purposes, of will. But it is not for psychology to deal with the inner life in its immediate ideological reality. This real life and its real inner connectedness demand for their understanding our interpretation and appreciation it is furnished for instance by the student of history or of philosophy. Psychology, on the other hand, is a science which aims at description and explanation of inner life, a logical attitude which is artificial. Psychology considers the inner experience therefore, for its special purpose as a series of describable phenomena; it transforms the felt realities of will into perceivable objects, into contents of consciousness. Through this transformation the real purposiveness, yes, the whole inner connection of

the will acts is eliminated; the psychological phenomena as such have no intentions and no significance any more but are merely bits of lifeless mental material, complexes of unphysical objects made up of elements which we call sensations. And this material which, through the objectification, has lost all its inner teleological ties, has not even the chance to enter into any direct causal connections. The physical phenomena can and must be conceived as causally connected, the psychical not. There cannot be causality where the objects do not last but are destroyed in the very act of their appearance; just this is characteristic of all psychological contents. The world is physical, in so far as we conceive it as identical with itself in ever new experiences, and to elaborate this self-identity of the material universe is the meaning of the causal treatment. The object is psychical just in so far as it is not identical in new experiences, but is created anew in every act. Therefore there is no direct causal connection of the psychologized inner life; therefore there is only an indirect causal explanation of psychical phenomena possible in so far as they can be conceived as accompaniments of physiological processes. In short, even the full conscious mental facts do not really hang together when viewed from a psychological point of view and are thus unfit to explain any results through their causal interplay; they are epiphenomena, and the causal working of the objectified conscious facts goes on in the physiological substratum. How misleading, therefore, to invent and to construct subconscious psychical phenomena for the express purpose of producing causal results instead of leaving that to the safe action of the cerebrum. The only motive for doing it is the popular confusion, —certainly not unfrequent even among psychologists,—which does not discriminate between the psychological material as part of the world of phenomena and the teleological significance of our inner life in the world of meaning. The will as purpose binds by its meaning the facts of immediate life together and enters as such into ethics or law or history, but the will as psychological content of consciousness does not bind anything and does not point to anything beyond itself; it is simply a passing phenomenon. And yet only in this unreal form, constructed by abstractions and conceptions, the will can enter into the system of descriptive and explanatory science. In the explanatory system of psychology the purpose as such does thus not explain anything, just as astronomy has learned that the sixteenth century mixed the categories when the beauty of certain astronomical curves was taken as the actual cause for certain astronomical movements.

There is thus no reason to conceive a psychical fact existing outside of consciousness, —and that corresponds to the only significant meaning of consciousness. Consciousness is nothing which can be added to the existing mental facts, but it indicates just the existence of the psychical phenomena. Consciousness cannot do anything, cannot look here and there and shine on some ideas and leave others without illumination. No, consciousness means merely the logical relation point of its contents; the psychical phenomena are in consciousness as the physical phenomena are in nature; there cannot be physical phenomena outside of nature. Seen in this way the psychologist must sharply separate those pathological cases which really show positive abnormal phenomena in the conscious facts themselves and those which from the standpoint of consciousness present negative occurrences only,—blanks where ideas are expected. To the first class belongs, for instance, the alternating personality; that is an abnormal grouping of psychical experiences. To the second class belong all those various phenomena which give rise to the theory of dissociated or automatic subconscious psychical processes. The dissociated idea is psychologically not existent just as the ticking of the clock in my room does not exist for me when my attention is turned to my reading; the ticking reaches my brain and may there have after-effects, but the sound-sensation is inhibited. In this way all that which suggested the

theory of the mental subconscious becomes simply increased or decreased inhibition. Why the mental accompaniments of certain physiological processes are sometimes inhibited must of course itself be explained physiologically; everything seems to point to the relation between sensory excitement and the openness or closedness of the motor channels of discharge.

It is true that such physiological explanation gives small foothold for that mystical expansion of the theory which seemed so easily reached from the subconscious mental life. But it is not the least merit of the scientific physiological explanation that it obstructs the path of such pseudophilosophy. Psychology even if it takes in psychological phenomena which lie under the cover of the subconscious, can never be the starting point for a metaphysical view of reality because, as we pointed out, the psychological material has been reached by an artificial transformation of the real life experience. The psychological phenomena are as unreal as the atoms which mathematical physics constructs for its logical purposes. If we seek real philosophy we must go back to the true immediate will experience out of which the psychological constructions are shaped but which is as such not possible object of description. An interpretation and appreciative understanding of this real life, even in the most idealistic philosophy, can then never conflict even with the most radical physiological explanation of abnormal psychology. The physiological psychologist thus ought carefully to avoid the language of the subliminal self theory as it flows over too easily into antiphilosophy. But he has no reason to avoid the language of the dissociated-idea, theory—provided that the psychological word is taken as a short label for the very complex neural physiological process. If I had to write the history of Miss Beauchamp I should conceive all subconscious processes in physiological conceptions, but I should describe them, for clearness and convenience sake, as the master of our symposium has so masterly done, in the terms of psychological language.

CHAPTER TWO BY THEODORE RIBOT
Professor of Psychology, College de France THE question of the subconscious is so broad, so complex and so obscure that I shall be content if, in the brief remarks which follow, I succeed in throwing even a little light upon it.

In this question we must distinguish two sides: the positive, composed of facts; and the hypothetical made up of theories.

With regard to the facts, I find it advantageous to establish two categories: *First:* The *static* subconscious, comprising habits, memory and, in general, all organized knowledge. It is a state of conservatism, of repose (albeit relative), since representations undergo incessant corrosions and metamorphoses within themselves.

Second: The *dynamic* subconscious which is a latent state of activity, of incubation and elaboration. Authors who have treated this subject, have furnished examples of it in profusion. From this source comes inventive work, inspiration in all sorts of discoveries, improvisation and even—to a feebler degree and in a more modest form—sudden repartee and *bons mots;* in short everything which sparkles forth from us spontaneously.

Naturally, discussion and conjecture have focussed by preference upon the subconscious processes we call "dynamic," since these are the most varied and the most fertile in results.

On the nature of this subconscious activity, however, one finds only discord and obscurity. "Doubtless, one may maintain that, in the case of the inventor, everything goes on in the subconscious as it does ordinarily in consciousness itself, barring a message which does not reach the *ego;* that the work which one may follow in consciousness, with its advances and its retrocessions, is identical with what goes on without our knowledge. Such an hypothesis is possible, but far from proved.

Again, concerning the essential nature of subconscious activity, two diametrically opposed theories have been put forward:

The first (Myers, Delboeuf and other more recent authors) bears the stamp of a peculiar biologic mysticism. According to these authors, in certain men subconscious activity is invested with almost supernatural power, not only of a trophic and physiologic, but also of a psychologic order, and constitutes in the individual an intermediate link between the human and the divine.

The second, which has attained its most complete expression in Boris Sidis' book on suggestion, draws this picture of our subconscious, which is far from flattering: it (the subconscious) is stupid, uncritical, extremely credulous, without morality, and its principal mental mechanism is that of the brute— association by contiguity.

In my opinion two such hypotheses are not at bottom irreconcilable, since the above advantages and defects make an integral part of human nature taken in its totality, and since they are unequally distributed among men. A much more important question, however, is that of the ultimate nature of subconscious activity. Although many authors have tried to evade it by enveloping it in obscurity and doubt, it comes back to this inexorable dilemma,—psychologic or physiologic?

The psychologic solution rests upon an equivocal use of the word *conscious*. The conscious bears an unvarying stamp: it is an internal event, which exists, not in itself, but for *me* and in so far as it is recognized by *me*. Now, this solution admits that, if from the clear realm of consciousness one descends to the "marginal" consciousness and finally continues to go lower and lower to the unconscious, which only manifests itself by motor reactions, the primitive state thus impoverished continues to remain to the end identical in its essence with the conscious. Underlying the psychologic theory, in all its forms, there is the tacit hypothesis that the conscious is assimilable to a quantity which may decrease indefinitely without ever reaching zero. It is a postulate which nothing justifies. The experience of psychophysicians with regard to the "threshold" of the conscious, without

settling the question, would rather justify the contrary opinion: the perceptible *minimum* appears and disappears brusquely. This fact and others which might easily be pointed out seem to me unfavorable to the hypothesis of the increasing or decreasing continuity of the conscious.

The physiologic solution is simple and comprises few variants. It maintains that subconscious activity is purely cerebral; the psychic factor which ordinarily accompanies the work of the nervous centres is absent. I incline toward this hypothesis, without disregarding its shortcomings and its difficulties; but, at least, it seems to me not contradictory as is the adverse hypothesis. It has been established by numerous experiences (Fere, Binet, Mosso, Janet, Newbold, etc.) that unconscious sensations (not apperceived) act, since they produce the same reaction as conscious sensation, and Mosso has been able to maintain "that the testimony of consciousness is less reliable than that of the sphygmograph," but there are cases more complex. For instance, that of invention is quite different, for it does not merely suppose the adaptation to an end which the physiologic factor would suffice to explain; it implies a series of adaptations, corrections, and rational operations whose nervous action of itself furnishes us but few examples. In spite of everything, I am coming more and more to the side of the physiologic hypothesis and am quite in accord with the opinion recently set forth in America by Jastrow, and more clearly by A. H. Pierce in his "Studies in Philosophy and Psychology" (1906), in which he has presented in favor of the cerebral interpretation such an excellent plea that further attempts in this line seem to me useless.

There still remains the question of double personality, or to be more exact, of multiple personality.

At the present time the majority of psychologists admit that the *ego,* the person, is a synthetical complex, which in its normal state, is made up of relatively stable elements, in spite of incessant variations. In the abnormal cases,

when a new personality arises, one can scarcely doubt that the subconscious lends its aid to its formation; on the one hand, in its static form, by the resurrection of habits or of memories which seemed lost; on the other hand, in the apparition of intellectual or moral dispositions— higher or lower, good or evil,—which, latent until then, characterize the new *ego*.

This psychologic problem is nevertheless quite different from that concerning the nature of the subconscious. This new synthesis, of which the subconscious furnishes only the materials (and these only in part), depends upon profound causes, probably physiologic, having their roots in cenesthesia. Whatever opinion one may emit upon this last cause, it is a distinct study which begins here; subconscious processes play a role which is secondary and subordinate and are, properly speaking, a result, an effect.

CHAPTER THREE BY JOSEPH JASTROW *Professor of Psychology, University of Wisconsin* TO one who has devoted a volume to an exposition of subconscious phenomena, the invitation to contribute to a symposium is naturally interpreted as a request for a statement of the underlying and supporting conceptions of the work in question. The difficulty in meeting this request is inherent in the phenomena themselves; for it is the nature of these to require delicate shadings and gradings and all the complex blendings of a difficult chiaroscuro, in order to shape the resulting delineation into a significant picture. Yet when addressed to those who are familiar with the picture and its *genre,* and equally with the elements and

The Subconscious. Part three is especially germane to the considerations here presented.

the technique of the composition, a sketch with reenforced contours and unconcern for transitions and corrections will meet with ready interpretation.

I deem it a fundamental requisite of any adequate conception of the subconscious that it makes vital connection with the ordinary range of normal mental procedure, finding a natural place in an evolutionary interpretation of psychic function, and interpretable likewise in (general) terms of neural disposition. Such conception finds an equal obligation to discover and decipher within the range of normal fluctuations, a great diversity of relations,—of excess and abeyance, of distortion, temperamental facilitation and exaggeration and impediment,—that suggest unmistakably the minor abnormalities of subconscious function. It is difficult to overemphasize the significance of this intermediate realm. There are to be sought the sources of the streams, whose waters in turbulent confusion break through their normally confining channels in seeming *lusus naturae*. With these obligations fairly met, the conception may confidently yet tactfully enter the perplexing field of the abnormal, and in so doing will be disposed to emphasize once more the transitory, superficial, introspectively controllable procedures, that in their estrangement maintain some correspondence, —fragmentary, uncertain, elusive, or even incoherent in part though it be—with the normal home relations. Thus rooted firmly in normal procedure, the conception may undertake the special analysis of the complexly abnormal.

The aspect of the resulting conception would admittedly be seriously altered if it should prove necessary in order to account for the abnormal varieties of experience, to assume a system of psychic relations in enlargement or correction of those seemingly adequate for normal psychology, and then in turn to revise the current psychological conception by a restatement in the light of the abnormal. Those who feel themselves forced by logical considerations or impelled by temperamental or philosophical preference to have recourse to such a remodeling of psychological relations have for the most part—and with wide diversity among themselves—proposed some form of secondary consciousness, coordinate or subordinate *alter ego,* subliminal self. Finding, notably in cases of disordered personality, a system of mental possessions and fa-

cilities seemingly out of relation to those of the normal self, they have concluded that there must regularly be such psychic satellites in the orbit, the presence whereof is not created but only revealed by a favoring eccentricity. They point out the notable range of experience, difficult of explanation, which the supposition of such a psychic relation might illuminate; and argue that any supposition that dispenses with such a psychic co-partner must in turn resort to devious assumptions to include within its explanatory scope the aforesaid divergent experiences.

For the tendency of this "dualistic" hypothesis to make alliance with extreme and gratuitous assumptions, the scientific formulation thereof need not be held accountable.

"The argument from alleged supernormal powers in freedom from or violation of accepted physical and mental limitations, the psychologist is hardly called upon to consider; though its actual prominence in the literature will excuse the comment that such use of the hypothesis but imposes an additional burden to be borne, and does not contribute to the logical force of the argument. To one firmly convinced of the truth

The mass impression of the realm as of the detailed features, the entire trend of psychological investigation and of so much of insight as illumines psychic procedure, seems to me overwhelmingly and consistently to bear against any such assumption, even when most objectively and logically shaped. Here the ways divide. While investigation and accumulation of data may proceed profitably without raising this issue, systematic interpretation cannot go far without revealing the formative trend of the underlying conception. To me the subconscious is psychologically significant and logically defensible only under some form of concept that clusters about the organic unity of the mind, and from such a base surveys in orderly sequence of relation, the divergent realm of minor and major abnormalities.

The explanation of subconscious procedure under this unitary conception is

still beset with hypothesis; the sketch thereof made by any one artist inevitably reflects a favorite perspective, an allegiance of school and method. Fundamentally the range of subconscious function must find a place in the mental system by reason of fitness or use, reenforced and developed by evolutionary influences, ultimately of a highly intricate nature. The degree as well as the manner of feelingawareness that attaches to functions that may qualify for a place in the psychic system is conditioned by the value of such an accompaniment or privilege in the functional efficiency. Fundamentally the subconscious status of certain functions is an expression of the mode of their representation in the physiological and psychological economy. It is a fact that influences in the shape of all sorts and conditions of stimuli, play upon the neuro-psychic equipment and modify its expressive behavior. If the reactions to such stimuli demanded an equable distribution of feeling-awareness throughout their range, there would be no provision (or a very different one) for subconscious functioning. The distribution of awareness as attaching to higher and lower, reflex and simply automatic and of the "supernormal" data, the entire physical and mental world—quite as legitimately as the subconscious—may require an entire reconstruction.

'At times a neutral term without the inevitable implications of "consciousness" is useful. For this I suggest feeling-awareness.

' automatically familiarized behavior, sets forth this relation; as, again, direct experimentation by an "impressionistic" response to aspects of stimuli equalized beyond explicit differentiation or recognition corroborates the result.

The analysis of subconscious procedure acquires additional complexity through the inherent many-sidedness of acquisition and expression. Through the facilitation brought about by experience, a lesser degree of awareness, a suppressed variety of its presence, accompanies—the sensitiveness to and the interpretation of outer stimuli as well as the voluntary aspect of the response (initiative). An equally important determinant is the distribution of the attentive attitude, in itself a fundamental factor of the psychic procedure. Peculiarly prominent in all is the will-like, consenting aspect of the incorporative process, by virtue of its intimate affiliation with the personal flavor of conduct, as through the selection and direction and integration of experience, a self emerges, matures and expands.

When the direction of interest in subconscious functioning is shaped towards an inclusion of abnormal relations, there are other obligations to be met. My exposition indicates my conviction that the conception thus emerging from the study of the normal legitimately and fairly applies to the abnormal field. The most instructive variety of the domestic species revealing relatively pronounced or independent subconscious functioning, I find in the diversified lapses popularly termed absent-mindedness. Though evanescent and superficial, the disengagement of the normally accompanying "privileges" of complete consciousness presented in such cases, and again their amenability to analysis constitutes this domain a peculiarly instructive example of what is meant by the subconscious in working trim. It is equally fortunate for the comprehension of the abnormal that so intrinsically abnormal a procedure as dreaming should be so common; and this both as furnishing a familiar alteration of mental state (physiologically conditioned), and as revealing the normality of the easygoing, revery-like, streams of mental occupation that constantly and characteristically contribute to the psychic life. toxications, trance and hypnosis present analogies of release, impairment and rearrangement of function in further extension of dreaming and mental abstraction. Abnormality in these regions is a shifting matter and centers about the orientation of the subject to his environment. Such orientation is variously interfered with by the invasions of projections from the inner world (analogous to those of trance,

hypnosis, delirium, drug intoxication), or by the allied alternations and entanglements of rival syntheses of experience (multiple personality and the like). Such dissociations frequently betray their origin in subconsciously assimilated experience, and their growth by a like disenfranchised rumination, while differently instructive, are the more sudden curtailments of distortions of orientation in disintegrating lapses, not uncommonly of a "shock" origin. Throughout this series the type characteristics far outweigh in importance the vagaries of detailed manifestations, while the analyses of retention to loss, of one conscious synthesis to its rival (notably in the hysterical anaesthesias) are peculiarly significant in their revelation of the standard *modus operandi* of die abnormally subconscious, of die intercourse between dissociated groupings of function.

The variants of dream states, the drug in

The fundamental difficulties surrounding this aspect of the conception are two: (i) the synthesizing of the products of such functioning into seceding systems (not merely sporadic states); (2) with or without such synthesis, the extreme elaboration of the products in specialized directions. Popularly this dual difficulty appears in the willingness to admit that absent-mindedness, dreaming, and simple suggestion are amply accounted for by a normally related conception of subconsciousness, but that trance states (like those of Mile. Helene Smith) and conflicting personalities (like the case of Miss Beauchamp) remain enigmatic. Hence it is well that explanation should be addressed to the rational or imaginative elaboration, and to the "doubling" or rival, seceding, or detached synthesis. The inherent difficulty of each phase lies in its participation in the other. The creative effort in Mile. Smith's Martian extravaganza astonishes by its appearance as the work of a handicapped phase of her consciousness; the ingenious tantalizings of "Sally" are remarkable because directed against and concealed from another phase of her being. Yet once the dis-

sociated-mindedness be admitted, a further complexity of its application seems no serious obstacle to its admission; and particularly is it to be recognized that this pyschic synthesis can not only draw upon the reservoir of the common consciousness, but as well assimilate in like partial incorporation experiences of its own. The widening detachment (doubling) results accordingly from the capacity of the dissociated consciousness to shape its orientation (not alone its memory resources) by its own

'Tbe most baffling group of subconcious facilities of a clearly normal type are the operations of arithmetical prodigies and related proficiencies. The determination of the status of these is a definite obligation which psychology has not yet met There are beginnings and a few notable analyses; in the main, the results seemed to me so unsatisfactory that I was reluctantly compelled to all but omit them from my survey. I believe that in suitable cases the application of the methods used in cases of shifting personality, to the procedures in calculating prodigies, will reveal a more intimate insight into the subconscious facilitating steps, and that these will conform to the general conception here advanced. The investigation seems at all events desirable and promising. contracted model. I have attempted to show that the status thus resulting is of one type or another according (mainly) as the "fault" thus arising is genetic (Miss Beauchamp) or is disintegrating (Mr. Hanna),—the latter the more suggestive of definite physiological variation. In each the demonstrated though gradual and hard-won fusion points to the underlying unity despite temporary psychological (or physiological) barrier, as do also the occasional spontaneous intercourse between one realm and the other and the artificially encouraged *pour parlers* upon a neutral ground. In fine, the added complication of these admittedly perplexing embodiments of dissociated functioning do not constitute a warrant for a distinctive hypothesis, but suggest a warranted extension of the conception of dissociation as applied to more common and regular phenomena. That the conception of dissociation must be shaped to include these is obvious; and the chief importance of further data lies in the hope that they may render more precise and explicit the connotation of that uniquely significant term in modern psychology. While pleading for the regulative value of normal psychological conceptions for the study of abnormal psychology, I am as ready to derive from the latter pertinent applications to the former, in theory and practice alike. The dictum that the grosser and more pronounced abnormalities are but common deficiencies writ large works both ways. The frequent existence of restraining and impeding influences of a subconscious order in normal individuals follows directly from the central position. The release of these by appropriate mental therapeutics is thus justified as practical procedure by reference to the analyses and again to the practical results in pronounced and wayward hysteria and in genetic and disintegrating lapses of personality. In such justification lies a legitimate phase of popular and professional interest in the conception of the subconscious. Here as elsewhere, wise practice will wait upon sound theory.

CHAPTER FOUR BY PIERRE JANET *Professor of Psychology, College de France* YOU'have set me quite a difficult task and one which I hardly feel capable of accomplishing to your entire satisfaction. You ask me to take a stand with regard to the metaphysical theories which are developing today and which seem to have for their point of departure the study of phenomena formerly described by me under the name of the "Subconscious." These studies, already old, since I published them between the years 1886 and 1889, do not permit me to take part in this serious quarrel; they have a much more restricted and much less ambitious range. While the researches of the present day, whether they have a spiritualistic or a materialistic tendency, attain to the summit of the highest metaphysics, my old studies, very modest as they were, simply endeavored to throw light upon, describe and classify certain phenomena of

pathological psychology.

Disturbances of the notion of personality are freely met with in psychiatric studies. One finds not only disturbances in the conception which patients make of their own person, when they pretend to be a king or an animal, but also one very often meets with curious alterations in the assimilation, the incorporation of such and such a phenomenon with that feeling they have of their own person. Indeed, it is undeniable that there takes place in us a certain classing of psychologic phenomena; some are attached to the group of the phenomena of the outside world, others are grouped about the idea of our person. This idea, whether exact or not, which is probably in a great measure a product of our social education, becomes a center about which we range certain facts, while others are placed outside of ourselves. Without discussing the value and the nature of this distribution as it is brought about in the practically normal mind, I state simply the fact that certain patients attach badly to their personality certain phenomena, while others do not hesitate to consider the same facts as entirely per sonal.

In the delirium of typhoid fever one of my patients used to say to me: "Just think of my poor husband who has such a frightful headache; see how my children suffer in their stomachs, somebody is opening their abdomen." She attributed to other people the sensations of suffering which ordinarily we do not hesitate to attribute to ourselves. One meets much more often still with a somewhat different illusion in that large class of patients which I have described under the name of "psychasthenics;" many of them repeat incessandy such remarks as, "It is not I who feel, it is not I who eat, it is not I who speak, it is not I who suffer, it is not I who sleep; I am dead and it is not I who see clearly," etc.

It is easy to determine that in these patients their movements are correct, their diverse sensations are correcdy conserved, even their kinaesthetic and visceral sensations; but the subject nevertheless declares that he does not attach them to his personality; as far as he may

he acts as if he did not have them at the disposition of his person. A patient of this sort, recently described by Seglas, declared that he had no memory and acted as far as possible as if he had really lost all memory, although it was easy to prove that he had in reality forgotten nothing. The apparent trouble of memory just as the apparent antecedent trouble of sensation and movement was nothing more than a disturbance in the development of the idea and the feeling of the personality.

'Nevroses et idees fixes, 1898, II, p. 62; Obsessions et psychasthenic 1903, I, pp. 28 et 307, II, p. 40, 351.

Among these psychasthenics the disturbance of the personality is not total. It is clearly manifest in certain mental operations which may aptly be called superior,—that is to say, in the judgment of recognition by which the attention attaches the new mental content to the old, in language with reflection and in voluntary action. But elementary operations of the personality seem to be preserved; consciousness, that act by which a multiplicity and diversity of states is attached to a unity, seems to survive. The subject declares that it is not he who remembers this or that act, that it is not he who sees this or that tree, but he remembers it nevertheless and continues to see it. At least it is manifest to us that his mind continues to see the tree, since he describes the changes which takes place in it and tells us: "The tree is green, its leaves flutter, but it is not I who see it." The disturbance of the personal perception appears not to be profound.

'Journal de psychologie normale et pathologique, March, 1907, p. 97.

This incomplete character of the disturbances of the personality is found in all the accidents of these psychasthenic patients; they have obsessions but are not completely insane and always recognize the absurdity of their obsessing ideas; they have impulses but do not carry them out; they have phobias concerning acts but never real inability to perform acts, or real paralyses; they have interminable doubts but no true amnesias. It is the striking trait of their character that they never have any symptom in its completeness, and this incomplete character of the disturbances of their personality falls within a general law.

Now there is another psychosis, all the symptoms of which might easily be put in a parallel column with those of psychasthenics, and that is hysteria. This mental disease has for its essential characteristic exaggeration, the carrying to an extreme of all preceding symptoms. Instead of the preceding obsessions with doubt, there are in the mono-deistic somnambulism of hysterics fixed ideas which develop to the most extreme degree, with complete hallucinations and impulses; in place of doubt there is true amnesia; in place of phobias we meet with complete paralyses. It is, therefore, interesting to see the form which the trouble of the personality, just described as incomplete in the previously mentioned disease, will take in hysteria.

Doubtless certain hysterics at times express, with regard to certain sensations, judgments analogous to those of psychasthenics.

A patient formerly cited by Professor James used to say: "My arm is no longer a part of me, it is foreign to me, it is an old stump." This, however, is rather exceptional and most commonly one meets with a different order of facts. In the wake of certain crises in which fixed ideas have developed superabundantly and completely in the form of feelings, acts and hallucinations, which we have called mono-ideistic somnambulisms, the patient acts as if he were completely ignorant of what has taken place; he does not doubt his memories, he does not declare them foreign to his person; he does not speak of them at all, he ignores them. The same subject has both legs paralyzed for certain periods of time, and yet he does not merely say that it is not he who walks, he does not walk at all. If one pricks or pinches his motionless legs, he does not merely say that the sensation is foreign to him, that it no longer beldhgs to him, that it is not he who feels; he says nothing at all, for he does not seem to feel it in any way.

The loss which the personality suffers, the alienation of the phenomena seems to be more complete than in the preceding case. Shall we say, however, that the cases are in nowise comparable?

The psychasthenic still retained his memories, his voluntary acts, his sensations. It is true that he said, "It is not I who remember, I who move and feel," but he proved that he did feel by describing correctly objects placed before him.

In the hysteric these psychologic phenomena are merely suppressed, it is quite another disease, and that is exactly what I formerly tried to show, although in opposition to the opinion current at that time. With a little more precaution than is necessary with the psychasthenic but in the same way, by more carefully avoiding attracting of the patient to the expression of these phenomena, one may demonstrate perfectly their existence in as complete a form as in the so-called normal individual. Take the case of a young girl of twenty years who in her somnambulistic periods indulges in *fugues* of several days' duration, far from the paternal roof. After her *fugues* she appears to have lost completely all memory of them, although she seems incapable of telling you why she went away or where she went. Under distraction and while she was thinking of something else, I put a pencil in her right hand and she wrote me the following letter apparently without cognizance of what she was doing.—"I left home because mamma accuses me of having a lover and it is not true. I cannot live with her any longer. I sold my jewels to pay my railroad fare. I took such and such a train," etc. In this letter she relates her entire *fugue* with precision although she continues to contend that she remembers nothing about it. Another case, that of a man who seemed to have both legs paralyzed, rapidly traverses roofs during a somnambulism and even during the waking state makes with his limbs any movements one desires, if such movements are called for under favorable conditions. These people who seem not to see clearly or not to feel anything in their hands, describe to you in a sub-

sequent somnambulism or by means of the writing of which I have just spoken, or by still other methods, all the details of objects placed before their eyes or brought in contact with their hands. Are we not obliged to conclude as in the preceding case, that sensations are really conserved, although the subject tells us that he does not feel them? These are interesting though perfectly commonplace clinical phenomena, since it is easy to see that all hysterical accidents are fashioned on the same model. They are analogous to the depersonalizations of psychasthenics, but they are not identical with them. I tried to sum them up under the word "subconscious," which, from my point of view, simply designates this new form of the disease of the personality.

Since the time when I first began to employ the word "subconscious," in this purely clinical and somewhat prosaic sense, I must admit that other authors have employed the same word in a sense infinitely more ambitious. The word has been used to designate marvelous activities which exist, so it appears, within ourselves without our even suspecting their existence, and which become the source of our virtues, of our enthusiasms and of the divination of genius. This recalls that amusing saying of Hartmann: "Let us not despair at having a mind so practical and so lowly, so unpoetical and so little spiritual; there is within the innermost sanctuary of each of us, a marvelous something of which we are unconscious, which dreams and prays while we labor to earn our daily bread." I intentionally avoid discussing theories so consoling and perhaps true withal; I simply remind myself that I have something quite different to do. The poor patients whom I studied had no genius; the phenomena which had become subconscious with them were very simple phenomena, such as among other men are a part of their personal consciousness and excite no wonder. They had lost the power to will and the knowledge of self they had a disease of the personality, nothing more.

In connection with these same facts

and in making use of the same word, their theories have touched the great problem of the connections between soul and body, between thought and brain. Are cerebral phenomena always accompanied by psychologic phenomena? When psychologic phenomena diminish, when they are reduced to their simplest expression do they not tend to disappear, and may not one then say that nervous phenomena subsist alone? May not certain coordinate movements which are but ill perceived by patients during their convulsions, and in choreas, be attributed to simple cerebral phenomena without interjecting the notion of psychologic phenomena? If we were really determined to baptize these physiologic phenomena without thought of the name subconscious, might we not on account of the analogy of the name say that all the phenomena of somnambulism or of automatic writing is easily explainable "by phosphorescent shadows which flit across certain centers of the cerebral cortex"!

Far be it from me to discuss these fine theories which seduce certain minds by their scientific appearance, and which after all do probably contain some truth. I am content to remark, that that is quite another problem Doubtless the question of the connections between thought and brain may be discussed with regard to somnambulism as well as with regard to nearly every fact of normal life, but in my opinion there is no good reason why this great problem should be particularly raised in this connection. The assimilation of the conduct of the somnambulist, of the execution of the suggestion, of a page of automatic writing, with incoordinate convulsive movements is pure childishness. These diverse acts are identical with those which we are accustomed to observe in persons like ourselves and to explain by the intervention of the intelligence. Undoubtedly one may say that a somnambulist is only a mechanical doll, but then we must say the same of every creature. These are useless reveries. In our ignorance, we simply know that certain complex facts, like an intelligent reply to a question, depend upon two things

which we believe associated; superior cerebral mechanism and a phenomenon which we call an effect of consciousness. We find the same characteristics in the so-called subconscious phenomena, and we must suppose back of them the same two conditions. To be able to affirm anything else we should need to possess precise knowledge concerning the expression of superior or inferior phenomena of cerebral activity, concerning the loss of the association of consciousness with cerebral phenomena, knowledge which we positively do not possess. Certainly it ought not to be with regard to half understood symptoms of a mental disease that we should try to resolve these great problems of metaphysics. In my opinion, we have got other psychologic and clinical problems to resolve concerning the subconscious without embarrassing ourselves with these speculations. You see that I am today more occupied than formerly with the relations which exist between the depersonalization of psychasthenics and the subconsciouness of hysterics. We must study the intermediate types which are met with much oftener than I had thought. It is necessary to determine if certain characteristics of the one disease are not found in the other. Does not the hysteric herself possess a sort of insane belief which makes her relinquish certain phenomena? Up to what point is she sincere in her declarations of ignorance? Does she not to a certain extent deceive herself? By what steps does she arrive at the complete separation of phenomena which seem to exist in certain cases? Do the psychologic phenomena thus dissociated always retain their properties, are they not more or less transformed? The same problem presents itself in connection with the muscular phenomena, for in the hysterical contracture it does not seem to me exact to say that the muscular contraction remains absolutely what it was in normal movements. There are many other clinical problems of great importance which it seems to me must be studied None of these researches can be made without exact and long continued observations carried on under good con-

ditions, and the very least of them is to my mind more important than all the huge tomes full of speculations put together. It seems to me not difficult to gather from these few reflections the reply to your questions, or, at least, to certain of them. 1. What do you understand by the "Subconscious?"

The word "subconscious" is the name given to the particular form which disease of the personality takes in hysteria. 2. Does "doubling" (Janet) of consciousness ever occur whether normally or pathologically? If not, how would you explain the various so-called subconscious phenomena of abnormal psychology (automatic writing, speech, etc.)?

This word is not a philosophical explanation; it is a simple clinical observation of a common character which these phenomena present.

3. Does the subconscious always represent or depend upon the doubling of consciousness? If so, must there be a lack of awareness on the part of the personal consciousness for the second dissociated group of ideas?

'A series of ten questions were sent to each contributor to this symposium, suggesting points on which it was thought desirable to obtain expressions of views and to keep the discussion within certain limits. Professor Janet concludes with answers to eight of these questions. I have interpolated each question in brackets in his article before the answer in order that the latter may be understood.—Editor.

There exist all sorts of intermediate pathologic forms between the doubt of the psychasthenic and the subconsciousness of the hysteric.
4. Is there normally in every individual a second group of co-acting ideas of which the individual is not aware (a so-called secondary consciousness)? If so, are such ideas discreet or systematized?

It is possible, for all pathologic phenomena have their germ in normal physiology.
5. If doubling occurs, is it always pathological? If so, how do you explain automatic writing, post-hypnotic phenomena, like unconscious solutions of arith-

metical problems and similar phenomena in normal people?

Clear-cut phenomena truly comparable to the subconsciousness of hysterics are infinitely rare in the normal mind. When they are really noted by competent observers they must be regarded as unhealthy accidents of a more or less transient character, and in general, as I have always observed, of a somewhat sinister omen.

Furthermore, these discussions of the words, health and disease are absolutely puerile and recall the sophism of the Greeks about the bald-headed man. A phenomenon is morbid when it is most often associated with other symptoms of a well recognized disease and when it disappears with the disease. Such indeed is the characteristic feature of somnambulism and of automatic writing, which can no longer be evoked in hysterics when they recover from their disease.

6. Do you include under the term subconscious all conscious experiences that have been forgotten, and which are capable of being synthesized with the personal consciousness at any given moment regardless of whether the forgotten experiences are co-acting or not (Sidis)? (In this case subconsciousness becomes co-extensive with the forgotten and out of mind.)

It seems to me difficult to reply to this question when we know so little concerning the form in which our memories are preserved when they are not called forth.

7. Do you limit the term solely to the conscious states which are in co-activity at any given moment, but of which the subject is not aware?

The word "subconscious" seems to me rather to apply to this more clearly cut case.

8. Do you base the conception of the subconscious on the fact of awareness on the part of the individual for certain conscious states, so that there would be different degrees of subconsciousness corresponding to different degrees of awareness? For example, as in absent-mindedness and as represented by the theory of the "fringe of the focus of con-

sciousness."

There are evidently relations between all these phenomena, but we must avoid confounding them with one another; analysis compels us to establish some discontinuity between the facts.

So here, my dear Dr. Prince, you have the answers requested. I fear that they will hardly satisfy your readers. An investigation of this sort does not resolve the problems once and for all; it merely brings the different opinions into competition as they were before. I hope that it may interest at least some few and lead them to psychological observations which will be of lasting utility to science.

CHAPTER FIVE BY MORTON PRINCE *Professor of Neurology, Tufts College Medical School* IN the prefatory note to this symposium six different meanings in which the term "subconscious" is nowadays used were defined. All but the first and fourth of these meanings involve different interpretations of the same observed facts. In a symposium of this kind three of these only need to be considered; namely, those which Professor Miinsterberg has so clearly distinguished and explained, as the points of view of the layman, the physician and the theoretical psychologist. As the first of these three hangs upon the validity of the second, we need only take up for discussion the two last. These two offer interpretations of facts which are not in dispute. Let me state over again the problem:

According to the first of these two interpretations (Professor Munsterberg's and my second type), so-called automatic writing and speech, post-hypnotic phenomena like the solution of arithmetical problems and various abnormal phenomena, of the origin of all which the subject is ignorant, are the manifestations of dissociated ideas of which the subject is unaware and which are therefore called subconscious. Thus a "doubling" of consciousness results consisting of the personal self and the subconscious ideas. I prefer myself the term co-conscious to subconscious, partly to express the notion of co-activity of a second co-consciousness, partly to

avoid the ambiguity of the conventional term due to its many meanings, and partly because such ideas are not necessarily *sub*-conscious at all; that is, there may be no lack of awareness of them. The co-conscious ideas may be very elementary and consist only of sensations and perceptions which have been split off from the personal consciousness, as in hysterical anesthesiae, or they may consist of recurring memories of past experiences. Under certain conditions by a process of synthesizing these ideas and assimilation of them with a greater or less amount of the personal self, which is thereby attenuated, in its faculties, quite large dissociated systems of subconscious ideas may be formed and give rise to the complicated phenomena for which an interpretation is desired.

According to the opposing hypothesis, all these phenomena are explainable as the manifestations of pure physiological processes unaccompanied by ideas. The apparently intellectual and purposive acts as well as volition and memory are performed by brain processes alone to which no consciousness belongs. Such acts differ only in complexity from such other physiological processes which carry on the digestion and other functions of the body, on the one hand, and the spasmodic jerkings and twitchings, seen in chorea, epilepsy and other abnormal affections, on the other. "Unconscious cerebration, Carpenter called it years ago. Which of these two interpretations is correct? Professor Miinsterberg is absolutely right in saying "no fact of abnormal experience can by itself prove that a psychological and not a physiological explanation is needed; it is a philosophical problem which must be settled by principle before the explanation of the special facts begins." The principle is the existence of dissociated subconscious ideas. Are there such things?

With the meaning of this problem well before the mind it becomes manifest that before the fundamental principle of dissociated ideas is definitely established, it is the sheerest waste of time to discuss larger problems, such as the extent of the subconscious symptoms, whether they belong to the normal as well as the abnormal mind, whether they form a "self," a secondary self (third meaning), etc. These and others are important but secondary problems. Above all is it a wasteful expenditure of intellectual energy to indulge in metaphysical speculations regarding the existence and functions of a mystical subliminal self (Myers), transcending as it does all experience and everything that even a "subconscious self" can experience. The point then which we have to determine at the very beginning of the inquiry is this: Do ideas ever occur outside the synthesis of the personal self-consciousness under any conditions, whether of normal or abnormal life, so that the subject becomes unaware of these? Or, putting the question in the form in which it is prescribed to the experimenter: Do phenomena which appear to be the manifestations of a subconscious intelligence necessitate the postulation of dissociated ideas, or are these phenomena compatible with the interpretation that they are due to pure physiological processes without psychical correlates?

The only grounds which I have for believing that my fellow beings have thoughts like myself are that their actions are like my own exhibit intelligence like my own, and when I ask them they tell me they have consciousness, which as described is like my own. Now, when I observe the so-called automatic actions, I find that they are of a similar character, and when I ask of whatever it is that performs these actions, Whether it is conscious or not? the written or spoken reply is, that it is and that consciously it feels, thinks and wills the actions, etc. The evidence being the same in the one case as in the other, the presumption is that the automatic intelligence is as conscious as the personal intelligence. The alternative interpretation is, not that a physiological process is lying, because lying connotes ideas, but that in some way it is able to rearrange itself and react to another person's ideas expressed through spoken language exactly in the same way that a conscious intelligence

Ires I

The phenomena which occur in the neatest and most precise form and which, from the fact that they can be induced, modified and examined at will, are best adapted for experimental study, are so called automatic writing and speech. We will therefore take these for examination and see if they ever require the interpretation of a secondary intelligence of a psychical nature.

When automatic writing is produced in its mosdy highly developed form, the subject with absolutely unclouded mind, with all his senses about him is able to orient, think and reason as if nothing unusual is occurring. He may watch with unconcerned curiosity the vagaries of the writing pencil. In other words, he is in possession of his normal waking intelligence. Meanwhile his hand automatically produces perhaps long discourses of diverse content. But he is entirely unaware of what his hand is writing and his first knowledge of its content comes after reading the manuscript. We then have intelligence No. i and writing manifestations which may or may not be interpreted as having been produced by a conscious intelligence No. 2. But writing of this sort is not always produced with intelligence No. 1 as alert as this.

On the contrary, often and perhaps most frequently the writer falls into a drowsy condition in which he imperfecdy orients his surroundings, and if he is reading aloud according to the common method of conducting the experiment, he is only dimly conscious of what he is reading. This extinguishing of consciousness in intelligence No. 1 may go further and he may not hear when spoken to or feel when touched. He reads on mechanically and without consciousness of the matter he is reading. In other words, he has become deaf and factually anesthetic and blind to everything but the printed characters on the page before him, and for even these mind-blind. In this state then there is practically extinguishment of all sense perceptions and intellectual thought, and finally the impairment of consciousness may be carried so far that he

actually goes to sleep. Ask intelligence No. 2 what has become of No. 1, and the answer may be, "He has gone to sleep."

'This answer was given by a subject observed while this paper was being prepared.

In other words, intelligence No. 1 has disappeared, but intelligence No. 2 continues.

Now to interpret the automatic writing produced when this great impairment of intelligence No. 1 has taken place as subconscious phenomena and due to subconscious intelligence whether physiological or psychological is to overlook the facts as presented. These are not phenomena of a subconscious intelligence but of an alternating intelligence or personality. The complete suppression of intelligence No. 1 has left but one intelligence, that which had been under other conditions intelligence No. 2. Unless the physiological interpretation be maintained the writing has ceased to be automatic in the sense in which the term was originally used and has become what, for the time being, is the primary intelligence although a different one from that which was originally awake. I say different because if we examine the content of the writing we may find it is made up of memories of past experiences which were entirely forgotten by the original intelligence No. 1 and gives evidence of a personality differing in character, volitions, sentiment, moods and points of view, of a character differing in a large degree from that of the waking intelligence. The writing may be an original composition involving thought and reason comparable to that exhibited by a normal mind. Such compositions are of great interest from the light they throw upon the origin and development of secondary personalities, but with that we have nothing to do here. At present the only interest we have in such compositions is the evidence which they offer for the interpretation of such a personality. That is to say, whether its intelligence is the exhibition of physiological or psychological processes. To arrive at a satisfactory interpretation, we must study the behavior of the personality to its environment. If we speak to it, it answers intelligently in writing, though intelligence No. 1 fails to respond. If we prick the hand, we obtain a similar response and lack of response from intelligence No. 2 and No. 1 respectively, and the same with the other senses. It exhibits spontaneity of thought and its faculties are curtailed in the motor sphere alone in which it retains power only to move the muscles of the arm and hand; but even here in the motor sphere its faculties are not necessarily so limited for it may break out into speech and may exhibit various sporadic movements. It has lost only a general coordinating control over the whole body. In the motor sphere, therefore, its loss is not so great as that which has befallen intelligence No. 1. In fact, we have here a condition very similar to that of some persons in deep hypnosis. The main point is that now we have to do with an alternating intelligence, not a co-intelligence. Is it an alternating *consciousness*?

The next thing to note is that in passing from automatic writing, which is performed while intelligence No. 1 is completely alert, to writing which is performed while this intelligence is completely or nearly extinguished, we pass through insensible gradations from one condition to the other and *we must infer that the intelligence must be the same in kind, physiological or psychologicalyWhich produced the writing in the one case as in the other*. If the alternating intelligence in the latter case is psychological, the subconscious intelligence in the former must be the same, for there is no place where we can stop and conclude—here the physiological ends and the psychological begins.

'By this is not meant that it has the same degree of knowledge and capacity for intellectual thought possessed by the original personality, No. I, but only that it has all the different *kinds* of intelligence possessed by a normal person.

In the alternating intelligence producing automatic writing we have an alternating personality. We have here substantially the same condition that is observed, first, in some hpynotic states;

second, trance states; third, "fugues," spontaneous somnambulism and post-epileptic states; fourth a state not very different from normal sleep with dreams, forgotten on waking; and fifth, certain states of deep abstraction. In none of these has there ever been raised the doubt as to the conscious character of the intelligence. All are "alternating" states and some are alternating personalities. In the first group, suggestions requiring conscious intelligence are comprehended, remembered and acted upon; in the second, writing and speech are manifested which can only be interpreted as the product of thought; in the third and fourth, the thoughts and dreams can afterwards be regained by certain technical devices; and in the last the conscious processes are remembered.

Let us go further with our experiment and take a case exhibiting automatic writing where intelligence No. 1 remains unimpaired. We hypnotize such a subject. When asked what sort of intelligence it was that did the writing, he replies that he remembers perfectly the thoughts, sensations and the feelings which made up the consciousness of which intelligence No. 1 was not aware and that this consciousness did the writing. Still, it may be maintained that this in itself is not proof but that the hypothesis is permissible, that these memories are sort of hallucinations, and that in hypnosis what were previously physiological processes now have become reawakened and have given rise in the hypnotic synthesis to psychical memories. We shall then have to go further and seek for additional evidence.

Automatic writers may be divided into two classes; namely, those who at the moment of writing are entirely unaware of what the hand is writing; and those in whom at the moment of writing ideas corresponding to written words surge apparently from nowhere without logical associative relation into the mind. Mrs. H., for example, is an excellent automatic writer of the second class. At the moment when the pencil writes ideas which it is about to express arise at once in her consciousness so that she

is herself in doubt as to whether she writes the sentence volitionally, or whether it is written automatically entirely independent of her will. Sometimes while writing, the ideas come so rapidly that unable to express them with sufficient celerity with the pencil she bursts out into voluble speech. To test her doubt, she is given a pencil and told not to write. Then she finds herself without control of her hand, and, in fact, the pencil writes the more fluently the greater the effort she makes to inhibit it. In the midst of a suitable sentence I hold her hand and restrain the writing, and ask her to complete the sentence by word of mouth, which of course she could do if it was her own intelligence, that is No. 1, that was doing the writing; but she cannot complete the idea, showing that she does not really know what the hand was about to write.

Again, Mrs. B. in hypnosis is told to write automatically when awake, "three times six are eighteen; four times five are twenty." After being awakened she is given something to read aloud; while reading the hand begins to write as previously directed, but she stops reading saying, that she cannot because the, to her, absurd sums three times six are eighteen, four times five are twenty, keep coming into her head. She cannot understand why she should think of such things.

Now, are we to conclude that the mechanism of automatic writing in the second class of writers differs from that performed by the first class, and that when the writer is *aware* of the automatic thoughts the writing is done by psychical processes, and that when he is *not aware* of any automatic thoughts it is done by physiological processes? In every other respect, in content of writing and in behavior of the automatic personality to the environment, we find the phenomena are the same. It does not seem to me that such an interpretation is justifiable. As I view this question of the subconscious, far too much weight is given to the point of awareness or not awareness of our conscious processes. As a matter of fact we find entirely identical phenomena, that is identical in every respect but one—that of awareness—in which sometimes we are aware of these conscious phenomena and sometimes not; but the one essential and fundamental quality in them is automaticity or independence of the personal consciousness. Doubling and independence of the personal consciousness are therefore the test of the subconscious rather than wareness.

In the content of automatic writing we find evidence which it is difficult to reconcile with a physiological interpretation. This was briefly touched upon before. When studied we find that the writing does not consist of words, phrases and paragraphs which might be mere repetitions or memories whether physiological or psychical, of previous experiences, but even consist of elaborate original compositions. Sometimes in Mrs. Verrall's writing they consisted of original Latin or Greek compositions. Sometimes, as in those who are inclined to a spiritistic interpretation, of fanciful fairy-tale-like fabrications. Sometimes they exhibit mathematical reasoning shown by the solution of arithmetical problems. Sometimes they consist of ingeniously fabricated explanations in answer to questions. Sometimes they indicate a personal character with varying moods and temperaments. Feeling and emotion whether of anger, hatred or malice, kindness or amiability are often manifested. If such a document were presented as testamentary evidence in the ordinary course of human affairs, it would seem as if the burden of proof would lie with him who would insist upon interpreting it as without psychological meaning and as only the expression of a physiological activity of the nervous system without thought. 8 l?roc. S. P. R., Vol. XX, p't liii, 1906.

6

Suggestions in hypnosis may result in posthypnotic phenomena, which are manifestations of an intelligence which may be of a kind which cannot possibly be explained by physiological *habits,* as it exhibits logical readjustment of ideas of a high order; for instance, complex arithmetical calculations. The subject is only aware of the final result, being en-

tirely ignorant of the process by which it was arrived at. Later this process can be recalled in hypnosis as conscious memories. To assume that such a calculation can be performed by a brain process not accompanied by thought would seem to require the abandonment of the doctrine of the correlation of mind and brain. In some instances, as with automatic writing, the subject becomes aware of the automatic conscious process though ignorant of its origin. Are we to assume here again that the processes giving rise to the same manifestations, under the same conditions, differ in kind according as whether a subject is aware of them or not— in the former case being psychical, in the latter physiological?

The great variety of phenomena occurring in abnormal conditions are often explained by the patient in hypnosis as the manifestations of ideas (perceptions, hallucinations, memories, emotions, etc.), which are remembered as such, though unknown to the personal consciousness. This evidence does not differ in kind from that derived from automatic writing (3).

After all, as I conceive the matter, the one great difficulty in the minds of those who are unable to accept the psychological interpretation of subconscious phenomena lies in understanding how we can have states of consciousness of which we are unaware. Consciousness is represented as a functioning unity, and it is difficult to accept the notion that all states of consciousness are not so synthesized as to form part of that great system which we dub self-conscious. Thus, consciousness is confused with 5//-consciousness. This has come about because the onlyimmediate experience which anyone has of conscious states is with that which belongs to his self, which is only another way of saying with that of which he is aware. All conscious states, so far as we experience them, belong to, take part in, or help make up a self,—in fact, the expression, "We experience" implies a self that experiences. It is difficult, therefore, to conceive of a conscious state that is not a part of a self-conscious self. It seems queer then, to think of

a state of consciousness, a sensation, a perception, an idea floating off—so to speak—by its lonesome self and not attached to anything that can be called a self. It is difficult to conceive of anything worthy of being called a sensation or perception, excepting so far as there is a self to experience it; and yet it really is a naive conception to imagine that we are self-conscious of each and every conscious state that is aroused in correlation with out nervous system. Such a conception is very much akin to the naive notion of scientific materialism which assumes, for the practical purposes of experimentation or other reasons, that phenomenal matter really exists as such. Consciousness whether in an elementary or complex form must be correlated with an innumerable number of different physiological brain syntheses. If this is not so the whole structure of the psycho-physiology of the mind and brain falls. We have every reason to assume that some sort of a psychical state occurs when any one of these association-groups is excited to activity. (At any given moment the great mass of them is inhibited.) There is strong reason to believe that though ordinarily there is a harmony in the functioning of these association-groups, yet at times there is considerable disharmony and there is clinical evidence for believing that there may be some independence of activity, especially under pathological conditions (hallucinations, obsessions, etc.), of different brain syntheses.

Without being obliged to determine what brain synthesis belongs to the personal consciousness at any given moment, we are entitled to ask why must we necessarily be aware of all the conscious states which may belong to each and every brain association-group? Is this not a naive assumption? If it is true that dissociated brain systems can functionate (as in other parts of the nervous system), and if it is true that they have psychical equivalents, then whether we are self-conscious of any given state of consciousness must depend, it would seem, upon whether the brain process, correlated with it, is synthesized in a particular way with the larger system of brain processes which is correlated at a given moment with the self-conscious personality. And in so far as a brain process can occur detached from the main system of brain processes, so far can consciousness occur without self-consciousness. Unfortunately, we have scarcely a glimmer of knowledge of the nature of the synthesis, and therefore of the conditions which determine whether we shall be aware of any conscious state or not. This is a problem in psychology which awaits the future. Nor is self-consciousness a necessary element of consciousness. The naive character of the notion that we must be selfconscious of our consciousness is shown by introspective analysis in intense mental concentration or absent-mindedness. Here is no awareness of self, only a succession of ideas which adjust and readjust themselves. It is not until afterwards, on "returning to one's self," that these ideas through memory become a part of our self-conscious personality. It will be noticed that an essential element in the conception of the subconscious, as generally held by students of abnormal phenomena, is the absence of awareness of the personal consciousness for the dissociated ideas. A consideration of the facts in their entirety do not permit of so limited a view to which I am compelled to dissent. Theoretically, a conception so narrow prevents our obtaining a broad view of allied psychological phenomena, obscures our perception of the broad principles underlying them and hinders a correlation of closely related conditions. Dissociation, with activity, independent of the main focus of consciousness, does not necessarily imply or require absence of awareness on the part of the latter, and practically, as we have seen in discussing the phenomena of automatic writing, under the same conditions, a subject is sometimes aware of the dissociated ideas which are actively manifesting themselves and sometimes not. The same is true of post-hypnotic and abnormal phenomena. Indeed, even when there is absence of awareness on the part of the personal consciousness, the dissociated co-consciousness may,

per contra, be aware of the content of the former. For this reason, if for no other, co-consciousness is the preferable term. The one fundamental principle and criterion of the subconscious is dissociation and co-activity (automatism). When we get rid of this notion of awareness as an essential element, we are able to grasp the relation between the subconsciousness of hysterics and the disaggregation of personality of the psychasthenic, a study with which Dr. Janet says he is now occupied. The obsessions, the impulsions, the fears, in short, the imperative ideas of the psychasthenic are as much disaggregated from the personal consciousness as the same are in the hysteric, excepting for that amount of synthesis that gives awareness. Indeed, the hysteric may have a certain amount of awareness, or awareness for some and not for other ideas. The only difference then between an ordinary obsession and a "subconscious" obsession as commonly viewed, is that the subject is aware of the one and not of the other. Undoubtedly the condition of awareness alters considerably the resulting psychical content, as it brings into play various co-operative and modifying and in some measure adjusting ideas. This is not the place to enter into a consideration of the differences and likenesses between psychasthenia and hysteria, but I believe it important to insist that lack of awareness is not an essential fact or in the development of the subconscious, and furthermore that an appreciation of this fact will enable us to better correlate the different varieties of co-conscious activities not only in various diseased conditions but with facts of normal mental life.

Those who maintain the physiological interpretation seem to me to involve thmselves in difficulties far greater than any offered by the psychological interpretation. It is a fundamental interpretation of psycho-physiology that all thought is correlated with physiological activities. Whatever doctrine we adopt, whether that of parallelism or psychophysical identification, every psychical process is correlated with a physiological process and *vice versa.* We

cannot conceive of a psychical activity without a corresponding physiological one. How then can we conceive of a physiological process of a complexity and character capable of exhibiting itself as a spontaneous volitional intelligence without corresponding correlated ideas? Surely this needs explanation quite as much as does a lack of awareness of conscious processes. Yet with a certain modification of our conception of the meaning of the physical, it is possible to reconcile both interpretations. As a panpsychist I find no difficulty in accepting both a physiological and a psychical interpretation. For those who accept panpsychism there is no distinction to be made between conscious processes and brain processes of a certain order, excepting as a point of view. They become identified one with the other. The psychical is the *reality* of the physical. I cannot conceive of brain processes except as objective phenomena of conscious processes, and I cannot conceive of consciousness excepting as the reality or "inner life" of brain changes. So that we may indifferently describe automatic actions as manifestations of physiological activities, if we keep to one set of terms, or of psychical activities if we mix the terms. But in doing this let us not straddle and deceive ourselves as to our real position. In thinking in physiological terms we must not confuse ourselves and, by adopting a terminology, imagine that those physical brain factors are without psychical equivalents. To hold to a pure physiological explanation without the notion of anything psychical as a part of their real nature, is to postulate consciousness as a pure epi-phenomenon, something that we can shift in and out at our pleasure, when we have brain action, and juggle with as a conjurer juggles with his coins, —now you see them and now you don't.

It may be that the final explanation of many conscious processes, if we would avoid the entanglements of metaphysics, must be in physiological terms, because it must deal with that which belongs to experience. We can experience physiological "after effects," and by a simple inference go back to the physiological functioning forerunner, and thus perhaps explain memory, but, as Professor Miinsterberg so well points out, it is difficult to see how a comprehensible explanation of memory can be found in "mental dispositions," and on grounds, as I would state them, that such dispositions being out of consciousness we have no experience of them and can have no conception of what they are. They become nothing more than metaphysical concepts. For myself I cannot even think of a "mental disposition," meaning, for instance, a name or mental picture that is not at the moment a state of consciousness, whether subconscious or belonging to my self-conscious synthesis. However this may be, I not only say with Professor Miinsterberg that "the physiological cerebration is well able to produce the 'intellectual' result," but it *must* be able to do so. The only question is whether it is accompanied by, belongs to, or *is* another aspect of ideas. This can, to my way of thinking, only be settled by logical inferences from the observed phenomena, and I have endeavored in what has gone before to marshal the evidence so far as it exists today in substantiation of this interpretation.

CHAPTER SIX

The Conception of the Subconscious
BY BERNARD HART, M. B., M. R. C. S.
Assistant Medical Officer, Long Grove Asylum, Epsom THE conception of the subconscious has of recent years acquired a dominating position in psychiatry. The utility of this conception in the co-ordination of our knowledge, and its fruitfulness in suggesting new lines of research, have become so obvious, that the opposition which it at first aroused has been almost altogether overcome. Considerable disagreement, however, still exists as to the precise meaning to be ascribed to the term. What is the nature of a subconscious process—is it a physical or
"No fact of abnormal experience can by itself prove that psychological and not a physiological explanation is needed; it is a philosophical problem which must be settled by principle before the ex-

planation of the special facts begins."— Munsterberg. mental phenomenon? This and other similar questions constitute a fertile source of dispute, and the Symposium which recently appeared in this Journal showed the very divergent views held by some of the Leading psychologists and psychiatrists of the day.

The present paper is an attempt to investigate the essential nature of this conception, to determine its claims to a place in the structure of modern science, and the position which must be assigned to it within that structure.

It will be profitable to first consider the more important stages in the historical development of the theory of the subconscious. Our next step will be an enquiry concerning the characters which modern science demands that a conception shall possess in order to qualify it for admission within its portals. We shall then be in a position to consider how far the conception of the subconscious satisfies these demands, and to determine its place and function in psychology.

The history of all thought has been dominated throughout by an essential tendency of the human mind—the endeavor to obtain continuity. The mind abhors discontinuity as nature is said to abhor a vacuum. It strives to bring every new experience into line with the old, to do away with inexplicable gaps, and to reduce its world to a connected intelligible whole. Mythology, religion, and philosophical systems provide us with numerous examples of this constant endeavor. Science is nothing but the same trend of thought become coherent and articulate.

Now it was early seen in the history of philosophy that, among the contrasts to be observed between the physical and mental, one of the most prominent was the comparative discontinuity of the latter. The psychical life made its appearance in an irregular manner, in flashes of limited duration, and in the intervals between these flashes it appeared to altogether cease to exist. In contrast to this the material world seemed relatively continuous, permanent, and independent of the individual. Hence, if the

study of the mind was to be brought into line with the rest of our knowledge, an attempt had to be made to get rid of the apparent discontinuity and irregularity of psychical experience. Such an attempt has formed an integral part of most philosophical systems. The method adopted by the earlier philosophers, however, consisted mostly in imaginative and fantastic constructions, which aimed solely at internal coherence, and which had but little relation to the facts. It was only after the method of the inductive sciences had long demonstrated its utility in other branches of knowledge, that an endeavor was made to apply it to the sphere of psychology.

The first serious contribution to the filling up of the gaps in the psychical series was made by Leibnitz, who demonstrated that our conscious life contains small elements lying outside its main stream, but which nevertheless produce an effect by a process of summation and combination. Schopenhauer (1) thought that a large number of our sense perceptions were the result of unconscious processes of reasoning—and the same theory was propounded in a more exact form by Helmholtz (2). By this period, therefore, the attempt to bridge the intervals in the psychical series by processes of unconscious thought had taken definite shape.

The question of the subconscious first, however, became prominent with the publication of Hartmann's "Philosophic des Unbewussten," in 1868. The intense enthusiasm with which this work was greeted in the most varied quarters affords a striking demonstration of that hunger for continuity whose existence we have already noted. Hartmann conceived the subconscious as a second personality concealed beneath the surface of our ordinary consciousness, but precisely comparable to the latter in its structure and functions. He appeals to this hypothetical being whenever there is a gap in the chain of visible causation, and endows it with properties of a really startling kind. "Let us not despair," he says, "at having a mind so practical and so lowly, so unpoetical and so little spiritual; there is within the innermost sanctuary of each of us a marvellous something of which we are unconscious, which dreams and prays while we labor to earn our daily bread" (3). Hartmann's work is of historical importance on account of the stimulus it provided to further investigation, but his use of the concept of the unconscious was so unbridled that the value of his actual results is almost altogether nullified. James has described his theory as a "tumbling ground for whimsies," and Hoffding remarks, "We may say of it, as Galileo said of the appeal to an almighty will, it explains nothing because it explains everything" (4).

Some of the most important advances in the historical development of the subconscious have been furnished by the French School of Morbid Psychology during the latter part of the nineteenth century, initiated under Charcot and Ribot, and culminating in the work of Janet. In his classical "Automatisme Psychologique" the latter demonstrated that a large number of morbid phenomena can be adequately explained by assuming the existence of dissociated mental elements altogether outside the sphere of the personality.

Morton Prince has further developed Janet's point of view. He divides psychological material into that of which the individual is personally conscious, and that of which he is not personally conscious. Those experiences are personally conscious which are synthesized in the "personality." The experiences of which the individual is not personally conscious are further divided into co-conscious and unconscious. *Co-conscious* corresponds in the main to Janet's "subconscious" —actively functioning ideas dissociated from the personality. Under *unconscious* are included the phenomena of memory, and in general all the ideas, traces, etc., which are not at the moment actively functioning, and which are to be regarded as mere physiological residua. Any of these latter may at any time become conscious or co-conscious. Dr. Prince considers that the essential character of a co-conscious idea consists in the fact that it leads an autonomous existence,

and is not dependent upon the ego-complex. Co-conscious, therefore, does not necessarily imply that the ego is unaware of the idea in questoin. Thus, in the well-known case described in "The Dissociation of a Personality," one personality knows all the thoughts and actions of a second, but considers them to be those of another being whom, indeed, she regards with unconcealed dislike. This extension of the meaning of Janet's conception is very important, and enables us to throw more light upon the analogous manifestations occurring in paranoia.

The most modern development of the doctrine of the subconscious is to be found in the works of Freud, Jung, and the Zurich School. Their conception is totally different from those enumerated above, far more different than is generally supposed. This point will be better appreciated after a consideration of certain philosophical questions, which will subsequently be discussed.

We have seen that the concept of the subconscious mind has gradually developed as a result of the demand for continuity in the psychical series. This same demand for continuity has, however, led to an endeavor to solve the difficulty in an altogether different manner. Certain philosophers asserted that the psychical was unreal, a mere epiphenomenal product of the physical, and that nothing but the material existed. The brain was considered to secrete thought as the liver secretes bile. This school reached its zenith in the materialism of Moleschott and Büchner —a crude and naive philosophy now generally discredited. Later authorities, however, while admitting the reality of the psychical, denied that it could be made amenable to the method of science. Thus Karl Lange required that all psychological definitions should be replaced by physiological, and Münsterberg asserted that "mental facts, as they are not quantitative, cannot enter into any causal relation" (5). It will be seen, therefore, that these authorities consider that so long as we are dealing with psychical facts there can be no question of causation or of science. They must be first translated into physi-

ological terms, and it will then be possible to formulate laws concerning them, and thus to incorporate them into the structure of our knowledge. This school has been aptly described by Hoffding as virtually wishing to abolish psychology in order to convert it into a science. For the exponents of this theory the question of the subconscious does not exist—consciousness and subconsciousness are alike to be reduced to physiological terms, and the difference between them consists merely in a varying mode of combination of the cerebral elements.

Certain other authorities adopt a compromise—they are ready to consider consciousness psychologically, but the subconscious is for them nothing but an inappropriate name for brain processes which have no psychological accompaniment.

The main question at issue between these various schools is, therefore, whether the subconscious is to be regarded as a brain fact or as a mind fact, whether it is a subject for physiology or for psychology. The present paper endeavors to show that this question is in itself based upon a misconception and that its solution becomes at once obvious when the meaning of the terms is correctly apprehended.

As a preliminary measure it will be necessary to temporarily diverge from our main subject, and to shordy consider the general properties of scientific concepts.

The philosophical consideration of the groundwork of science is a growth of comparatively recent years. The earlier scientists contented themselves with practical results, and did not consider the foundations upon which they were building. During the latter part of the nineteenth century, however, the need for a precise formulation and definition of these foundations began to make itself felt. Hence there arose a school of critical philosophy unique amongst philosophical creeds in the fact that its exponents have been men eminent in the scientific world —'Clark-Maxwell, Ostwald, Mach, Karl Pearson. Pearson's "Grammar of Science" remains the finest vindication in the English language of the principles, aims, and methods of modern science. The short exposition which follows is an endeavor to cull the essential points from its pages. But limitations of space prevent more than a short summary of the principal conclusions being given, and for the demonstration of their validity the reader must be referred to the original work. Science is characterized, not by its content but by its method of investigation—it embraces the whole field of knowledge and is as applicable to history as it is to chemistry. It deals, not with a fabulous entity called "matter," but with the content of the human mind, and acknowledges its incapacity to deal with anything which forms no part of that content. The material of science is therefore human experience, what James calls "the flux of sensible reality." In other words, phenomena, of whatever sort or kind they may happen to be, constitute the material, while science is simply our method of treating this material. Now it is found that human experience does not take place in an entirely haphazard and chaotic manner, but that the events follow one another with more or less regularity and order. This is the principle of the uniformity of nature. The aim of science is to find a means of proceeding from one point of experience to another with the least exertion of mental energy, in other words to achieve an "economy of thought." Its method is, firstly, to take some portion of human experience and to classify the facts found therein into sequences; secondly, to find some simple treatment which will resume an indefinite number of sequences in a single formula. Such a formula constitutes a scientific law. The law is the more fundamental the wider the range of facts which it resumes. It is not a mythological entity, it is merely a construction of the human mind to enable it to deal better with its experience. If we examine any scientific law in order to determine its essential nature, we find that it has no immediate reference to sense impressions, or, in other words, to phenomenal reality, but is purely ideational

or conceptual in character. The meaning of this statement will be made clearer by taking an example, e. g., Newton's law that "every particle attracts every other particle." Now a particle is not a sense-impression; it is defined as an infinite "ly small portion of matter, that is to say, a pure idea, formed by carrying what is given in sense impressions to a conceptual limit in the mind. "Newton is here dealing with conceptual notions, for he never saw, nor has any physicist since his time ever seen, individual particles, or been able to examine how the motion of two such particles is related to their position" (6). Similarly geometry, with its points, straight lines, and surfaces, is dealing with entities which are frankly acknowledged to be conceptual in character, and to have no real existence in the world of sense impressions. The physical conceptions of the atom and the ether are precisely analogous in their nature. We find, therefore, that science does not profess to mirror some hypothetical universe lying altogether outside the human mind, but simply to provide a conceptual model, a "conceptual shorthand," by aid of which we can resume our sense impressions and predict future occurrences. "The physicist forms a conceptual model of the universe by aid of corpuscles. These corpuscles are only symbols for the component parts of perceptual bodies, and are not to be considered as resembling definite perceptual equivalents. We conceive them to move in the manner which enables us most accurately to describe the sequences of our sense impressions. This manner of motion is summed up in the so-called law of motion" (7). We therefore reach the conclusion that science is simply a mode of conceiving things. The justification of science lies precisely in the fact that it does enable us to resume our sense impressions and predict future occurrences; its value as truth lies in its value as a working hypothesis by which we may become the masters of phenomena.

Now there may be more than one mode of conceiving the same things, and which mode we adopt may depend on the practical necessities of the mo-

ment. Thus the mathematician insists on regarding bodies as bounded by continuous surfaces, whereas the physicist is compelled to regard them as bounded by discontinuous atoms. Neither of these modes is more true than the other; the question is merely which one has the greatest practical value in the particular sphere of thought in question.

Armed with these conceptions let us now direct our attention to those fields which more particularly concern us, and firstly let us consider the problem of the physical and the mental. What, in fact, is the difference between physics and psychology? We are usually told that there are two orders of phenomena, the physical and the mental, two series which are so qualitatively different that the passage from one to the other is unthinkable. Concerning the relation between these two series innumerable philosophical battles have been waged, and science must approach the question with a due regard for the metaphysical quicksands which await her on every side. It was pointed out by Bishop Berkeley that sense impressions are the only things of which we have any immediate knowledge, and modern science, having with some difficulty duly digested this fact, has discarded the pretence that it is engaged in a research into "things in themselves," and has relegated the latter to the limbo of useless figments. Being entirely pragmatic in its ideals, and having a criterion of validity measured solely by utility, it recognizes that its field is the content of the human mind, neither more nor less. The modern scientist cannot therefore be accused of sharing the vulgar conception that "reality" consists of "material substance," which by means of "energy and force" acts on "spiritual substance," giving rise in the latter to "sensations" which mirror the external reality. What, then, does he mean when he distinguishes between the mental and the material? The answer is that he means two different modes of conceiving human experience. On the phenomenal plane the physicist and the psychologist are dealing with precisely the same entities, sense impressions; the distinction between them lies in their different conceptual methods of resuming these sense impressions so as to express them in simple formulae. The physicist resumes his sense impressions by means of a conceptual model involving space and time, whereas the psychologist regards them as actual or potential constituents of a consciousness. As Mach (8) puts it, there is a "change of direction" in their methods of research. The ultimate goal of the physicist is a complete description of the universe in terms of motion or mechanism, the ultimate goal of the psychologist is "personality." Neither method is in itself better, more perfect, or more real than the other, both have an equal right to be incorporated into the structure of science, comparison between them can only be made on the grounds of utility. We are only entitled to ask by which method we are better enabled to resume our experience of the past and to predict our experience of the future. And the only answer to this question which it is possible to give in the present state of knowledge is that both methods are of value, and that neither can be abandoned in favor of the other.

For the present the physiologist and the psychologist must be allowed to proceed along their respective roads. But there must be no jumping from one mode of conception to the other. The physiologist must not introduce a psychological conception into his chain of cause and effect, nor must the psychologist fill up the gaps in his reasoning with cells and nerve currents. The former error is comparatively rarely met with, the latter is unfortunately only too common. No physiologist would consent to admit "ideas" as active elements in the sequence of changes which take place in the nervous system. He simply points out that he has no use for such a conception, and that, so far from helping him in his explanation of phenomena, it vitiates his reasoning, and destroys the validity of all his former concepts. The psychologist, on the other hand, is a weaker vessel; he less commonly belongs to what James has termed the "tough-minded" school of philosophy.

He is usually prepared to humbly admit that the phenomena of memory are adequately explained by the potential physical energy of a brain cell, and does not venture to suggest that the potential psychical energy of an idea is a conception just as valid, and with precisely the same claim or lack of claim to real existence.

The distinction between the phenomenal and conceptual which underlies the principles

This exposition of the method of science is mainly extracted from a paper by the author, entitled "A Philosophy of Psychiatry" *(Journal of Mental Science,* July, 1008), which contains a more detailed investigation of the scientific basis of Psychiatry. The term "sense-impression" has been used for the sake of simplicity. It can no longer be maintained, however, that the mind contains nothing but sensory elements. Thought and emotion involve factors which cannot be reduced to terms of sensation, in the proper meaning of that word. To be strictly accurate, "element of experience" should be substituted for "sense-impression" in the above description. given above, is of fundamental importance. Anything which can be experienced is a phenomenal fact—a scientific concept is a construction of the mind which cannot be experienced at all. A nerve fibre is a phenomenal fact, the nerve current which traverses it is a conception. The nerve current is not a portion of our experience, we only experience the results which we ascribe to it; in other words, we invent the nerve current to explain the phenomenal result. Similarly colors, chemical substances, falling bodies are phenomena; ether waves, atoms, the force of gravity are conceptions. Precisely the same distinction is met with in the scientific treatment of the psychological series, a fact which we shall hope to subsequently demonstrate.

It is only within recent years that morbid psychology has become amenable to the method of science. It was necessary that objectives should replace introspective psychology, and that the presence of certain external signs

should be regarded as indicating the presence of certain conscious processes, a deduction from analogy which every man makes when he talks to any other man. Without this assumption any scientific treatment of the mental processes of the insane was obviously impossible. It is needless to point out that psychology must also postulate the existence of an absolute determinism within the psychical series. The law of causation forms the essential basis of the method of science.

Our conception of the nature of science, and its relation to psychology, may therefore be summarized as follows: (1) The psychical and the physical are two different modes of conceiving human experience.

(2) From the point of view of science we are compelled to postulate an absolute determinism within each of these modes. (3) The method of science is applicable to either mode. It consists in the more or less arbitrary division of phenomenal experience into artificial elements, and the construction of laws regulating the interaction of these elements. The sole justification of these laws consists in the fact that they enable us to resume and predict our experience, and hence to achieve an "economy of thought." (4) Science does not claim that the elements with which it deals necessarily have perceptual equivalents, and it may ascribe properties to certain of these elements which are even contradictory to all perceptual experience, e. g., a weightless and frictionless ether. The constructions of science are therefore largely conceptual in character, and must be sharply distinguished from the phenomena which constitute our actual experience. (5) The various elements entering into a conceptual construction must all be of the same mode, they may be either physical or psychical, but cannot consist in a mixture of the two.

We are now in a position to return to our main theme, and to consider in the light of first principles the various doctrines of the subconscious so far enunciated.

It is at once obvious that we must fundamentally disagree with those authorities who regard the subconscious as a brain fact and not as a mind fact. Such a view involves that jumping from one mode of conception to the other, from the psychological to the physiological which we have seen to be incompatible with the method of science. A conception must be in the same terms as the phenomena which it is designed to connect. We cannot conceive cells and fibres as the connection between two ideas. The conceptions of psychology must all be constructed within the psychical series. Only in this way can psychology have the same air as its sister sciences, the construction of a conceptual model which will enable us to resume our past and to predict our future experience. The conception of the subconscious has been devised by the psychologist to explain certain psychological phenomena—it must be regarded as a psychological conception.

For the same reasons *memory* must also be regarded as a psychological conception, a conception constructed to fill up the gaps in the phenomenal psychic series. It is, of course, true that memory is not itself a phenomenal psychic fact, we only experience the recurrence of a certain mental process—we assume, in order to satisfy our demand for continuity, that it has in some way existed during the interval, and we invent the conception of memory to explain this continued existence. To the reader who has not adequately grasped the essential principles of the modern philosophy of science this may appear to be a very unsatisfactory explanation of memory. He may object that if this is all that psychology can say in the matter he would prefer to adopt the physiological point of view, and to regard memory as the conservation of traces in the brain. But he will find that the physiological conception of memory is no more a phenomenal fact than the psychological. He will find himself using such terms as "nervous energy," "permeability of paths," and other purely conceptual ideas, and he will finally begin to realize that his "conserved trace" is merely a conception invented to resume the fact that a certain brain phenomenon is

capable of repeating itself. Translating memory into the physical series does not make it a phenomenal fact, it must inevitably remain a conception. And if memory from both points of view is merely a conception, then surely if we are talking of the recurrence of mental phenomena it is a psychological conception. Both in this case and in that of the subconscious no useful purpose is served by suddenly jumping into the other series, and all hope of discovering a comprehensive scientific law is *ipso facto* abolished. To maintain that the subconscious is a brain fact and not a mind fact is precisely analogous to maintaining that the law of gravity is a psychological conception and not a physical conception.

Munsterberg (see Chapter One) has objected that "Those who insist that the memory idea presupposes a lasting mental disposition and cannot be explained by physiological after-effect, only forget that the same logic would demand a special mental disposition also for each new perception. The whole mystery of an idea entering into consciousness presents itself perfectly every time when we use ous eyes or ears." We cannot admit that this is altogether true—the logical extension of the doctrines enunciated above would be simply that every new sensation *might* be also due to a previous "mental disposition." But science demands of its conceptions that they should satisfy the criterion of utility. We construct a conceptual memory and a conceptual subconscious in order to explain our experience—the conception of a previous mental disposition for each new sensation would serve no useful purpose whatever. We have to admit that sensations appear in a mind without any antecedents in that mind, and there can be no scientific objection to such an admission. Such an objection could only have force if we postulated a law of conservation of psychic energy for each individual consciousness analogous to that holding in the material world. If we adopt panpsychism we may assert the existence of psychic antecedents to every sensation, but these would not, of

course, exist *us* '

The example of memory shows us that psychology, like its sister sciences, has its phenomena and conceptions. This is only a reiteration of the fact that sciences do not differ in their method, but only in their material. For the sake of simplicity we have so far spoken of the subconscious as if it were also conceptual in character, but this position now requires considerable qualification.

It is of fundamental importance to recognize the fact that different authors when they speak of the subconscious not only speak from different points of view, but speak of totally different things. Morton Prince has pointed out that "the term subconscious is commonly used in the loosest and most reprehensible way to define facts of a different order, interpretations of facts, and philosophical theories" (9). Hence it is meaningless to predicate any statement of the subconscious as a whole without first defining the sense in which we are employing the term. Dr. Prince has enunciated its various meanings in his prefatory note. By Stout and others the term is used to denote those marginal portions of the field of consciousness which are not at the moment in the focus of attention. Here subconscious merely means "dimly conscious." Myers ascribes to the subconscious various supernatural properties which take his conception altogether beyond the limits of science. We have already dealt with Hartmann's picture of the subconscious as a second self comparable in all respects to the personal consciousness. The remaining meanings are best illustrated by the doctrines of Janet and Freud, and we must now proceed to examine these at some length.

in the *individual* consciousness. In the present state of our knowledge such a speculation takes us beyond the limits of utility, and therefore of science. Panpsychism may, however, be regarded as the Utopia of the psychologist. We have actual experience only of our own conscious phenomena—we deduce the conscious phenomena of others by means of analogy in two ways, directly from what they tell us through the medium of speech, indirectly from their actions. Now the subconscious

It may be maintained that our knowledge of the conscious phenomena of others is therefore really conceptual in character, as we ourselves have no actual of Janet and his followers does not differ in its essential nature from any "conscious phenomena of others" with which we are acquainted—its existence is deduced on precisely the same grounds. This fact has been ably demonstrated by Dr. Prince in his contribution to the symposium. If we hold a conversation with a patient whose hand at the same moment writes of matters which are unknown to the personality, we speak of the subconscious phenomena attending the writing for the very same reason that we speak of the conscious phenomena attending the patient's conversation. The distinction of the subconscious lies solely in the fact that it is dissociated from certain other "conscious phenomena of others," which we designate as the personality. The subconscious of Janet is, therefore, a phenomenal fact. It may be reduced in complexity to even a single idea, but it remains a phenomenon. Janet himself has remarked, "These diverse acts are identical with those which we are accustomed to observe in persons like ourselves and to explain by the intervention of intelligence. Undoubtedly one may say that a somnambulist is only a mechanical doll, but then we must say the same of every creature. The term 'doubling-of-consciousness' is not a philosophical explanation; it is a simple clinical observation of a common character which these phenomena present." (10) experience of them. If conceptual is taken in an indefinitely wide sense this is of course true. But such deductions are on an altogether different plane from the conceptions of science. Relatively to the conceptions of science they are phenomena, just as helium in the sun is a phenomenon—and both science and everyday life are compelled to treat them as such. To refuse to subscribe to this point of view would involve the adoption of Solipsism.

If, however, we now turn to the views of Freud and Jung, we meet again with the phenomenon of dissociation, but we find added thereto a mass of conceptions of an altogether different character. Limitations of space prohibit any adequate description of these doctrines, and we must therefore assume that our readers are already acquainted with their main features. We are here only concerned with the general conceptions underlying Freud's teaching, and these may, perhaps, be described in our own terminology as follows: The subconscious *unbewusstsein)* is regarded as a sea of unconscious ideas and emotions, upon whose surface plays the phenomenal consciousness of which we are personally aware. These unconscious ideas are agglomerated into groups with accompanying affects, the systems thus formed being termed "complexes." These complexes are regarded as possessing both potential and kinetic energy, and thus are capable of influencing the flow of phenomenal consciousness according to certain definite laws. The nature of their influence is dependent upon the relation they have to each other and to the normally dominating or ego complex. The complex may either cause the direct introduction into consciousness of its constituent ideas and affect, or its influence may be distorted and indirect. The indirect effects may be of the most various types—symbolisms, word forgetting, disturbance of the association processes, etc. A single idea or image in consciousness may be conditioned (constellated) by a multiplicity of unconscious complexes.

All this is surely very different from anything that we have hitherto considered. In what does this difference consist? What is an "unconscious idea"—is not this a meaningless self-contradiction? Has anybody ever experienced an "unconscious complex"? The answer to all these questions is simple—we are no longer on the phenomenal plane, we have ascended to the conceptual. Unconscious ideas and complexes are not phenomenal facts, they are concepts, constructions devised to explain certain phenomena—they have not been found, they have been made. The implicit assumptions in Freud's doctrines may be expressed as follows: If we imagine certain entities which may be described as unconscious ideas and complexes, if we ascribe certain properties to these entities, and assume them to act according to certain laws—then we shall find that the results thus deduced will coincide with the phenomena which occur in actual human experience. This train of thought is the analogue of that underlying all the great conceptual constructions of physical science—the atomic theory the wave theory of light, the law of gravity, and the modern theory of mendelian heredity

We thus owe to Freud the first consistent attempt to construct a conceptual psychology. The attempt is, moreover, a legitimate employment of the method of science, the construction of a conceptual model which will enable us to resume our experience. It is, of course, true that conceptions have to be employed therein which cannot even be conceived as having a phenomenal existence. But we have seen that the same statement is equally true of the conceptions of physics. An unconscious idea is a phenomenal impossibility just as a weightless, frictionless ether is a physical phenomenal impossibility. It is no more and no less unthinkable than the mathematical conception-1. But objections of this kind do not in the least vitiate the use of phenomenal impossibilities as scientific concepts; the utility of such conceptions in physical science will surely suffice to demonstrate this. It is only necessary to clearly understand that we are speaking of concepts and not of phenomena.

Similarly when we speak of "complexes" we mean that it is convenient to conceive that ideas are bound together into systems, that these systems persist in the mind, although we are not conscious of them, and that they exert an influence upon the flow of phenomenal consciousness of which we may or may not be aware. The complex may be said to be the psychological analogue of the conception of force in physics. Strictly speaking, it can never itself become a fact of experience, a portion of phenomenal consciousness. Certain ideas, affects, and conative tendencies belonging to the complex may become facts of experience, we may be aware that we possess the complex—but the complex as a whole and as a directing force can never be actually experienced, it is a pure conception. This may be seen, for example, in what may be termed the "political complex." When the party politician is called upon to consider a new measure, his verdict is largely determined by certain constant systems of ideas and trends of thought which we refer to as his "political complex." He may be honestly convinced that he is influenced solely by an unbiased consideration of the pros and cons of the measure in question, but the psychologist knows that this is not really so. Even if the politician is aware that he is biassed, this complicated system we have described can hardly be present as a whole to his mind. The "political complex" is not conscious, and it is equally impossible that it can be co conscious. It is merely a conception which enables us to explain the fact that when a certain man is confronted with a political situation he will tend to act in a certain constant direction.

We cannot agree with Dr. Prince when he says, "What is it that binds the mental experience of an emotional railroad accident, an obsession, or of a subject or mood complex, or whatever kind of association it be into a system? The answer must be sought in the nervous system, not in the mind" (n). We should prefer to say that it must be sought in the conceptual sphere, not in the phenomenal.

The conception of the complex is not, except in name, an altogether new departure in psychology. James's description of the various "selfs" (12) which determine a man's action can be immediately translated into the language of complexes. Similarly Hoffding, when discussing the theories of the Associationists, has pointed out that "in the process of association it is the connected whole which exercises its powers over the single ideas" (13) The lack of a perceptual equivalent to many of Freud's conceptions is very striking

when we peruse such a work as the "Traumdeutung." Here the individual dream image is conceived as being constellated by a large number of unconscious complexes—as a result of the combination and interaction of these complexes the single image emerges into consciousness. Can we form any idea of a state of mind in which all this mass of mental elements is actually and phenomenally present? We have no evidence whatever of their phenomenal existence, such evidence as we had, for example, in the case of automatic writing previously considered. Freud has himself remarked on this point, "How can one picture to oneself the psychical condition during sleep? Do all the dream thoughts (subsequently elicited by analysis) actually exist together, or after one another, or do they constitute different contemporaneous streams finally coalescing? In my opinion, there is no necessity for us to attempt the construction of a picture of the psychic state during dream formation. We must not forget that we are speaking of unconscious thinking, and this may quite possibly proceed altogether differently from the conscious thinking with which we are acquainted" (14). Similar considerations apply to Freud's description of the mechanism of word-forgetting, mistakes in speaking, etc.

It is this very aspect of Freud's teaching which has aroused so much opposition, because the introduction of conceptual psychology has seemed so strange to those who have been accustomed to leave psychology its phenomena, but to hand over its concepts to physiology.

All these difficulties vanish at once when we remember that we are speaking of concepts and not of phenomena. We are no more called upon to picture what a mass of simultaneous unconscious ideas may be like, than a physicist is called upon to picture what an ether without weight and without friction may be like. It is of the utmost importance that the phenomenal and conceptual should be sharply distinguished when dealing with these questions. The neglect of this principle has, we believe,

led to that confusion of terminology and treatment stigmatized by Dr. Prince in his communication upon the Subconscious at the recent Geneva Congress. It is best to limit the term subconscious to the phenomenal facts demonstrated by Janet, and to speak of Freud's conception as the "unconscious," the literal translation of the German *Unbewusstsein*.

Scott (15) has objected that Freud's doctrine has revived an atomistic theory of psychology—but all sciences are compelled to more or less arbitrarily divide phenomenal continua into artificial elements. They demand, in fact, a "continuity of conception together with a conceived discontinuity of the material. " The conceptual theory of the unconscious is, moreover, constructed on an altogether different plane to the philosophical system of the old Associationists, in which the elements were regarded as real, and the unity of the whole as unreal.

It must be definitely understood that we are making no attempt to demonstrate the validity of Freud's conceptions. Such an aim lies entirely outside the scope of the present paper. Our sole concern is to show that his conceptions are cast within the legitimate framework of science, and that they have all the properties which science demands that a concept shall have. But if this be so, then the validity of Freud's theories must be tested by the method which has established all the conceptions of science, the method of experiment and verification. They cannot be proved or disproved by *a priori* considerations. The conceptions must be applied, and the results thus deduced must be compared with the results which are actually found. The truth of a scientific conception is neither more nor less than its utility in enabling us to resume and predict our experience.

We must now proceed further and endeavor to determine the relation between Janet's *subconscious* and Freud's *unconscious*. This relation is often held to be one of rivalry, but if our analysis of the two doctrines is correct, this view must be erroneous. There can be no rivalry between a description of the phenomenal facts, and a conceptual model constructed to resume these facts. The phenomenon of dissociation has not been disputed by Freud—on the contrary, it takes a prominent place amongst the circumstances which he desires to explain. His work lies on a deeper plane, his aim is not a description of the facts, but the conceptual explanation of these facts. We have here, in fact, that progression by which the method of science is invariably characterized. Firstly, the collection and classification of facts, represented here by the co-ordinated description of the phenomena of the subconscious or co-conscious; secondly, the construction of a conceptual model to explain these facts, represented by the theories of Freud. Precisely analogous advances are to be found in the history of physics. Kepler, for example, by classifying the successive positions in space of the planets, demonstrated that each moved in an ellipse, one of whose foci was occupied by the sun. Newton subsequently explained this fact by the construction of the law of gravity. It must be carefully observed that we have spoken throughout of the relation of Freud's doctrines to Janet's conception of the subconscious, not to Janet's work as a whole. There can be no question that this larger relation is to a considerable extent one of conflict. But this conflict only arises when Janet leaves the phenomenal plane and proceeds to construct conceptual generalizations. Thus his views on the essential nature of hysteria and psychasthenia, the separation of the latter as a distinct entity, the origin of obsessions, and other similar points—these cannot be reconciled altogether with the teaching of Freud. But whatever the ultimate verdict on these theories may be, Janet's indestructible monument will always be his vindication of the psychological method, his demonstration of the phenomena of dissociation, and a description of the facts of hysteria which has never been excelled in the history of psychiatry.

We are now in a position to summarize the results of our investigation: The word *subconscious* has been used by various authors to denote facts belonging to altogether different categories, and it is necessary in the interests of clearness that a terminology should be devised which will obviate this confusion. Excluding those speculative interpretations which do not enter into the field of science, these facts may be grouped under three heads. Firstly, the marginal elements of phenomenal consciousness (the *subconscious* of Stout), secondly, dissociated portions of phenomenal consciousness (the *co-conscious* of Morton Prince, and the *sub-conscious* of Janet), thirdly, a non-phenomenal conceptual construction designed to explain the facts of phenomenal consciousness (the *unconscious* of Freud). All these form part of the material of psychology, none of them form part of the material of physiology.

BIBLIOGRAPHY 1. Schopenhauer. Satz vom Grunde. 2. Helmholtz. Die Tatsachen in der Wahrnehmung. 3. Hartmann. Das Unbewusste, quoted by Janet, Journ. Of Abnorm. Psychol., June, 1907. 4. Höffding. Hisory of Philosophy, p. 583. 5. Münsterberg. Psychology and Life, p. 127. 6. Pearson. Grammar of Science, 2d ed., p. 281. 7. *Ibid.* 8. Mach. "De la Physique et de la Psychologie," L'ann£e Psychologique, 1906. 9. Morton Prince. "The Subconscious," Comtes Rendus, Geneva Congress of Psychology, 1909. 10. Janet. "The Subconscious," Journ. Of Abnorm. Psychol., June, 1907. 11. Prince. "The Unconscious," Journ. Of Abnorm. Psychol., Oct., 1908. 12. James. Principles of Psychology, Vol. 1, p. 291. 13. Höffding. The Problems of Philosophy, p. 18. 14. Freud. Die Traumdeutung, p. 205. 15. Scott. "An Interpretation of the Psycho-analytic Method in Psychotherapy," Journ. Of Abnorm. PsyChol., Feb., 1909.

CPSIA information can be obtained at www.ICGtesting.com
Printed in the USA
LVOW03s1221190515

438918LV00031B/396/P

9 781230 239835

RACING POST
ANNUAL 2017

Racing Post One Canada Square, London E14 5AP. 020 7293 2001
Irish Racing Post The Capel Building, Mary's Abbey, Dublin 7. 01 828 7450

Editor Nick Pulford
Art editor David Dew
Cover design Jay Vincent
Other design Peter Gomm, James Pugh, Daniel Hill, Paul Fielder, Andrew Pennington, Ross Clarke
Chief photographers Edward Whitaker, Patrick McCann
Other photography Dan Abraham, Morhaf Al Assaf, Alain Barr, Debbie Burt, Gerry Cranham, Mark Cranham, Steve Davies, Getty, John Grossick, Julian Herbert, Caroline Norris, Louise Pollard, Matthew Webb
Picture editor David Cramphorn
Graphics Samanatha Creedon, Stefan Searle
Picture artworking Nigel Jones, Stefan Searle
Feature writers James Burn, Scott Burton, David Carr, Graham Dench, Steve Dennis, Andrew Dietz, Alastair Down, Katherine Fidler, Nicholas Godfrey, Jack Haynes, Daniel Hill, David Jennings, Tom Kerr, Richard Lowther, Jack McCarron, Tony McFadden, Keith Melrose, Lee Mottershead, Julian Muscat, Lewis Porteous, Nick Pulford, Stuart Riley, Mark Scully, Brian Sheerin, Mark Storey, Alan Sweetman, Peter Thomas
Contributors Mark Bowers, Steve Mason, John Randall, Peter Scargill, Martin Smethurst, Sam Walker

Advertisement Sales
Racing Post: One Canada Square, London E14 5AP.
020 8263 0226 Cheryl Gunn, cheryl.gunn@racingpost.com

Archant Dialogue
Advertising Sales
Gary Stone, 01603 772463, gary.stone@archantdialogue.co.uk
Advertising Production Manager
Kay Brown, 01603 772522, kay.brown@archantdialogue.co.uk
Prospect House, Rouen Road, Norwich NR1 1RE. 01603 772554
archantdialogue.co.uk

Distribution/availability
01933 304858 help@racingpost.com

Published by Racing Post Books
27 Kingfisher Court, Hambridge Road, Newbury, Berkshire RG14 5SJ

ISBN 978-1-910498-73-6 [UK]
ISBN 978-1-910498-74-3 [Ireland]

Printed in Great Britain by Buxton Press. Every effort has been made to fulfil requirements with regard to copyright material. The author and publisher will be glad to rectify any omissions at the earliest opportunity.

www.racingpost.com/shop

Welcome to the Racing Po
'It was some year, w

The headline is a quote from Nicky Henderson as he reflects on Sprinter Sacre's magnificent comeback in a moving and revealing article in this book, and he might have been talking about 2016 as a whole rather than simply from his own perspective as the proud trainer of a popular hero who rose again to great acclaim.

Welcome to the Racing Post Annual, which once again is packed with the best horses and stories of the year. This is our sixth year and, as usual, we hope this book captures the essence of the racing year – the memorable moments and the horses and people who made them happen.

We start with a blank canvas of 208 pages each year but this sport's enduring capacity to excite, entertain and enthral soon brings colour and life to these pages. On the very first day of 2016 came two significant news items – Sir Anthony McCoy's knighthood in the New Year's Honours (see pages 20-21) and racing's move from Channel 4 to ITV starting in January 2017 (pages 138-140) – and by the end of the year we are bulging with great stories.

Brilliant photography, too, from the Racing Post's Edward Whitaker and Patrick McCann, whose pictures adorn our pages. Their images capture the heart and soul of the sport from the racecourse to work mornings, as well as the great bond between horses and people.

Nowhere was that bond more evident this year than between Henderson and Sprinter Sacre, who lit up the jumps season with his rediscovered brilliance. In the article starting on page 22, the trainer hails that comeback as the standout achievement of his career. Other great training feats included Aidan O'Brien's Arc 1-2-3 (pages 4-9), Dermot Weld's Derby first with Harzand (pages 112-115) and the title battle between Paul Nicholls and Willie Mullins (pages 38-41).

Racing success, thankfully, is never restricted to the big yards and we also celebrate the achievements of Laura Mongan with Harbour Law (pages 116-119), Cheltenham Festival first-time winners (pages 102-108), Michael Dods with Mecca's Angel (pages 142-143), Kerry Lee (pages 158-159) and John Bridger with the ageless Megalala (pages 166-167).

All the equine stars of the year are here, including Annie Power (pages 48-53), Don Cossack (pages 54-58) and Thistlecrack (pages 94-98) over jumps and Minding (pages 12-14), Almanzor (pages 16-17) and Postponed (pages 18-19) on the Flat. Stories of human interest too, from first-time champions Richard Johnson (pages 30-36) and Jim Crowley (page 14) to the Queen's Royal Ascot triumph (pages 66-70) and the emotional backgrounds of National-winning trainer Mouse Morris (pages 84-90), Adam Kirby (pages 60-65) and Brodie Hampson (pages 162-163).

As usual, we look ahead with relish to the new year with the Annual 20, our regular selection of horses and people to watch in 2017. May the next year be as good as this one.

Nick Pulford, Editor

CONTENTS

60

84

128

116

199

ARC OF TRIUMPH

By Peter Thomas

NO sporting accomplishment, however mighty, will last forever – sic transit gloria mundi, and all that – but where some can be aptly contained within an annual of this nature, so others require a more permanent memorial to do them justice. For the exalted few, inclusion in the Racing Post Centennial will in time be no more than they deserve.

Thirty-three years on, Michael Dickinson's Famous Five is still spoken of in tones of hushed awe. Wherever racing people are gathered together around a tap-room table, the prodigious feats of Dr MV O'Brien are discussed with the reverence usually reserved for an especially good Pope.

Lester Piggott is afforded just such veneration, along with his magnificent counterpart Frankie Dettori, but the number of the called who are ultimately chosen is a tiny one, and admission into that number requires a momentous body of work capped by an achievement that will endure across generations.

Aidan O'Brien had long since been recognised as one of the great trainers of the age, even before the events of October 2, 2016. Historically – or at least since he started training at Ballydoyle in 1996 – the son of County Wexford had assembled such a cast of high achievers at his Tipperary yard that names and dates seemed almost to merge into each other in an unending blur of accomplishment.

From Australia to Rock Of Gibraltar and from Johannesburg to Camelot, the names and places filled the history books of Irish and British racing – not to mention an entire atlas of other Turf jurisdictions – to the extent that this year we even began to talk of unofficial world records.

O'Brien, still a couple of weeks shy of his 47th birthday, was hailed as the most prolific trainer of Group 1 winners of all time. Had his moment of overarching glory in Chantilly not arrived when it did, 2016 might have been

▸▸ *Continues page 6*

Aidan O'Brien's 1-2-3 in the Prix de l'Arc de Triomphe was a feat to rank alongside Dettori's Magnificent Seven, Dickinson's Famous Five and Piggott's nine Derby winners

remembered as the year of his hot pursuit of Bobby Frankel's mark of 25 Group 1 wins in a season.

But O'Brien's 19th, while it represented no statistical landmark, lighted out for new territory in the same way that his namesake Vincent had done five decades earlier.

****

BEFORE the first Sunday in October, Aidan O'Brien's season had been a proverbial curate's egg: good in parts but a bit off in some of the areas where it mattered.

Minding's two Classics and four Group 1s had lit up the summer, but her defeat in the Irish Champion Stakes had to wait until Champions Day to be avenged by glorious victory over the colts in the QEII.

The Classic colts, meanwhile, had their limitations exposed far earlier in the campaign, with only The Gurkha's Poule d'Essai des Poulains victory to show for their efforts after US Army Ranger and Idaho had been swept aside by Harzand in the Derby.

Steadily, however, the seeds of glory were being sown, although not necessarily in ground that had looked to be the most fertile. The filly Found was not by any stretch of the imagination a Coolmore superstar as the autumn set in, having seemingly peaked with her Breeders' Cup Turf win of 2015 and landed a sole Curragh Group 3 in the spring before five times finding one too good for her as the season progressed, including in the Irish Champion behind Almanzor.

Suggestions of any unwillingness to succeed were not ventured within earshot of O'Brien, of course, but she was beginning to reach the stage where defeat had become the rule rather than the exception.

Highland Reel had already paid his way by landing the King George at Ascot, but that was a race shorn of the talents of Postponed, who soon put the pretender in his place when they met at York the following month, as did Almanzor at Leopardstown.

Likewise Order Of St George had done his bit by landing the Ascot Gold Cup, but while the Irish contingent were no doubt happy to celebrate the Queen's 90th birthday in

such fitting fashion, the same colt's defeat at 1-7 in their domestic St Leger would have done little to convince them they had a genuine Group 1 middle-distance performer on their hands.

To compound matters, Ryan Moore had, rightly or wrongly, spent a rare spell in the stocks for his rides both in the Irish Leger and on Minding in the Irish Champion, and although it wasn't as if Ballydoyle was about to implode with under-achievement, O'Brien went into the Arc with a side that looked a little more Europa League than Champions League.

****

O'BRIEN had been forced to wait an age for his first Prix de l'Arc de Triomphe win in 2007, after Kieren Fallon had charted an uncompromising course through the field to score by a head from Youmzain, prompting interminable deliberations among the French stewards.

Nine years later he was still waiting for his second, and standing in his path was the formidable figure of four-time Group 1 winner Postponed, who unlike the Ballydoyle contingent
▶ Continues page 8

▶Road to the Arc: (clockwise from left) Order Of St George wins the Ascot Gold Cup; Found is second to My Dream Boat in the Prince of Wales's Stakes; Highland Reel after winning the King George VI and Queen Elizabeth Stakes; (below) O'Brien's first Arc winner Dylan Thomas

'EXTRAORDINARY'
WHAT THEY SAID ABOUT O'BRIEN'S ARC 1-2-3

"It's one of those unique things, like Frankie's seven and Dickinson's five. The first three in an Arc is quite incredible – to get all three there in top shape and beat the best around. It's the hardest race to win in Europe every year" *Ryan Moore, rider of Found*

"These things can't happen but sometimes they do. It was an amazing training feat. He's a master trainer, without any doubt" *Michael Tabor, part-owner of Found*

"How could you say anything is higher than this? It's the most difficult race. For that to happen is incredible" *Aidan O'Brien*

"It's an extraordinary achievement, absolutely phenomenal" *Freddy Head, trainer and four-time Arc-winning jockey*

"I'm part of history – I was one of the three. I don't think we'll see that again in the Arc. To have the first, second and third is amazing" *Frankie Dettori, rider of Order Of St George and four-time Arc-winning jockey*

"It's possibly the most extraordinary achievement ever on the Flat. To have the first three in the toughest race is absolutely magic. The man is a genius" *Henry Candy, Group 1-winning trainer on Arc day*

THE LEADING SIRE IN AMERICA
2014 | 2015 | 2016

RANKED #3 ON THE TURF SIRE LIST IN 2016
AMONG ACTIVE SIRES IN NORTH AMERICA

2016 GRADE 1 WINNERS INCLUDE
FROSTED, CREATOR, TIME AND MOTION,
SWEET LORETTA AND PRETTY CITY DANCER

2017

TAPIT | EMPIRE MAKER | TO HONOR AND SERVE
KARAKONTIE | TAPIZAR | HAT TRICK
AFLEET ALEX | BIRDSTONE

www.gainesway.com

FOUND: IRON LADY AND ARC WINNER

Aidan O'Brien once had the Iron Horse, Giant's Causeway, who ran and ran through the 2000 season with ten races from April to November, including nine consecutive Group or Grade 1 contests.

A decade and a half later he has Found, the Iron Lady, and in some ways she is even more remarkable. Whereas Giant's Causeway went through the Classics, into all-age competition and ultimately to narrow defeat on dirt in the Breeders' Cup Classic before retirement at the end of his three-year-old campaign, Found has demonstrated her iron constitution in not just one but two tough seasons.

Having also finished up at the Breeders' Cup – after eight races as a three-year-old – Found not only managed to conquer America with her Turf victory at Keeneland, she also did something else Giant's Causeway did not: she came back to do it all over again.

By the time she reached the Prix de l'Arc de Triomphe, she was on her eighth race of the year and a remarkable 12th Group 1 contest since the start of 2015. Of course, she had become known as a serial loser at the top level – nine times second in her last 11 Group 1s – but she had just run the race of her life behind Almanzor in the Qipco Irish Champion Stakes (122 on Racing Post Ratings) and was almost guaranteed to be on her game again at Chantilly.

'Almost guaranteed' because the one poor run of her life – the only time she had finished outside the first three in 18 starts – had been her ninth place in the 2015

Arc. A troubled passage through the race had been blamed then and there were concerns over whether the draw would compromise the O'Brien trio (in stalls 11, 12 and 16) at Chantilly, but Ryan Moore was always well placed this time. "I had the horses I wanted around me in my sights," he said afterwards.

Moore led two furlongs out, putting more faith in Found's resolution than many punters, and this time she would not find one too good for her. She was too good for all the rest.

"She's been frustrating sometimes, but this was probably the main aim all year, she was in the best shape today," Moore said. "She was back to a mile and a half, it was an evenly run race, and she showed what she's capable of. At her best she's a very hard filly to beat."

This was Found at her best, with Racing Post Ratings upgrading her again to a career-high 124. That still made her the joint-lowest-rated Arc winner in the history of RPRs alongside Urban Sea (1993) and Solemia (2012) – some distance off top-class female winners such as Treve (131 at her peak in 2013) and Zarkava (129 in 2008).

With Found, however, it is not all about the ratings. The other figures that count are the number of times she turned out on the big stage and fought her hardest, against all manner of competition and over various distances.

While Solemia is already fading from memory and Urban Sea is lauded more for her achievements as a broodmare than a racemare, Found's durability and her moment of triumph in the Arc will not be easily forgotten.

arrived at the top of his form with six consecutive successes behind him, stretching back to the 2015 King George.

The 15-8 favourite had still to convince some pundits he was the real deal, but in regular bridesmaid Found he was facing a brave but clearly beatable 6-1 shot, while Almanzor, the pick of the French, had been withdrawn from the race by Jean-Claude Rouget and the best of the rest of the home team appeared to be Andre Fabre's 12-1 shot New Bay.

Japanese raiders always attract interest these days, but there seemed to be none of the mania behind Makahiki that had followed the likes of Deep Impact across the globe, and it was left to Derby hero Harzand to fill the berth of second favourite at 11-2, while Highland Reel at 20-1 and Order Of St George at 14-1 occupied the middle ground.

Clearly it wasn't the best Arc field ever assembled, and the change of venue forced by the razing and rebuilding of Longchamp left some turfistes disorientated, but Chantilly, a grateful benefactor and gracious host, was rewarded with a full-blooded bout of racing history.

Against the fittingly regal backdrop of the famous Chateau de Chantilly and the Great Stables, the Aga Khan's Vedevani set a generous pace for Harzand and ploughed into a clear lead three furlongs from home, hotly pursued by Frankie Dettori on Order Of St George.

Postponed had tracked the leader closely, if a little widely, and seemed well placed to mount a fierce challenge, but his effort petered out as quickly as it had begun; New Bay's threat on the outer proved to be an empty one; and Harzand was shuffled backwards into a lacklustre ninth. As they floundered, Ryan Moore, always handy on the rail tracking The Grey Gatsby and Highland Reel, threaded the eye of the needle to take the lead on Found with almost two furlongs to run.

There was to be no doubting Found's resolution as she was urged on by the world's finest big-race practitioner, and in behind her the full extent of the drama began to reveal itself.

Highland Reel, lacking the pace to

go with Found as she made her thrust, persevered down the outer under Seamie Heffernan, passing Postponed with unlikely ease; Dettori, having been similarly tapped for toe, followed the winner down the rail and stayed on resolutely to see off Siljan's Saga for third. As he watched, O'Brien might have felt similar emotions to Dickinson as his Famous Five galloped into history. "Come on my boys," Dickinson had yelled; the difference for O'Brien was that the one out in front was a girl.

****

THAT the fourth-placed horse was able to finish among the principals at odds of 100-1 perhaps took a little of the gloss off the status of the event, but such quibbles were an irrelevance to a feverish crowd of visiting fans and those academics sharpening their quills to rewrite the annals.

Aidan O'Brien had saddled the first three home in Europe's biggest Flat race. Where the extents of Group 1 tallies across hemispheres and centuries remain unofficial and quite possibly unresolvable, this was a feat that was utterly measurable and definitively unique.

For Moore, the only blemish on an otherwise flawless ride came when he allowed himself to be outmanoeuvred after the post by Dettori, who caught

him unawares and delivered a very public kiss, smack on the mouth of his good friend, in full public view, on horseback.

For O'Brien, however, there was no downside at all. His genius, formerly measured in terms of quality and quantity down the years, was suddenly encapsulated in a single race, set in the transparent amber of history for the benefit of generations to come.

On paper it was a length-and-three-quarters success for a bold filly in yet another top-grade race, the like of which O'Brien has won in time zones the world over; but in the eyes of the world this was a distillation of what it means to be the trainer who now wears the mantle of the greats.

It can be argued that with the ammunition O'Brien has, it's no wonder he has the winners he does, but the sheer volume of his success is surely enough to ward off such

▶ Happy day: Found in the winner's enclosure at Chantilly after leading home stablemates Highland Reel and Order Of St George in the Arc; Ryan Moore is congratulated by Aidan O'Brien (top right) and in more unexpected fashion by Frankie Dettori

negativity. Yes, he may have filled the first three slots in the Arc with three offspring of the mighty Galileo, but these were no bluebloods among mules – they were each-way shouts needing to be delivered cherry ripe after campaigns that could hardly be said to have been tailored to the occasion.

They were, in short, the contemporary equivalent of a Famous Five or a Magnificent Seven and will be remembered as such.

O'Brien declared his team's achievement as "incredible" and added, to nobody's surprise, that he was pleased for "the lads"; trainers of the calibre of Dermot Weld and Freddy Head queued up to pay tribute to a phenomenon; even Moore was effusive in his praise of the feat; but for the mot juste we should turn to Dettori, a man who knows a thing or two about sporting immortality. "I'm definitely part of history," he said. "I don't think it will be done again."

If it is, it may be done by the icon's son Joseph O'Brien, such is Aidan's ability to prepare the best to achieve the most; or it may be another young buck, perhaps as yet unborn, or at least unknown to all but his closest family.

But one thing is certain, when it is done, it will be a great trainer that does it.

'On paper it was a length-and-three-quarters success, but in the eyes of the world this was a distillation of what it means to be the trainer who now wears the mantle of the greats'

PACESETTER

Ryan Moore led his rivals
a merry dance in the
King George with
a masterclass of
front-running on
Highland Reel

By Graham Dench

TOWARDS the end of a glorious season for Ryan Moore in his association with Aidan O'Brien, the jockey was rated the world's best by a clear margin in a new set of global rankings. The standings, based on statistical analysis of the top Flat jockeys, were confirmation of what O'Brien already knew when he linked up with Moore and what racegoers around the globe have come to realise in recent years.

The rankings, developed by international website Thoroughbred Racing Commentary, use results from nearly 1,500 Group and Graded races staged each year in the major racing nations and have Racing Post Ratings as a key element. Moore came out top ahead of Frankie Dettori and other high-ranked European jockeys were Christophe Soumillon in fourth and Pat Smullen in ninth.

Nobody would have been surprised to see Moore at the top, especially not in this annus mirabilis for the jockey and his main stable. Time after time, on Found, Minding, The Gurkha and so many others, Moore delivered big-race successes for O'Brien. One of his most accomplished rides – seemingly simple yet brilliantly executed – brought victory in the King George VI and Queen Elizabeth Stakes on Highland Reel.

Some might argue there was nothing special about it. After all, Highland Reel had form as good as any in what was by no means a vintage field following the scratching with a respiratory infection of 2015 winner Postponed. With Postponed taken out of the field, so was his pacemaker. That meant there was every chance that Highland Reel, who at three had dictated throughout in the Secretariat Stakes at Arlington Park and also been happy to lead when winning the Hong Kong Vase, might not face too much pressure up front.

Yet what struck home after the race was that Moore had made it

Winning team: Aidan O'Brien and Ryan Moore collect their trophies after the success of Highland Reel (main picture) in the King George

all look almost routine. Yes, so routine that Britain's foremost middle-distance race, sponsored by Qipco and worth just short of £700,000 to the winner, was Moore's 70th top-level victory, and his 29th for O'Brien in a relationship that first flowered with the 33-1 success of Beethoven in the 2009 Dewhurst Stakes and has truly flourished in the last three seasons.

O'Brien has long recognised there is no better big-race jockey than Moore, whose tactical masterclasses have become his stock-in trade in the ten years since his career-first Group 1 win on Notnowcato in the 2006 Juddmonte International Stakes.

Taking Notnowcato across to race against the hedge on the stands side in the 2007 Eclipse, despite ground that was perceived to be drying out fast, was an early example of Moore's willingness to think outside the box and spring a surprise. The Derby winner Authorized was a 4-7 chance and widely expected to win, but Moore had walked the course and come up with a plan to thwart him.

On the other side of the world, in the 2014 Cox Plate, he dropped

Adelaide out at the start, from what many dismissed as an impossible draw, and then circled the field round the final bend before launching him with an irresistible challenge. Even the most partisan among the Australian press had to concede that Moore was a rare talent. Any number of other excellent rides, in Europe, America or Japan, have confirmed as much.

Clarity of thought characterises Moore's best rides and he showed it again on Highland Reel. While not showily impressive, it was a highly efficient piece of riding that gave his mount the best chance of success while at the same time reducing the percentages for his rivals.

Although Highland Reel's best form matched that of any of his six rivals, it certainly did not stand out, and at four he had been beaten already at Meydan, Sha Tin and Royal Ascot, most recently in the Hardwicke by the Queen's Dartmouth, who many expected to repeat the trick.

Dartmouth was favourite following Postponed's withdrawal in midweek, but the big hitters got stuck in to Highland Reel on

raceday and they never had much cause for concern.

Moore, whose only previous success in six rides on Highland Reel had come when the colt beat the older Flintshire at Sha Tin the previous December, knew exactly what was required and orchestrated affairs to perfection, with no need for the assistance that some might have been expecting from Seamie Heffernan on stable companion Sir Isaac Newton.

Jumping Highland Reel straight out in front from stall three, Moore was able to establish an easy lead without apparent effort. The colt raced a couple of lengths clear of John Gosden's three-year-old Wings Of Desire and French challenger Erupt, enjoying himself as he bowled along at just a steady pace with his ears pricked.

Pressing on running into Swinley Bottom, Highland Reel had suddenly stretched that lead to nearer five lengths over Wings Of Desire and, although his rivals were not panicking, they surely knew they had allowed the leader an advantage that would not be easily recovered.

Five furlongs from home Highland Reel came back to the

field, but Moore was just giving him a breather. The advantage over Wings Of Desire was no greater than two lengths turning for home, and the rest were close enough, but the writing was already on the wall.

Approaching the two-furlong marker, as Dettori attempted to launch his challenge on Wings Of Desire and Olivier Peslier angled out on Dartmouth, Moore kicked again and Highland Reel responded. Wings Of Desire got within a length or so, but Moore had saved plenty and Highland Reel was not holding back under hard driving.

Highland Reel passed the post a length and a quarter clear of Wings Of Desire to give O'Brien a fourth King George success, following those with the colt's sire Galileo, Dylan Thomas and Duke Of Marmalade.

Dartmouth, bidding to give the Queen a second win in a race she took in 1954 with Aureole, snatched third late on, but he was beaten a further two and three-quarter lengths and had never looked like getting on terms.

Nobody can say for sure that Postponed would have repeated his 2015 King George success had he been fit to race, but the evidence of the form book strongly suggests he would have done.

Postponed had beaten Highland Reel by more than four lengths into fourth when the pair had first met in the Dubai Sheema Classic at Meydan in March and he beat him fair and square once again, albeit by a reduced margin into second, less than four weeks after Ascot when they both dropped back in trip for York's Juddmonte International.

However, Highland Reel could do no more than beat those who were put before him at Ascot. Was he a great King George winner? Clearly not. But was it a great King George ride? Most definitely.

RACING POST ANNUAL 2017 11

In a glittering year for Aidan O'Brien, a relentless campaign that ended in QEII triumph showcased the wide-ranging talents of both the trainer and his filly

MAGICAL
MINDING

By David Carr

TEAM GB demonstrated perfect timing with 27 golds and 67 medals overall in Rio, the country's best in an overseas Olympics. Time after time, in event after event, British competitors showed their best form when it mattered most. Whether it was a cyclist or a rower, a gymnast or a diver, they all seemed to peak at exactly the right time in a four-year cycle.

Team A O'B – that's Aidan O'Brien's immensely strong Ballydoyle set-up – do things slightly differently. Yes, they can lay out a horse for the date that counts but they also have an uncanny knack of getting their best horses to peak time after time, not choosing between targets but grabbing them all.

The latest in a long line of tough as well as talented competitors that includes Giant's Causeway, Rock Of Gibraltar and Found is Minding, whose verve and versatility shone throughout the season. First she came through a busy Classics programme with spellbinding victories in the Qipco 1,000 Guineas and the Investec Oaks, and then she stepped up to beat the older fillies and mares. That was plenty, but O'Brien asked her another question in a red-hot Qipco Irish Champion Stakes, where she was third behind Almanzor and Found, and yet another by dropping her to a mile in the Queen Elizabeth II Stakes.

The QEII was her seventh Group 1 assignment of the year, five and a half months after the first, and she was back at a mile for the first time since May. That seemed an incredibly tough ask, even if she was 7-4 favourite on merit, yet O'Brien's judgement proved spot on once again.

He knew that last-time-out defeat in such a high-quality race was nothing to lose sleep over and he could see Minding was thriving, not wilting. "Her usual work rider got off her recently and said she couldn't believe the piece of work Minding had just done," he revealed after the QEII.

O'Brien was talking after being thoroughly vindicated by a performance from Minding that brought enormous satisfaction even in such an incredible season for his team. The QEII was a genuine championship event, contested by the winners of both Newmarket Guineas, both Irish Guineas, the Prix Jacques Le Marois and the Celebration Mile.

Yet Minding brushed her rivals aside, bursting clear well over a furlong out and quickly putting a couple of lengths between herself and the field. The fact that Ribchester had narrowed that margin to half a length at the line did not reflect the superiority of a filly who never looked in any danger of defeat.

Victory made Minding the first of her sex to land Britain's most important mile race since Milligram beat fellow three-year-old filly Miesque in 1987. She was succeeding where top-notchers such as Bosra Sham, Ridgewood Pearl and Kooyonga had failed in the interim. Just as notably, it was a first Champions Day success for Ryan Moore.

Yet the really remarkable aspect was that such a peerless display should come as the final flourish in a year already jam-packed with achievement.

There had been no gradual start to the season, taking things quietly with an eye to the future. Minding, favourite for the 1,000 Guineas since winning the Moyglare Stud Stakes and Fillies' Mile at two, went straight to Newmarket without a prep run and galloped to an imperious victory by three and a half lengths. In landing his third win in the race, O'Brien served notice of what was to come in 2016 by making it a 1-2-3 as Ballydoyle and Alice Springs filled the places behind their stablemate.

Short-odds backers had a reminder that there is no such thing as a certainty three weeks later when Minding was sent off 4-11 favourite for the Tattersalls Irish 1,000 Guineas. She banged her head coming out of the stalls, never looked quite as happy in the
▸ *Continues page 14*

▸ Girl on film: Minding after her victory in the Queen Elizabeth II Stakes (left) and (from top) winning the 1,000 Guineas, Oaks, Nassau and QEII

desperately testing conditions as Newmarket ninth Jet Setting and was beaten a head by that mudlark.

Minding shaped as though she would get a mile and a half, but where next? The Investec Derby trials failed to throw up a compelling contender from Ballydoyle among the colts, leading to speculation that the filly could be supplemented for the race, and she was favourite – 'with a run' – in some lists. It is fascinating to note with hindsight that Minding's peak Racing Post Rating of 123 – over a mile – ranks her higher than Epsom winner Harzand (124) once the 3lb fillies' allowance is taken into account.

The final decision to stick to the Oaks proved far from an easy option, even in a race weakened by the absence of main market rival So Mi Dar. Moore's mount was brought virtually to a standstill in scrimmaging at the top of the straight and dropped back to eighth and it was testament to her talent that she could produce the turn of foot needed to get herself out of trouble and catch Architecture in the final 300 yards for an ultimately comfortable triumph.

That burst of speed was again in evidence as she ran down the enterprisingly ridden Bocca Baciata in the Pretty Polly Stakes at the Curragh and again when she made short work of her rivals in the Qatar Nassau Stakes at Goodwood. After the QEII, O'Brien – like the rest of us – marvelled at her versatility. "To go from a mile, to a mile and a quarter, then a mile and a half, and then come all the way back to a mile for an all-age Group 1, they have to be very special to do those things."

The good news is that we should see Minding again in 2017. She has already won seven Group 1 races – matching the great Miesque as only the second filly to reach that total by the end of her three-year-old campaign – and a tantalising target is Australian sprinter Black Caviar's tally of 15. Such is her versatility that she could be aimed at the Lockinge, the Eclipse, the King George or the Champion Stakes next season. Such is her durability that Minding might take the lot and still come back for more.

HARD WORK PAYS OFF FOR CROWLEY

Jim Crowley almost achieved the impossible nearly two decades ago when he teamed up with a history-maker at Wetherby at the spring bank holiday meeting in 1998.

Nobody ever won on the legendary Quixall Crossett, who retired with a record 103 defeats to his name, yet that afternoon Crowley got nearer than anyone ever did, forcing the perennial loser into second place at 33-1 – going down by just two lengths on a chaser who usually did well to beat the ambulance home.

From being a bit part in a tale of historic failure, Crowley has been transformed into a huge success story and made history himself this year. On a rather more recent visit to the north-east of England, Crowley wrote two huge names out of the record books by scoring on Castleacre at Newcastle on the evening of September 30. It was his 46th winner of the month, passing the mark of 45 set by Fred Archer and Sir Gordon Richards.

That pretty much clinched a first Flat jockeys' title for Crowley, with 2015 winner Silvestre de Sousa soon admitting defeat and hailing one of the more surprising champions.

The surprise was not because of Crowley's origins as a jump jockey. Several have made a successful switch from jumping to Flat in recent years, with Dougie Costello the latest to make it to the Group 1 winner's enclosure in 2016 thanks to Quiet Reflection.

Instead, this was a tale of the unexpected because for much of the season it did not look as though it was going to be a good year for Crowley. Having switched from jumping in 2006, he was established as a top-ten jockey – top six in 2015 – but made a slow start to the latest campaign and did not get into that bracket until mid-July.

Yet having started the season as a 66-1 outsider he began to focus on the title after riding a treble at Glorious Goodwood that took him to within two of De Sousa. His 38 winners in August, during which he hit the front for the first time, would be considered remarkable were it not for what happened the following month and he ended the title race 16 clear with a total of 148.

Crowley, 38, was quick to pay tribute to the efforts of Tony Hind, having signed up the agent of former champions Ryan Moore and Richard Hughes with the express intention of gunning for the crown himself. Yet it was the jockey, not his rides-booker, who put in the hours in the saddle – and on the motorway – with a herculean effort that meant he ended the season with some astonishing statistics to his name.

With no huge stable backing him, he rode for no fewer than 143 different trainers, none of whom provided him with more than 18 winners individually. He rode on all bar four of Britain's Flat tracks and was successful on 25 of them. It was entirely typical that on the day after he had become mathematically certain to land the championship, he made the 600-mile round trip from his Sussex home to take six mounts at Redcar on the eve of Champions Day.

Crowley drew a rare blank there and on the final afternoon but was a thoroughly deserving recipient of the trophy presented by Olympic gold-medal-winning showjumper Nick Skelton at Ascot – just a few furlongs from where the jockey was born and brought up.

Despite the gruelling schedule that took him to the crown, he stressed that he had "enjoyed every minute" of the fight. "It's amazing, truly amazing. This is beyond my dreams," he said at Ascot. "You used to see McCoy going to Sedgefield for one ride. His work ethic rubbed off on me a bit. The harder it was, the better it was for me. I thrived on the workload."

SHADWELL STALLIONS

Muhaarar
Oasis Dream - Tahrir

£30,000 (1st JAN, SLF)

Mukhadram
Shamardal - Magic Tree

£7,000 (1st JAN, SLF)

Nayef
Gulch - Height Of Fashion

£5,000 (1st JAN, SLF)

MAN WITH A PLAN

Jean-Claude Rouget set his sights on a Champion Stakes double with Almanzor and was vindicated as the exciting colt proved himself the king of Europe

By Scott Burton

LITTLE more than half an hour before a climactic Qipco Champion Stakes, Jean-Claude Rouget lapses into 'manager speak' in the Ascot paddock. Rouget has been in Britain for most of the week since overseeing Almanzor's final work in Deauville and has been calmly repeating the mantra – mostly in English – that he is respectful yet not overawed by the opposition. Now, with a French camera crew looking for a final few *bon mots*, Rouget says: "The horse is well . . . I am quite calm . . . you must treat all races the same . . ."

In contrast to the colourful interviews Rouget has given during this miraculous season, filled not just with Almanzor but the unbeaten La Cressonniere and Royal Ascot winner Qemah, this is unusual for being restricted to what his countrymen routinely refer to as 'la langue du bois' ('wooden language').

In fact, Rouget, in common with racing professionals and fans alike, does not consider the imminent rematch with Found as just another race. Yet his calm facade does reveal the Frenchman's absolute conviction that

Almanzor has already come out on top in the race of the season when sweeping past Found and Minding at Leopardstown five weeks earlier.

Having decided to miss the Prix de l'Arc de Triomphe with Almanzor and come to Ascot instead, Rouget is about to be vindicated in spectacular style.

****

ROUGET hatched the plan to target the Champion Stakes double in the weeks following Prix du Jockey Club success for Almanzor, whose progress he admitted afterwards had been glimpsed out of the corner of one eye as he tracked shorter-priced stablemate Mekhtaal through his binoculars.

"I thought they had similar chances beforehand, though Almanzor was better drawn," he said at Chantilly. "I could see he had a good position but I spent most of the race watching Mekhtaal and it was only when it became obvious he wasn't going to pick up that I switched back."

Winning jockey and Rouget stalwart Jean-Bernard Eyquem had been the story that day, having been handed the ride when Christophe Soumillon was claimed to partner Zarak for the Aga Khan. Eyquem smothered his mount away on the rail and was able to take a pull, so well was Almanzor travelling, before taking his mount out four wide to launch what would, by the end of the season, come to be recognised as the colt's trademark finishing burst.

"At 400 metres I began to let him go," Eyquem recalled. "At 300 I felt he had loads left and by 250 metres out I knew I was going to win my first Jockey Club."

Zarak ran a brave race in second and his presence at Deauville in Rouget's choice of warm-up for the Irish Champion ensured that Eyquem was given a second opportunity. Once again Almanzor flew home.

So far so good. But a sizeable slice of the conventional wisdom held that Almanzor was at the head of a so-so crop of three-year-old colts in France, while even Rouget recognised that the Irish Champion was in an entirely different league. In no particular

order his colt would face the winners of the Epsom and Irish Derbies; the 1,000 Guineas and Oaks; the Eclipse; the King George and Hong Kong Vase; and the 2015 French Derby.

Soumillon was finally available to ride Almanzor and, at least publicly, was unwilling to venture a bolder prediction than an each-way chance in what was widely regarded as the race of the season. Such advance billing can often be counter-productive but Leopardstown delivered on that burning promise as Almanzor – with Soumillon motionless and Piggott-high in the saddle – and a Frankie Dettori-inspired Found swept through from well off a searing pace to leave rivals and spectators breathless after a thrilling finish.

Often reduced to tears at the moment of his biggest triumphs, Rouget gave a passable impression of a punter who had had his maximum on, rhythmically slapping his racecard against his palm and screaming at the top of his lungs before being

engulfed in victory celebrations by the rest of the Almanzor clan.

With the presentations done and at least part of his voice gone out and away somewhere in the direction of Grafton Street, Rouget said: "Of course I was delirious, that's normal. I could see he was going to do it and, although Found fought hard, he was always going to come out on top."

In this moment of great triumph, two opposing views began to crystallise. Here was a brand new star who appeared to hold any race in Europe at his mercy and Soumillon was adamant: "If you don't go to the Arc with a horse like this, you'll never go."

But Rouget's long career has made him wary of how fast you can run out of horse at the end of a hard season, as well as how difficult it is to back up such a performance three weeks later.

Told of Soumillon's comments, he remarked without a hint of rancour: "He is the jockey but I am the trainer."

Every swirl and eddy around Almanzor in the intervening five weeks would send fresh

⏵⏵ True champion: Christophe Soumillon pushes Almanzor clear in the Champion Stakes at Ascot, sparking celebrations in the winner's enclosure with trainer Jean-Claude Rouget (below)

waves crashing against the rock of Rouget's resolve. Injury to La Cressonniere revived the Arc debate and, although that was resisted, there was more talk after Found stormed to success on the first Sunday of October while Almanzor stood in his box up at Deauville.

****

TWO weekends later here is Rouget at what he frequently confesses to be his favourite venue, seemingly indifferent to the pressure of proving he was right to miss Chantilly and come to Ascot instead. Deep down, the 63-year-old is convinced this will be a more straightforward task than in Ireland.

With Ryan Moore back aboard Found, Soumillon is in no mood to showboat and commits early enough to ensure the suspense is not prolonged. Almanzor scores impressively by two lengths from Found, almost trebling the margin of victory in the Irish Champion. That is reflected in a Racing Post Rating of 129, a 2lb improvement on Leopardstown.

Suddenly there are French men and women everywhere as Almanzor surfs into the winner's enclosure on a wave of delighted connections. There are tears and double kisses but amid the joy Rouget has swapped delirium for quiet, professional satisfaction, gratefully receiving the congratulations of Aidan O'Brien, trainer of the runner-up.

"He doesn't have the pace for a mile and I have my doubts about his reserves for a mile and a half, so I think I made the right choice," Rouget says. "This is his trip and there are a lot of good races to be won over this distance at four."

Rendezvous for the Prince of Wales's Stakes at Royal Ascot next June, morning suit obligatory. Rouget is not likely to be changing his plans.

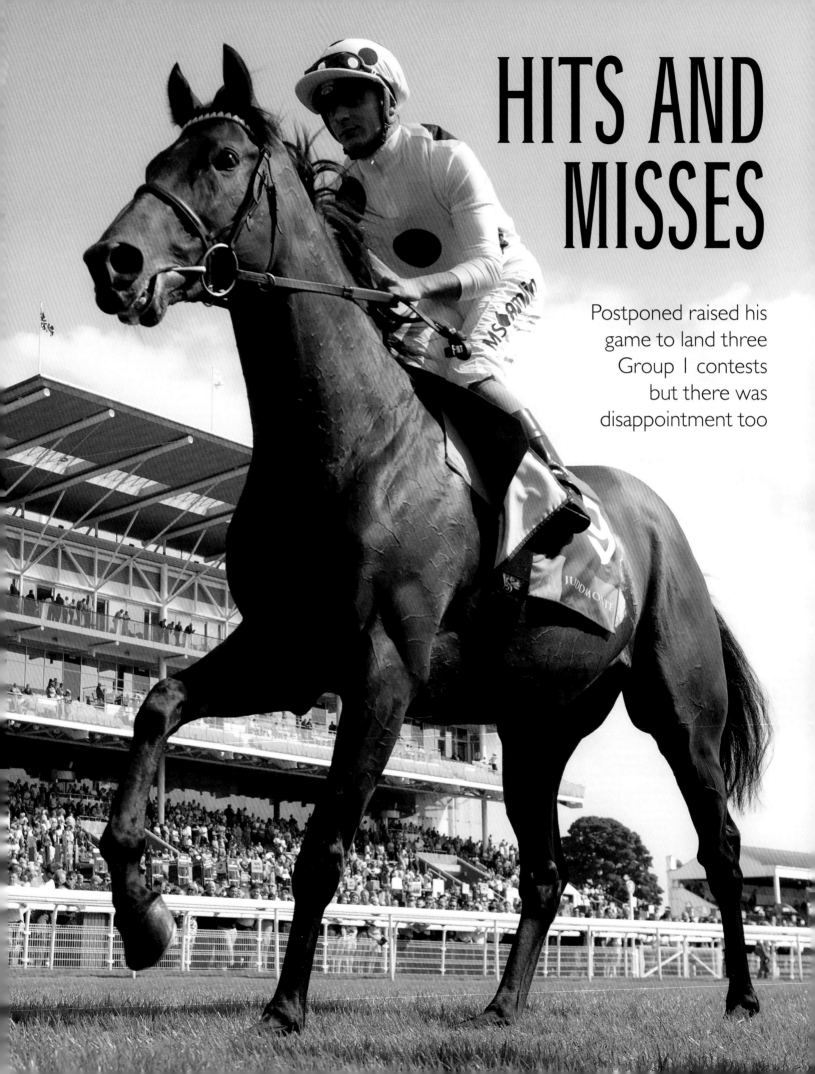

HITS AND MISSES

Postponed raised his game to land three Group 1 contests but there was disappointment too

By Nick Pulford

▶▶ Winning spree: (clockwise from top left) Postponed lands the Dubai Sheema Classic; another decisive victory in the Coronation Cup; in the York winner's enclosure after the International with owner Sheikh Mohammed Obaid, trainer Roger Varian, jockey Andrea Atzeni and Varian's wife Hanako

FOR a snapshot of any racing year and its main players, the most famous and prestigious races might be the first place to look. Over fences it could be the Cheltenham Gold Cup and the King George VI Chase; on the Flat the top middle-distance older horses might be identifiable from the results of the King George and the Prix de l'Arc de Triomphe. In which case Postponed would be missing from the picture of the class of 2016.

From early spring to midsummer, Postponed was unstoppable in high-level middle-distance races with four straight wins, including the Dubai Sheema Classic, the Coronation Cup and the Juddmonte International. Yet it was his misfortune that when it came to the two biggest races of the year he was missing either in body or spirit, denying him the opportunity to put his irrefutable stamp on the division.

The son of Dubawi had first arrived as a Group 1 force with victory in the 2015 King George VI and Queen Elizabeth Stakes and a repeat success appeared likely when he entered race week as the red-hot 1-2 favourite after an unbeaten 12 months. Three days before the race, however, he was ruled out with a respiratory infection and victory went to Highland Reel, who had been beaten by Postponed in Dubai and would be again at York.

That was one opportunity lost, but there was still the Arc. Again Postponed was favourite and this time he did line up, but he was not in the form that had seen him reach a career-high of 126 on Racing Post Ratings for his Group 1 sequence at Meydan, Epsom and York. He was a dull fifth, six and a half lengths behind Found, and that was rated 117 on RPR.

Roger Varian, his trainer, gave a typically cool-headed assessment a few days later. "There was a combination of variables regarding Postponed's performance in the Arc. He got a bit upset beforehand by the sport horse who was leading the parade and got a bit colty, which was not like him. He was also awkward around the bend in the race and didn't find what we expected in the straight."

The disappointment was intense, even if the reasons were valid after a season that had started for Postponed with a Group 2 prep-race win at Meydan on March 5, three weeks before Dubai World Cup night. In his Stable Tour with the Racing Post in April, Varian had named four races as possible targets: the Coronation Cup, Eclipse, King George and Arc. Postponed won the first of them but missed the next two and was below par in the fourth.

Timing is everything, and with Postponed it was the sense of disappointment that was left freshest in the memory at the end of the season. That was a shame because before that he had been the dominant force.

He had beaten the winners of the 2016 Arc, King George and Eclipse, sometimes more than once, and those who had written their names on the 2015 roll of honour in the International, Breeders' Cup Turf, St Leger, Hong Kong Vase and Japanese Derby. He was beating many of the best around, and beating them well.

The winning run started in the 2015 King George and continued on Arc trials day a few weeks later, but he did not run again that year. Nor did he run again for Luca Cumani following the decision of owner Sheikh Mohammed Obaid to move Postponed – and 34 other horses – across Newmarket to Varian's Kremlin House Stables.

That was a controversial decision but in this situation Varian could only get on with the job – "you can't afford to feel guilt," he said – and he did it impressively well. Postponed won his prep at Meydan by three lengths in his first outing for Varian and then was equally clinical in the Sheema Classic with a two-length victory over Japanese challenger Duramente, with Highland Reel beaten more than four lengths in fourth.

That was already a step up on his King George performance – 2lb better on RPR – and he continued at that level on his return to Britain. Varian took him to Epsom's 'Breakfast with the Stars' to give him a taste of the track before the Coronation Cup and was pleased with the response.

"The work got his blood pumping and he will have grown an inch," he said.

On his return to Epsom 11 days later for a race renamed in honour of the Queen's 90th birthday, Postponed proved Varian's point as he powered clear to leave Found four and a half lengths behind. Although Found had a reputation as a near eternal second, this was the furthest she had been beaten as a runner-up and it was achieved off a go-stop-go tempo by Postponed's pacemaker that did not seem ideal for the favourite.

The Eclipse was swerved to keep Postponed at a mile and a half for the King George but, after he was forced to miss Ascot, Varian dropped him in trip for the Juddmonte International over 1m2½f. Highland Reel and Hawkbill, having won the King George and Eclipse, were joint-second favourites at 6-1, with Postponed 15-8.

The betting reflected concern over the health of Varian's string – the stable star had been odds-on at Meydan and Epsom – but there was no stopping Postponed again. He took control almost three furlongs out and, despite edging across third-placed Mutakayyef, never looked likely to be beaten, with Highland Reel a length and a quarter behind in second.

"I'm not sure this is as spectacular as some of his other wins," Varian admitted, "but off the back of having had a setback and coming back in trip against a pretty deep field, he stamped himself as by far the best horse in the race."

With the doubts over the pace at Epsom and whether he was absolutely at his peak for York, there was reason to hope Postponed might produce his best performance of the year in the Arc but instead it was the worst. Never mind, there is always next season as he will stay in training as a six-year-old with the Sheema Classic as his first big target again.

Ultimately, Postponed could not stamp himself the clear leader in a division that lacked great quality and depth. In 2017 he will have another opportunity to claim the undisputed crown.

Arise, Sir Anthony as jump racing legend receives knighthood

As 2015 turned to 2016 came the news that 20-time champion jump jockey AP McCoy had been awarded a knighthood in the Queen's New Year's Honours list in recognition of his services to horseracing.

McCoy, who rewrote the record books during an extraordinary 23-year career in the saddle, spoke of his knighthood as being "the greatest honour that can be bestowed upon you".

Having been given the title Sir Anthony McCoy OBE, he was only the second jockey in history awarded a knighthood after Sir Gordon Richards in 1953.

"This is the pinnacle in terms of awards. It's a great honour for me and for my family. Mum and Dad are very proud," McCoy said.

"It's also great for the sport and great for jockeys. I know quite a lot about Sir Gordon Richards – I did get a bit obsessed with him for a period of time during my career – and it just goes to show what jockeys can achieve."

McCoy, 42, received his knighthood from the Princess Royal at Buckingham Palace on June 22.

After the ceremony McCoy, who was accompanied by wife Chanelle and children Evie and Archie, said: "It was a very special day for myself and my family as we all felt very honoured and privileged.

"It was absolutely great that the Princess Royal put the sword on my shoulder as we've known each other for a very long time. It's the only time in my life I've ever felt nervous in front of her." McCoy said she had told him she was "very honoured" to be conducting the ceremony.

He joked about his new title, saying: "It's only my close friends who I'm going to make call me Sir Anthony. I think everybody else can call me Tony or AP or whatever they like."

McCoy retired at the end of the 2014-15 jumps season with a career tally of 4,348 jumps winners, comprising 4,204 in Britain and 144 in Ireland.

He joined an elite band from racing who have been awarded a knighthood, alongside Richards, Sir Cecil Boyd-Rochfort, Sir Noel Murless, Sir Peter O'Sullevan and Sir Henry Cecil.

Sir Michael Stoute was knighted in 1998, but he received the honour in recognition of his services to tourism in his native Barbados, rather than for racing. Sir Mark Prescott is a hereditary baronet.

McCoy was appointed MBE in the 2003 Queen's Birthday Honours and OBE in the 2010 Birthday Honours for his services to racing.

Pictures: PA

Once the undisputed champion, Sprinter Sacre came back from the depths to land two knockout blows and regain his title in thrilling style

THE FIGHTER

By Steve Dennis

THE champ sat on his stool, his head low, his mind in a daze, blood from a cut above his eye running down his face like tears. Another round like the last one and it was all over. His cornerman moved in close, whispered in his ear. "Come on, champ. We can still win this. We don't quit in the corner. You're the king of the world, remember?" He reached for the towel and a gasp rose around the ring until the crowd saw he wasn't going to throw it in but use it to wipe the blood gently from his fighter's face. "Come on champ, one more round. Just like old times." And the bell rang, and the champ stood up.

Sprinter Sacre had been in the wars. First the health goes, then the reputation follows. In the summer of 2013 he had a ten-race winning streak over fences to his name and a Racing Post Rating that elevated him to greatness. Before the year was out his career had been wrecked by a heart problem, atrial fibrillation, a fast and erratic heartbeat. He spent a year in the wilderness, and when he finally returned to action he resembled a ghost from the past, the same name but not the same horse. He was all washed-up, a has-been, glass-jawed, heavy-legged, easy to hit. Finished.

"We don't give up easily in our neck of the woods," says trainer Nicky Henderson. "I thought he ran okay at Sandown at the back-end [of the 2014-15 season]. Our biggest hope was his vet, Celia Marr. She said that what happened at Kempton, the heart problem, would leave a mental scar, it wasn't a nice experience.

"So how long does it take a horse to get over it? It can take a long time. So maybe another summer might clear his memory of what happened.

"There was no pressure from Caroline [Mould], she was brilliant at a very tough time for her, the first season after [husband] Raymond died,

▸ *Continues page 24*

but Sprinter's rather ceased to be simply her horse and is pretty much public property really. That's why the downhill slide was so horrible because we were dealing with something that wasn't entirely ours.

"We did say that he would have to tell us he was all right, it would have to happen on a racecourse. If that hadn't happened, that would have been it. Retirement. And some would have said about time too. But there was always just that something there, something that said 'keep trying'."

The champ returned home to Lambourn after his summer holiday and Henderson's horseman's heart lifted immediately. One day, somewhere in the future, there would be a television montage to the tune of that hymn to indefatigability The Impossible Dream, and it was here that Henderson began to dream.

"He did look different when he came in, he looked fantastic, he'd had a great summer. The previous year he didn't look like he used to look. And he is this amazing specimen. He's a male model.

"The whole thing was for him to regain his confidence, his self-belief. That was at the heart of everything we did before he ran again. He came back to us looking like he was in a better place with himself and he did a lot of long, slow work on our new Wexford sand gallop, which seemed to help him a lot, he obviously enjoyed it, it built him up well.

"And then, on the grass, from mid-October, we purposely did much less fast work with him. The horses who were leading him, or following him, we took them down a whole two degrees, lesser horses, not horses he'd been working with before. I didn't want him going out with the A-team – I wanted him to feel like he was the boss again. Go and murder that, boy, and feel better about yourself.

"It was all about not stressing him in any way. Put two ordinary horses together and Sprinter comes along behind, all he does is cruise on past them. Normally I would hate the idea of anyone thinking they've won a gallop, a gallop isn't about that, it's about trying to make horses feel good. They've got to do some work but complement each other at the same

FOLK HERO
SPRINTER SACRE SEASON BY SEASON

2009-10 Two wins from two runs in bumpers as a four-year-old

2010-11 Sole season over hurdles ends with third place behind Al Ferof in the Supreme Novices'

2011-12 Five-race unbeaten campaign as a novice chaser capped by seven-length Arkle win over Cue Card with an RPR of 176

2012-13 Another five-race unbeaten season, all in Grade 1s, culminating in a hat-trick at the Cheltenham, Aintree and Punchestown festivals and taking him to an RPR of 190

2013-14 Pulled up on reappearance in the Desert Orchid Chase at Kempton, after which he is found to be suffering from an irregular heartbeat and does not run again for 13 months

2014-15 Runner-up on return at Ascot but then pulled up in the Champion Chase before another second at Sandown, with a best RPR of 170

2015-16 Triumphant return to the top with a four-race unbeaten season including roof-raising wins over Un De Sceaux at Cheltenham and Sandown

▶▶New lease of life: Sprinter Sacre (right) enjoys his summer holidays with stablemate Jenkins at David and Juliet Minton's Mill House Stud in Much Wenlock, Shropshire, and (below) with groom Sarwar Mohammed after returning to Seven Barrows last autumn

time – two horses finishing nicely together, I love that. But this was different, so he sat in behind two lesser horses and went easily past them. We tricked him, basically."

It's an old trick. Find a patsy, and let the champ knock him over. Sign him up to the 'Bum of the Month' club and let him loose, let his ego swell at the same rate as his muscles. Before you know it, the champ's feeling like a champ. And the gym work goes on apace.

"We worked on his jumping too. I mean, he'd always been so spectacular, and his jumping was never a problem but after his time off it was never as slick as it had been, he wasn't as deadly over his fences. His mind wasn't right, and maybe his body wasn't right either. We had to build them both up again.

"Tony Gilmour is our 'back man' – I call him

▶▶ *Continues page 26*

INTO MISCHIEF

A **leading sire** in North America

Grade 1 winners include
PRACTICAL JOKE,
a multiple Grade 1-winning 2yo of 2016

Half-brother to multiple
Eclipse Champion
BEHOLDER

" Into Mischief has **rapidly developed** into one of North America's **most exciting** young sires. "

—ALAN PORTER
Pedigree expert

SPENDTHRIFT

The Breeders' Farm
859.294.0030 | spendthriftfarm.com
2017 Fee: US$75,000 S&N

Barbara Livingston photo

that, but he's much more than that really. [Orthopaedic expert] Buffy Shirley-Beavan was a great help too. It was about building up the muscles in his loins and back – behind the saddle he was missing a bit.

"The previous season I hadn't been desperate to take his rugs off at the races, I wasn't particularly proud of the way he looked, but when it came to the Shloer I couldn't wait to get his rugs off and let everyone have a good look. And it was worth looking at. The last time he'd looked as good as that was at Punchestown, before the problems started."

****

THE Shloer Chase at Cheltenham in mid-November, a race that bears the name of a fizzy drink, would be the test of whether Sprinter Sacre still possessed his own effervescence. He had been in the doldrums long enough to have lost his penalty for winning Grade 1 races and he was receiving weight from horses who would not have seen which way he went when he was in his pomp. It would be a good test, an eliminator before the old champ could begin to consider a crack at the title again. Another knockdown, though, would be the end.

"We knew he was looking good, and we knew his work was good, but of course we hadn't asked him any kind of question. I didn't want to. It had to happen now, and it would have been retirement day if it hadn't gone right."

It happened. The old slugger, fed on a diet of easy meat, his body in fighting trim, his ego bolstered by all those undemanding bouts at home, rolled his shoulders and rolled back the years. The dream was not looking so impossible.

"It all happened in ten strides, like it used to. They were going up the hill and suddenly he took off, jumped the fourth last, and was gone. I told Nico [de Boinville] that if at any stage the horse wanted to get on with it, let him. Don't say whoa, say go. Don't disappoint him. It was just a bit further out than I'd wanted, because of the fitness aspect.

"He went into the fence three lengths down, came out three lengths

A DIFFERENT CHAMP

THE RATINGS VIEW

Sprinter Sacre became a champion again in 2015-16 – officially the best over two miles in the end-of-season Anglo-Irish Classifications – but he was around a stone below his magnificent peak of 2013.

As a seven-year-old, Sprinter Sacre earned a Racing Post Rating of 190 with his 19-length victory in the 2013 Queen Mother Champion Chase (below) and hit the same mark again when he beat Cue Card by four and a half lengths at Aintree over two and a half miles.

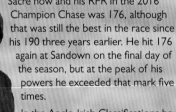

That put Sprinter Sacre second only to Kauto Star – who recorded 191 in the 2009 King George VI Chase – in the history of Racing Post Ratings.

Those heights are well out of reach for Sprinter Sacre now and his RPR in the 2016 Champion Chase was 176, although that was still the best in the race since his 190 three years earlier. He hit 176 again at Sandown on the final day of the season, but at the peak of his powers he exceeded that mark five times.

In the Anglo-Irish Classifications he was the champion two-mile chaser on an official rating of 175, well below the 188 that gave him the title three years earlier but still the best in the division since then.

up. Gone. Goodbye. That's the moment I knew he was back. What a moment."

When Sprinter Sacre returned to the winner's enclosure a 14-length winner he was greeted like a prodigal son. To many there it felt similar to a festival welcome, but this outpouring was born simply of sheer relief. Henderson, who confesses with a wide smile his propensity to easy tears, was not the only one fumbling for his handkerchief. The public had their horse again, and so did he. It was time to step back, regroup, breathe.

The next step involved a return to Kempton – the scene of his darkest hour – for the Desert Orchid Chase. "I suddenly realised – I rang Celia, asked her whether we should be going back to Kempton if he's supposed to forget about what happened?" It seemed, though, that Sprinter Sacre had finally put the past behind him. He ground out a game victory over Sire De Grugy – "It had been all so easy for him in the past, but he really had to fight there, maybe his first real battle" – a hard-fought win on points that pointed the way onwards.

"Nico said he wasn't the same horse as at Cheltenham, said he felt flat. It was slightly disappointing, but the good thing about it was it told us what to do. If we could get him that well for Cheltenham first time, we could do it for the festival. We'd keep him away from soft ground and go straight there. We didn't need to use

the Game Spirit, didn't need to go anywhere, just be much happier doing it our own way.

"We took a pull with him in January, as we would anyway. Everything went very smoothly, we were lucky because if you do it that way you can't afford for him to have four or five days off, a temperature, a stone bruise, any little niggle throws it all out of whack when you're following a tight schedule."

****

HENDERSON pursued his impossible dream. Somewhere within that song's lyrics is a line about fighting the unbeatable foe, and now Sprinter Sacre would face such a horse. Un De Sceaux had won 14 of his 16 races, had failed only when falling with a clear advantage, had never actually, physically, been beaten. No pundit would countenance the victory of the past over the future.

Henderson recalls with glee a rowdy Cheltenham preview night in the Sydney Arms in London when his affirmations of his horse's chance were shouted down. "In your dreams, they said," he remembers. In your impossible dreams, Henderson. And in the cold, clear light of day, he saw the scale of the task awaiting his old fighter, back in the ring to take another swing at the title against an

▶▶ Float like a butterfly, sting like a bee: (from left) Sprinter Sacre puts in an almighty leap in the Shloer Chase; on his way to winning a hard-fought duel with Sire De Grugy at Kempton; some quiet time in the woods in the build-up to the festival; Nicky Henderson acknowledges the appreciative crowd after the Shloer

opponent no-one had laid a glove on.

"At no stage did we ever say he was back to where he was, that ratings pinnacle of 190. We knew he was mortal after all. He was unbeatable before, but we knew he wasn't like that any more. We were trying to do something that was impossible, that wasn't realistic. He was 5-1, Un De Sceaux was 4-6. It was a dream, the sort of thing you lie awake with in the small hours, thinking of what might happen. But when I took his rugs off that afternoon, he looked unbelievable."

It was a good word to sum up the day. And everyone loves the comeback kid, don't they? With three to jump, Un De Sceaux was in front, going well, in a position from which no horse had ever bested him, well ahead on points, the referee waiting patiently before lifting his arm in triumph yet again. Yet Sprinter Sacre got up from his stool, found from somewhere reserves both mental and physical, and hit the champ with all he had, the ghost from the past, the ghost with a hammer. Knockout.

"They came off the top of the hill, and for three strides, maybe four, Un De Sceaux went to go and I thought 'this is over', Nico was clicking him along and it wasn't happening. Those four strides seemed like four minutes.

And then the next four strides, oh bloody hell.

"He's done it, he's changed the race, and they won't come back at him. The silly fool didn't jump the last properly, the showoff. But it didn't matter. My father [Johnny Henderson, chief executive of Racecourse Holdings Trust, which bought Cheltenham in the 1960s and saved it from the developers] put the roof on the grandstand and my horse nearly blew it off. Quite good fun."

Weights and measures. Sprinter Sacre beat Un De Sceaux by three and a half lengths, regained his Champion Chase crown after three years away. The impossible dream? No, not with this horse. King of the world, again.

The racing world paid its dues with deep and unadulterated delight. There is an unofficial list of great Cheltenham Festival celebrations – Dawn Run, Desert Orchid, Imperial Call, Istabraq – and Sprinter Sacre went into it, somewhere near the top. You could probably have heard the cheers in Cheltenham town centre.

"I never thought we'd be part of a scene like that. I remember Istabraq coming in from his third Champion Hurdle, my horse Blue Royal led over the last and finished third, and his owner Lynn Wilson said it was the privilege of his life to be standing in the unsaddling enclosure on that day, to be part of that. I think Sprinter doubled it. It was quite extraordinary.

▶▶ *Continues page 28*

"That was the day of my career. It has to be. You've got to have the horse, of course. He has to have a sublime talent. But as a trainer that was above the likes of See You Then, and all that harrowing the gallops at 2am. It was unique."

****

THEN, of course, as tradition demands it, the rematch. Sandown, a febrile final day of the season, Sprinter Sacre v Un De Sceaux II, the 'rumble in the commuter belt'. Henderson wasn't keen.

"I would have given anything not to run him again. What was there to be gained? We had just had the most incredible day, he'd blown the world away, why in the world did we need to go and do it all again five weeks later? Yes, it was a valuable Grade 1, but we weren't doing all this for money, were we?

"Ten days before Sandown I was looking for the smallest excuse to take him out, I must have weighed him ten times in five days, I was looking for anything. Corky [Browne, Henderson's legendary, long-serving right-hand man] was killing me about it – why are we doing this?

"But there's no doubt he was better at Sandown than he was at Cheltenham. I knew that going in, he was roaring, I told Caroline that I simply couldn't not run him. He was unreal – he very nearly was as good as ever at Sandown, as good as he once was. He tanked it. Nico couldn't hold him at the last of the Railway fences. The crowd was unbelievable."

The crowd was on its feet, rattling the roof again as Sprinter Sacre bullied Un De Sceaux, had him on the ropes from a long way out, put him down and out in the almost casual manner he was once renowned for, a flick of the wrist. He cantered in by 15 lengths, the undisputed champion. Bring 'em on.

Henderson pauses, brings us back up to date. He will never be able to top the life-affirming, life-defining story of Sprinter Sacre's revival, but his boy is back in the gym, working on the heavy bag, sweating off his summer holiday, ready to defend his hard-won crown again.

"He looks unbelievable again. He

▸▸Title regained: Sprinter Sacre powers up the hill to take back the Queen Mother Champion Chase crown after a gap of three years, with devoted rider Nico de Boinville in the saddle this time

came in at 630kg, that's heavier than he's ever been, although we're stripping it off him now. He'll likely just go to the Tingle Creek at Sandown in December, then the Champion Chase, only two races. After that, we'll see.

"Because he's only got to say once that it's not what he's up for, and that'll be it and he can go and open supermarkets instead. We're just his curators, just looking after him for his public.

"Look, people probably think I overdo the 'this is killing us' schtick, although it shouldn't be underestimated. It can take you to some very dark, tough places. But what happened with Sprinter Sacre last season is why we do it, why we put ourselves through it all. It was some year, wasn't it? Some horse."

Sprinter Sacre: The Impossible Dream is published by Racing Post Books. Buy it at the discounted price of £15 at racingpost.com/shop

WORTH THE WAIT

When Sprinter Sacre won his first Queen Mother Champion Chase in 2013, Nico de Boinville was best known as his work rider. It was an important job, one he had taken on when Sprinter Sacre arrived in Nicky Henderson's yard from France. The horse was a three-year-old, the rider was 19; they grew up together.

Then an amateur, De Boinville had to give up his seat on Sprinter Sacre to Barry Geraghty on racedays throughout the glory days of 2012 and 2013 but things had changed by the start of the 2015-16 season. Geraghty had become JP McManus's retained jockey, while De Boinville was a Gold-Cup winning jockey after his triumph on Coneygree.

Although Sprinter Sacre was not the prized mount of old, he now became De Boinville's to ride on the racecourse as well as at home, and their understanding of each other was integral to a great revival.

The high point of a perfect season came when Sprinter Sacre took back the crown in the Champion Chase and, having had to watch in 2013, De Boinville revelled in his own moment of glory. "This is unbelievable. It's definitely on a par with winning the Gold Cup. Sprinter Sacre gave me his all. It's an absolute privilege to ride him," said the rider, who just a month earlier had lost his 59-year-old mother Shaunagh to cancer.

Reflecting on his partnership with Sprinter Sacre, De Boinville said: "I've been a very lucky boy from the word go, the moment I entered Seven Barrows, that the guvnor let me even sit on this horse, and now I'm allowed to take the reins on the track. The guvnor has shown so much faith in me and so much in the horse."

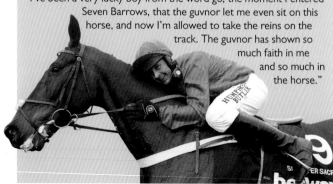

Looking for
Classic winners...

BBAG graduate ISFAHAN
wins the German Derby, Gr.1

KNIFE EDGE leads home a 1-2 for
BBAG graduates in the Group 2
German 2.000 Guineas,
with DEGAS a close second.

Spring Breeze Up Sale:
Friday, 26th May 2017

Premier Yearling Sales:
Friday, 1st September 2017

October Mixed Sales
Friday, 20th October and Saturday, 21st October 2017

KING RICHARD THE FIRST

AP McCoy's retirement left the jump jockeys' crown vacant and Richard Johnson, for so long heir apparent, seized his moment. In the summer, as he set the pace again, the new champion reflected on a job well done

By Peter Thomas

THERE was a time towards the end of last season when, given the very public outpouring of goodwill towards Richard Johnson, it was possible to believe that his bid for a first jump jockeys' title would be carried over the finish line by a tidal wave of approval, regardless of what happened on the track.

Owners rallied to the cause; familiar trainers redoubled their efforts on his behalf while unfamiliar ones joined the fray; journalists fell over themselves to proffer gushing yet heartfelt words of encouragement; the walk from weighing room to paddock became an obstacle course strewn with racegoers eager to slap the back of the man who would be king.

For a while it seemed almost as though, even in the weighing room

– that other-worldly inner sanctum where steely self-interest co-exists easily with camaraderie – Johnson's colleagues were willing him to succeed where for 20 years he had failed. If the quotes were to be believed, the rider that beat him to the championship risked the kind of opprobrium previously reserved for the evil twin of the man who shot Bambi – but the gnarly 39-year-old himself was never fooled.

He had been rabidly chasing down the untouchable AP McCoy for too many seasons to think for one second that any of his rivals would defer to his rank or reputation. Aidan Coleman snapped at his heels for an uncomfortably long spell at the outset and it soon became apparent that only a full-throttle 'Dickie' could be sure of prevailing. Luckily, full throttle is the only way Dickie knows.

"Last season perhaps there was a feeling that there was some justice in what I managed to do after two decades of trying," he concedes, reassured by the sight of the trophy on his mantelpiece, "and the support was amazing, even from the other riders.

"But once we leave the weighing room we're all as keen as each other to ride winners and if Aidan had been able to keep up the good run he had at the start of the season, he definitely wouldn't have been easing up to let me by at the end of the season.

"Being champion is the ambition of every jockey in the weighing room, the same as it was for me for 20 years and still is today, so last year was a fight and it'll be a fight to hang on to what I've got. Riding winners is what gets us all out of bed in the morning and nobody will be going

▶▶ *Continues page 32*

THE CHAMP IN NUMBERS

out of their way to be nice to me on the track, that's for sure."

In the final analysis, the 2015-16 jump jockeys' championship was a fairly bloodless affair, with the name of McCoy being replaced on the silverware by that of Johnson, almost as a matter of routine. Trainers who had wanted McCoy now wanted his great rival, the new best jockey in the country, to the extent that 41 of them provided him with at least one winner in his final tally of 235.

Along the way he reached the 3,000-winner mark that would have been an absolutely staggering milestone were it not for the fact that McCoy had already passed it and added another 1,358 for good measure before he retired.

It's the story of Johnson's working life. Having watched Richard Dunwoody better the 'unsurpassable' feats of Peter Scudamore, he went on to eclipse Dunwoody in the same way a planet might eclipse a medium-sized grapefruit, but still he found himself only the second-best jockey of his generation. Yet for all the 16 seasons he was runner-up in the

▸▸ Sharing the moment: Richard Johnson walks through a guard of honour at Sandown on the day of his coronation and (left) with the trophy and his children, sons Percy and Caspar and daughter Willow

title race, he began each new campaign with the same zest and ambition, seemingly oblivious to the unceasing fruitlessness of it all.

He perfected the art of ploughing a furrow that deviated not one millimetre as a result of extraneous influence or distraction. His ambition – stated by many but stated convincingly by few – was and remains simply to take each race as it comes, to treat each new contest as he has treated every other in his career, regardless of the fast-receding McCoy on the horizon in front of him, the hullabaloo of the chasing pack or the constant hum of admiration that ended in a crescendo at Sandown on the final day of last term.

McCoy's records – the 289 winners
▸▸ Continues page 34

39 age (born July 21, 1977)

1 champion jockey title (2015-16)

16 times runner-up to AP McCoy

234 winners in 2015-16, a career-best

3,058 career wins in Britain and Ireland at end of 2015-16

20 Cheltenham Festival winners

1 Gold Cup winner (Looks Like Trouble, 2000)

1 Champion Hurdle winner (Rooster Booster, 2003)

1 Champion Chase winner (Flagship Uberalles, 2002)

1 Stayers'/World Hurdle winner (Anzum, 1999)

20 Grand National rides without winning, a record

2 seconds in Grand National (What's Up Boys, 2002; Balthazar King, 2014)

£174,000 richest win (Rooster Booster, 2003 Champion Hurdle)

177 RPR of top-rated mount (Gloria Victis, 2000 Racing Post Chase)

POINT OF ENTRY

DYNAFORMER – MATLACHA PASS, by SEEKING THE GOLD

▶ *The Next* *Global Sire*
DYNAFORMER'S
MOST ACCOMPLISHED SON AT STUD

▶ **FIVE GRADE 1 WINS ON TURF**

▶ **SOUGHT AFTER 1ST YEARLINGS**
1st Crop Yearlings for
$275,000, $150,000, $140,000,
$140,000, $135,000, $130,000,
$130,000, $100,000, $100,000, etc

$275,000
SOLD

"The pedigree to become Dynaformer's heir."
– Avalyn Hunter

Ⓐ

ADENA SPRINGS KENTUCKY

CLASSIC
BLOODLINES

CLASSIC
PERFORMANCE

AWESOME AGAIN ▶ GHOSTZAPPER ▶ MACHO UNO ▶ MUCHO MACHO MAN ▶ POINT OF ENTRY
Jack Brothers +1-859-509-0879 ▶ Cormac Breathnach +1-859-552-4345
www.AdenaStallions.com
PHOTO © SKIP DICKSTEIN, PHOTOS BY Z

in a season or the 4,358 in a career – lie tantalisingly within, or perhaps just beyond, his grasp, but they won't affect his outlook one jot as the defence of his title continues.

"We had three days without any racing when last season was over and we went away for a couple of nights, just my wife Fiona and me," he recalls, "and it was nice to be able to take some quiet time to look back on it all, how nice people were, how smoothly it went, how Menorah winning on the last day made it a perfect finish, but that feeling doesn't last long.

"You've had a long season but realistically, even before Sandown, all you're thinking about is the following Thursday and trying to get back on the scoreboard and off nought winners as soon as possible.

"What you're most focused on is what's ahead rather than what's gone by. The main thing again is the championship and now I've won it once, it makes me want to do it again and again. Nice horses are lovely to have along the way – and you learn very quickly that you have to enjoy them when they come along, because they don't come along very often – but the only way to the title is through consistency."

In short, the world will not shift on its axis as a result of the sea-change that occurred last season. Johnson can treat winning and losing in the same implacable manner on the basis that he puts the same effort and mindset into both, so the presence of just one Grade 1 winner on last term's roster – Native River for Colin Tizzard in the Mildmay Novices' Chase – is incidental to his outlook.

For as long as we could all remember, he had done the same thing year after year, hoping to defy Einstein by coming up with a different result; this season he will do the same thing again, regardless of his new-found status as champion, although the defence of his crown may feel a little different to years of unavailing pursuit.

"I know sometimes I'll feel under pressure when I've had a frustrating day and I'll know everybody's chasing me, breathing down my neck, but it's

still a nicer feeling to be in front than to be ten behind and wondering how you're going to make up the ground.

"What it does is make you realise how much pressure AP had to put himself under every year to keep his momentum for so long. I've only managed to do it once and already I know how hard it is to keep up that pace and that relentless routine.

"Last season I was everywhere all the time, and this season will be the same, but I'm no different to the other lads in that respect – we all want to ride the best horses we can, wherever that may be. Sitting in a car for five hours isn't that bad if you've got the prospect of a winner at the end of it, so that will be the plan, to travel wherever I have to for the best rides available."

If Johnson has the mind of a champion it is the natural affinity for the struggle that defines it. An end-of-season break with the wife is all well and good, but far from

▶▶ Road to success: (clockwise from top left) Richard Johnson taking things easy in the Taunton weighing room; celebrating his 3,000th winner in Britain and Ireland on Duke Des Champs at Ascot in January; signing autographs after his 200th victory of the season on Cheat The Cheater at Warwick in February; with long-time ally Philip Hobbs and that all-important piece of silverware

collapsing in an exhausted heap in the hiatus between hostilities, the lad from Herefordshire – who claims to have rejected a career in farming as being "too much like hard work" – is ever keen to get back on the hamster wheel as soon as possible, which is just as well given the nature of the modern jumps calendar.

Once back in the saddle, he has both eyes on his next ride, albeit with a biologically unlikely third on the prize and a freakish fourth on the opposition. He claims to have had words with Nigel Twiston-Davies, asking him to suggest to son Sam that he might take it easy for a week or two, but is expecting nothing other than ferocious opposition from this, and every other, quarter.

"There are people who say we should have more of a break," he smiles, "but for me the best thing to come out of summer jumping is that with it being so competitive and there
▶▶ *Continues page 36*

SMART CALL rated 121
(Liesl King)

SOUTH AFRICA - the secret's out!

2017 MAJOR RACES

The Sun Met

Kenilworth Racecourse   28 January   Cape Town

SA Derby

Turffontein Racecourse   29 April   Johannesburg

Vodacom Durban July

Greyville Racecourse   1 July   Durban

2017 PREMIER YEARLING SALES

Cape Thoroughbred Sales

Cape Premier Yearling Sale   21 - 22 January   Cape Town
For the full Sale's Calendar and latest news:
www.capethoroughbredsales.com

Bloodstock South Africa

National Yearling Sale   26 - 28 April   Johannesburg
For the full Sale's Calendar and latest news:
www.tba.co.za

JB McIntosh Drive • Summerveld
Shongweni • KwaZulu-Natal
South Africa
Tel: +27 (0)31 769 2961/63
Mobile: +27 (0)83 406 4881
Email: info@racingsouthafrica.co.za

www.racingsouthafrica.co.za

XPRESSIONS ADV & DESIGN

being so many runners these days, you don't have a chance to get fat any more.

"When we had six or eight weeks off in the summer it was hard for us as jockeys, both financially and as athletes. You'd get unfit, almost out of the swing of things, and it would take you a good while to get back into the routine. Staying active all year round means we don't have that problem, but it means the title race is a long one.

"I'll be making no assumptions about winning a second title, that's for sure, but fortunately there's no sign that people have given up supporting me after last season. There was always a chance that the sympathy vote might have dried up, but Gordon Elliott has been fantastic and the likes of Charlie Longsdon and Jonjo O'Neill, the ones I picked up last year after AP finished, are still putting me up and Philip [Hobbs, his oldest ally] looks to have a great team of young horses to go to war with.

"[My agent] Dave Roberts always keeps me busy and tries to send me to the right places – which isn't always as easy as you might think – and the only noticeable change is that where I used to like to get to 100 by Christmas, that was in the days of AP and from now on I'll want to be hitting that mark a fair bit earlier.

"It was my first 200 last year, so that will be the aim again, and if I can ride 15 or 20 winners a month the numbers will take care of themselves. After that it's up to the rest of them to catch me."

The flow of goodwill may be a little less of a torrent now that Johnson finally has his name on the roll of honour, but any thoughts that his inner steel might be compromised by success or his eternal fire doused by relief are indisputably wide of the mark.

Any trainer in need of the best jump jockey in the country will still look no further than Johnson, and any jockey looking to muscle past him in the rankings will find himself locked in mortal combat. Dickie may be nice, but he's not that nice.

AT HOME WITH THE JOHNSONS

Richard Johnson on his wife

It's only on my days off that I realise how much work she actually does for us all. With three kids you don't have a spare moment, so it feels a bit unfair sometimes that, now I have a driver, I can have three hours' kip in the car on the way up to, say, Perth, read the paper, get a bit of peace and quiet, while Fiona's at home working flat out.

On the rare occasions I have a day off, there's no let-up and I'm quickly reminded that being a parent is a full-time job. I'm probably there less than most fathers, which is hard for me, but it's harder for her, looking after the office work and the kids and all the other things I don't do – which is quite a lot.

It's also tough for her having to explain to the kids that I won't be home until they've gone to bed and I'll be gone by the time they wake up, every day for a fortnight sometimes, and it's lucky she was from a racing family because it's hard to explain the hours and the lifestyle to someone who isn't. She knows what it's all about and she's incredibly supportive.

'He's very OCD when it comes to the dishwasher'

Fiona Johnson on her husband

Where did you go on your first date – and who paid? We went to the White Hart in Winchcombe – and he paid, like a gentleman.

How did he propose? Oh, it wasn't an incredible surprise, because we'd gone to look at the rings together, bought them together, there was no grand gesture or anything.

How is Richard different now from when he was riding for your dad? I don't really remember him riding for Dad [Noel Chance] but people have told me he's a lot more level-headed now, things don't get to him too much. If he's had a bad day he can leave it at the door. His best friend Richard Burton says he used to get through a lot of phones, throwing them around and that.

How do you both relax after racing? We'll go for dinner or do something with the family. If he gets home early from the races – quite a rare thing – we'll all sit down for dinner at the table together, and the children love that.

He can win a jockeys' championship, but how would he fare on Masterchef? He can make cheese on toast and does very good scrambled eggs. The trouble with him is that he doesn't push himself, he's probably more capable than he thinks he is.

Did he do his fair share of feeding and nappy changes when the children were younger? He was really good, very hands-on. If he's at home he'll do bath-time and put the children to bed.

What's his worst habit around the house? Oh, there's some serious OCD with the dishwasher. It's all very structured, if something's been put in the wrong way round it'll all have to come out and be started again. It's a running joke when friends come round, they daren't help stack the dishwasher because they won't get it right.

How does Richard cope with a disappointing day on the track? He's very level-headed, and he can't be in a mood for too long because the children soon take him out of it. He says that however bad his day has been, someone else has had it worse, and he soon gets over it.

Away from racing, what is Richard's greatest strength? He's a real do-er of things, very busy, even on a day off he gets on with what he needs to do, never leaves things until tomorrow. Not too much fazes him, you know.

How confident was Richard about winning the title at the beginning of last season? He was hopeful, but not confident. He put himself under a lot of pressure and there were lots of people telling him that this was his year.

How much does it mean to him, to have done it at last? Everything, a huge, huge amount.

What do you think annoys Richard most? Rudeness, probably. He always says it costs nothing to be polite.

Do you think Richard would rather win a second Gold Cup or a first Grand National? That would be very close, if I had to pick one then maybe a second Gold Cup.

How many more seasons do you think Richard will ride for? I expect he'll continue for another three or four years. He'll keep going while he still enjoys it.

When he retires, do you think he'll have any trouble adapting to life out of the saddle? No, I don't think so. We've got horses at home and he'll be on the farm – as long as there are horses around him he'll be fine.

2017 Racing Dates

McCARTHY INSURANCE GROUP RACEDAY
SATURDAY 7th JANUARY (NH)

CORK'S REDFM STUDENT RACE DAY
THURSDAY 23rd MARCH (NH)

SUNDAY 2nd APRIL (F)

RACING HOME FOR EASTER FESTIVAL
SATURDAY 15th APRIL (F)
SUNDAY 16th APRIL (NH)
MONDAY 17th APRIL (BH) (M)

START OF SUMMER 2 DAY MEETING
FRIDAY 5TH MAY (E) (NH) (BBQ)
SATURDAY 6TH MAY (F)

FRIDAY 19TH MAY (E) (F) (BBQ)

FATHERS DAY MEETING
SUNDAY 18TH JUNE (F)

MALLOW TOWN SUMMER RACE EVENING
FRIDAY 14TH JULY (E) (NH) (BBQ)

2 DAY BANK HOLIDAY FAMILY MEETING
MONDAY 7TH AUGUST (BH) (NH)
TUESDAY 8TH AUGUST (E) (F)

2 DAY WINTER MEETING KICK START
SATURDAY 14TH OCTOBER (F)
SUNDAY 15TH OCTOBER (NH)

THE PADDYPOWER CORK NATIONAL
SUNDAY 5TH NOVEMBER (NH)

SUNDAY 19TH NOVEMBER (NH)

THE KERRY GROUP HILLY WAY CHASE
SUNDAY 10TH DECEMBER (NH)

Get your heart racing...

- Premium Level Restaurant Package
- Premium Level Barbeque Package
- Social Package
- Premium Level Admission
- General Admission
- Children go FREE

Book your tickets today

corkracecourse.ie

t: +353 22 50207

@corkracecourse

Cork Racecourse Mallow

corkracecourse

CLASH OF

Paul Nicholls had to fight tooth and nail to retain his British title under a concerted challenge from Irish champion Willie Mullins

By Mark Storey

WHEN Paul Nicholls went without a winner at a Grand National meeting marbled with triumphs for Willie Mullins, the battle for the 2015-16 British trainers' title looked finished. The bookmakers made Mullins, basking in a lead of £183,000 in prize-money with just a fortnight of the season to go, as short as 1-10 to deny Nicholls a tenth title win in 11 years.

The momentum was firmly with Mullins. The perennial Irish champion, fourth behind Nicholls the season before, had launched his first all-out assault on the British crown. He had the will and the weaponry, and at Cheltenham and Aintree he had come out with all guns blazing.

Somehow, against the odds, Nicholls stayed in the fight. He had been on the retreat for weeks, losing important battles along the way, and yet he refused to believe the war was lost. He marched his army north, to Ayr, and scored a morale-boosting victory with Vicente; then he turned back south, to Sandown, for the final clash. The Nicholls side found one last burst of strength and victory was theirs.

Nicholls was jubilant. "Ten is just a magic number," he declared. "Going home after Aintree I thought I had no chance. I didn't think the horses would suddenly start running as they did. Vicente gave us a big day last week and the

NICHOLLS

Prize-money £2,439,560

Winners 122

Runners 568

Strike-rate 21%

Grade 1 wins 2

Biggest earner
Vicente £147,810

Earners in top 25 3

Best performer on RPR
Silviniaco Conti 175

Horses in RPR top 25 2

Figures in Britain in 2015-16

THE TITANS

horses have been running well. We stuck in, worked hard and got some great results."

The final margin was £97,825.50 in favour of Nicholls, a small amount amid the near £5 million amassed by the two sides over the course of the season. Mullins had the quality (13 Grade 1 winners in Britain to Nicholls' two) while the defending champion had the quantity that goes with home advantage (568 British runners to Mullins' 159). Between them, they produced a duel of epic proportions.

****

THE Cheltenham Festival dawned with Nicholls odds-on for the title. Mullins had a raft of favourites for the meeting but Nicholls, buoyed by a Grade 1 win with Silviniaco Conti in the Ascot Chase, still had a £1.2m cushion over his rival.

That did not last long once the Mullins gang got to work on the opening day.

Douvan strolled to victory in the Arkle, Annie Power stepped in for injured stablemate Faugheen and made off with the Champion Hurdle and Vroum Vroum Mag took the Mares' Hurdle. By the end of the day, when Nicholls' highlight was Bouvreuil's second in the novice handicap chase, Mullins had cut the lead to £740,000.

On the Wednesday, Nicholls got on the scoreboard with Diego Du Charmil in the Fred Winter Juvenile Hurdle, but by then Yorkhill had swaggered off with the Neptune Novices' Hurdle for

Mullins, who also had a pair of valuable Grade 1 seconds, trimming the gap between the pair at the end of play to less than £600,000.

Twenty-four hours later and Mullins was up to second in the table, just £257,000 behind Nicholls, after a St Patrick's Day when all his favourites delivered: Black Hercules in the JLT Novices' Chase, Vautour in the Ryanair Chase and Limini in the Trull House Stud Mares' Novices' Hurdle.

Mullins was unable to add to his seven festival scorers on the final afternoon but second and third for Djakadam and Don Poli in the Gold Cup – along with a disappointing run in the Triumph Hurdle by Zubayr, one of Nicholls' most fancied runners of the week – put him within £30,000 of the reigning champion as the Channel 4 cameras went off air.

It was then, with the stealth of a burglar, that Nicholls struck. The 2016 festival was already defined, catalogued and headlined, but as the final two handicaps were run, back on to the stage came the man with the keenest eye for the importance of marginal gains.

The Martin Pipe Handicap Hurdle was the scene for Ibis Du Rheu to triumph at 14-1. Then, at double those odds, Solar Impulse took the Johnny Henderson Grand Annual Chase. The odds

▶ *Continues page 40*

MULLINS

Prize-money £2,341,735

Winners 27

Runners 159

Strike-rate 17%

Grade 1 wins 13

Biggest earner
Annie Power £361,374

Earners in top 25 7

Best performer on RPR
Vautour 180

Horses in RPR top 25 9

Figures in Britain in 2015-16

didn't matter to Nicholls, but the combined prize-money of nearly £95,000 did.

"Putting the blinkers on was a last-minute decision and they made a massive difference," said Nicholls about Solar Impulse. "You have to go with your gut sometimes." It was the type of move that separates a great trainer from a good one, and for Nicholls that extra breathing space was crucial at a time when he was feeling the suffocating presence of Mullins.

****

WHILE Mullins had one British runner in the three weeks between Cheltenham and Aintree, Nicholls had 39, with ten wins helping to extend his lead to £246,000. But it was Mullins who was backed for the title after his post-Cheltenham declaration that it was "all to play for" and he would "probably run a few more at Aintree than usual". He was still available at 5-4 after Cheltenham but the money poured in as the strength of his Aintree arsenal became clear.

The previous year Mullins had sent nine runners to the Aintree races, bar the Grand National; this time he had 30. There had always been doubt about how important winning the British championship was to him. Now there was none.

Inevitably, the Mullins winners piled up. On day one came Grade 1 victories with Annie Power in the Doom Bar Aintree Hurdle and Apple's Jade in the Betfred Anniversary Juvenile Hurdle, and at the end of the following day he overtook Nicholls when Bacardys and Battleford finished first and second in the Grade 2 bumper.

On paper that seemed a turning point, but the outcome of the day's big race ultimately proved more significant. Vautour, sent off at odds of 1-5, crossed the line first in the Grade 1 JLT Melling Chase, but he was riderless, having left Ruby Walsh on the turf at the ninth fence. The £112,788 first prize, which had seemed Mullins' for the taking, instead went to the Tom George-trained God's Own.

Even so, the winners kept flowing in Mullins' direction. Neither of the

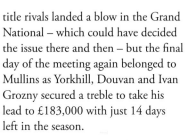

title rivals landed a blow in the Grand National – which could have decided the issue there and then – but the final day of the meeting again belonged to Mullins as Yorkhill, Douvan and Ivan Grozny secured a treble to take his lead to £183,000 with just 14 days left in the season.

****

THE assault on Aintree appeared to define the season. Rather than save his best for Punchestown three weeks later, Mullins had loaded up a fleet of horseboxes in County Carlow and sent a wave of top-class performers across the water to Merseyside. As he racked up the winners, the Nicholls cause appeared increasingly forlorn. The arch-competitor had the desire and the skill to retain his crown, but not, it seemed, the ammunition. There were few glossy names in the yard and a sizeable lead in the title race had been built up over the winter chiefly by an army of more everyday performers, brilliantly trained and expertly deployed.

'Putting the blinkers on was a last-minute decision and they made a massive difference. You have to go with your gut sometimes'

Then came the Mullins tide in the big-money events at the major festivals and Nicholls, as much as he plotted and planned from his Somerset headquarters, was swamped. By the end of Aintree, his lead had been washed away – and then some.

Nicholls was now a 5-1 chance and opportunities were drying up. But the determination remained, running right through his Ditcheat yard, and he was not finished yet. After a double in the Fontwell rain the following Friday, his new assistant trainer, Harry Derham, said: "We have to have a big weekend but we have some good runners at Ayr. We certainly won't be giving up."

A drip-drip of small winners had narrowed the gap, but Nicholls needed a magical Scottish Grand National day at Ayr. Things started well with Vivaldi Collonges winning the first and got even better when Le Mercurey took the second. Nicholls' horses were flying and £42,000 had been trimmed from the lead.

The Mullins-trained

Measureofmydreams lined up as joint-favourite for the Scottish Grand National, worth £119,595 to the winner. But he fell at the third and instead it was Vicente, a 14-1 chance for the reigning champion, who carved through the field under Sam Twiston-Davies and powered away to win. Nicholls was back in front and, after Gibbes Bay completed the four-timer in the bumper, his lead over Mullins was more than £33,000.

"We're back in the game," Nicholls declared. Seven days to go, and it was all to play for.

****

SANDOWN'S season finale loomed, and the battle went right to the wire as Nicholls notched four more winners at Wincanton and Mullins took three at Perth. At the start of the final day, Mullins was £53,000 adrift and in need of a game-changer.

Lining up in the opener for the Closutton team was Voix Du Reve, who had looked in command in the Fred Winter before falling at the last

and opening the door for Nicholls to grab a one-two. The Mullins juvenile was beaten again at Sandown, with Nicholls taking third, and it was the same story in the Oaksey Chase as odds-on shot Valseur Lido misfired.

Victory for Un De Sceaux in the Celebration Chase would put Mullins back in front, and the market struggled to split him with Sprinter Sacre. The outcome, though, was a comprehensive 15-length victory for Sprinter Sacre and the game was almost up.

Mullins still had a fancied runner in Measureofmydreams for the bet365 Gold Cup, but his fall at Ayr was hardly the ideal preparation and as they came up the Sandown hill it was Nicholls to the fore as Just A Par was narrowly outgunned by Neil Mulholland's The Young Master.

It was all over. Second place, and £31,800, topped up by stablemate Southfield Theatre's £7,950 for fourth, was enough for Nicholls. With three races of the season left, he could not be caught.

▶▶ Blow for blow: Willie Mullins takes Aintree by storm with victory for (clockwise from bottom left) Yorkhill, Annie Power and Douvan before Paul Nicholls and Sam Twiston-Davies strike in the Scottish National at Ayr with Vicente (main picture). The title could have gone either way as the trainers went into battle on the final day of the season (top right) but Nicholls finally emerged on top after an epic battle

"Well done, great season," said Mullins as he shook Nicholls' hand after the closest finish to the trainers' championship for more than a decade. A shade under £98,000 separated them at the finish. But what united them meant just as much: two men invigorated by battle, sending charged particles through the jumps season.

Nicholls described it as "far and away the best" of his title wins, a view informed by the intensity of the struggle and his recovery after all had seemed lost. "There was a lot of pressure because this time the title created a lot of interest. It was almost like Team GB against Ireland."

Mullins, who had gone so close to becoming the first Irish trainer since Vincent O'Brien in 1954 to take the British title, is sure to try again. "If we're in the same position after Cheltenham next year we'll definitely give it another go. We'd be mad not to," he said.

If that is a gauntlet thrown down, Nicholls will be happy to pick it up and take on the fight again.

By David Jennings

REWIND to February 18, 2015. Willie Mullins is like a rugby ball in the middle of a scrum as reporters try to get possession of some crucial Cheltenham clues. It is the annual media visit to Closutton before the festival and Ireland's champion trainer is being thrown from one hack to another with names of horses and races bouncing around all over the place. The answers are arriving with refreshing honesty.

Annie Power is sticking to her own sex and going for the Mares' Hurdle despite a public desire to see her battle with the boys; Douvan is destined for the Supreme; Faugheen, Arctic Fire and Hurricane Fly will take each other on in the Champion Hurdle; the JLT Novices' Chase has been chosen for Vautour. The Don Poli dilemma has yet to be solved, though.

"I nominated the National Hunt Chase for Don Poli back in November but I think the Gigginstown team and Bryan Cooper are favouring the RSA," Mullins says. "A lot will depend on what they want to do as they have a lot of horses in both races. I look at his style of running and think the four-miler will really suit him. I love his style of racing and, since they changed the conditions, I think the four-miler is becoming a classier race."

And where will Drinmore winner Valseur Lido show up? "I thought he was an RSA horse but I think connections want to go for the JLT. They also have Very Wood for the four-miler and one or two others, so it'll depend on where they go. I feel the further he goes, the easier he's going to do it, so it would be the RSA for me."

Mullins lost both arguments. Don Poli ran in the RSA. He won it too. Valseur Lido ran in the JLT. He was third to Vautour, beaten 15 lengths.

Fast-forward to September 28, 2016. Ireland's biggest owner and Ireland's biggest trainer part company. Sixty Gigginstown House Stud horses are taken away from Closutton and sprinkled out among Gordon Elliott, Henry de Bromhead, Mouse Morris, Jessica Harrington, Noel Meade and Joseph O'Brien. Why? It was all over money, apparently. You make up your own mind.

"We're parting company. It's basically over fees," Mullins revealed. "I put up my fees for the first time in ten years and Gigginstown chose not to pay them. That's it, we're just parting company. I'm not willing to try to maintain the standards I have without putting the fees up, so that's the way it is.

"Everyone that comes into my yard is treated the same. We have evolved our methods of training, which obviously costs a lot, and we're not prepared to sacrifice that. They have been very good to us over the years, they've bought some fantastic horses and there's a fantastic team of horses going to whoever is going to get them. Whoever gets the horses will be a big challenge to me being champion trainer."

A big challenge indeed, especially since his main rival in the title race was the chief beneficiary of the reshuffle. Elliott, who started the season by winning the Galway Plate and both the Kerry and Munster Nationals,

▶ Continues page 44

▶ Magnificent seven: Willie Mullins had another incredible haul at the Cheltenham Festival with (clockwise from top left): Douvan, Annie Power, Vroum Vroum Mag, Yorkhill, Black Hercules, Vautour and Limini

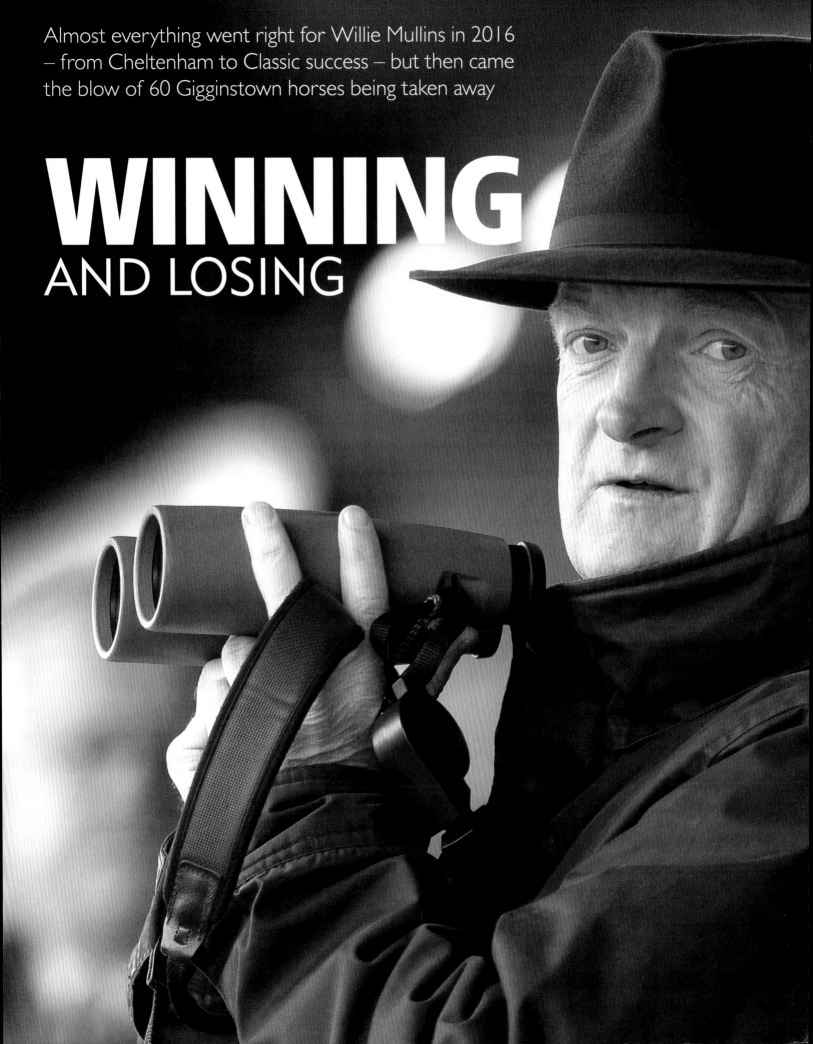

Almost everything went right for Willie Mullins in 2016
– from Cheltenham to Classic success – but then came
the blow of 60 Gigginstown horses being taken away

WINNING
AND LOSING

gobbled up Apple's Jade, Don Poli and Outlander.

Paddy Power initially felt the move was big enough to make Elliott 8-11 favourite to topple Mullins in the trainers' title race but they had a quick rethink, perhaps prompted by support for the defending champion, and the market soon had a more familiar look.

But can Mullins maintain his dominance without some of his best players? If Barcelona let Suarez, Neymar and Pique join Real Madrid, La Liga would surely look very different at the end of this season than it did at the end of the last one, wouldn't it? Mullins' magic wand will need to conjure more tricks than ever before if he is to rule supreme in Ireland once more.

****

JUST last season the Scottish National was all that ultimately came between Mullins and a first British trainers' title. On the second-last Saturday of the season in Britain, Mullins arrived at Ayr with a lead of £110,000 over Paul Nicholls. Another cracking Cheltenham, thanks to the victories of Douvan (Arkle), Annie Power (Champion Hurdle), Vroum Vroum Mag (Mares' Hurdle), Yorkhill (Neptune Novices' Hurdle), Black Hercules (JLT Novices' Chase), Vautour (Ryanair) and Limini (Mares' Novices' Hurdle), saw him move closer to emulating Vincent O'Brien, who was the last British champion jumps trainer from an Irish base.

An all-out assault on Aintree had strengthened Mullins' position and Measureofmydreams was 8-1 joint-favourite for the Scottish showpiece following a fine third to Minella Rocco in the National Hunt Chase at Cheltenham. Victory would have ended the title race a week early. There would have been no way back for Nicholls.

But Measureofmydreams crashed out at the third fence and the x-rated viewing did not end there for Mullins, who was forced to watch Vicente, Nicholls' sole runner, claim the £119,595 first prize.

The Scottish National swayed it but so too did Vautour's shock departure at the ninth fence in the Melling Chase at Aintree when 1-5 favourite.

Had he stayed on his feet and gone on to the expected victory, it would have been an extra £112,788 in Mullins' account.

The near-miss in the British title race was one of the few times Mullins was thwarted in his ever-expanding ambitions. The major target is always the Cheltenham Festival and in 2016 he took top trainer honours for the fourth season in a row, and the fifth time in six years, in moving to a total of 48 festival winners – eight ahead of Nicholls and now just seven behind Nicky Henderson.

He also came out on top at the Grand National meeting, where Yorkhill, Douvan, Ivan Grozny, Bacardys, Apple's Jade and Annie Power all won, and at Punchestown even though his usual strength there was depleted by his earlier big-meeting raids in Britain. He was

▶▶Aintree aces: (clockwise from top left) Bacardys, Apple's Jade, Douvan, Yorkhill, Ivan Grozny and Annie Power score at the Grand National meeting; (below) Mullins with Gigginstown's Don Poli in the winner's enclosure after landing the Lexus Chase

champion trainer in Ireland for the tenth time – matching Nicholls in Britain – and his prize-money haul was approaching double Elliott's total, and with 185 winners to Elliott's 123.

The strength in depth of the Mullins team is incredible, even with the loss of the Gigginstown horses. Six of the 20 jumpers who recorded a Racing Post Rating of 170-plus in 2015-16 were trained by Mullins, giving him nearly one-third of the best talent in Britain and Ireland. None of the six wore the maroon and white of Gigginstown; the best in their colours was Don Poli, who recorded 168 with his third in the Timico Cheltenham Gold Cup and again when second to Cue Card at Aintree.

****

ON the eve of the final day of the British season, Mullins reflected that "these are

▶▶ Continues page 46

NOBLE MISSION (GB)

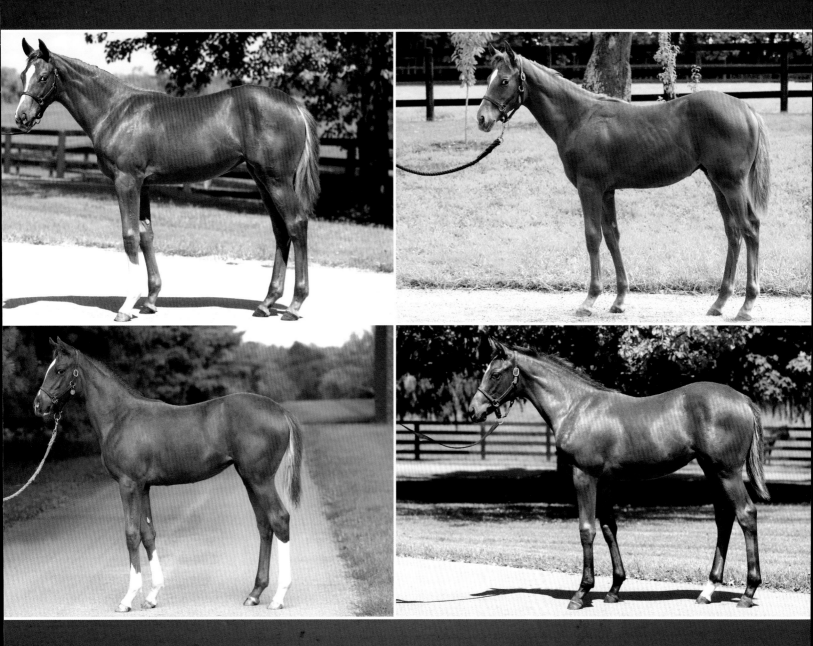

3X GROUP 1 WINNER
including Champion Stakes, Tattersalls Gold Cup and Grand Prix de Saint-Cloud

CARTIER CHAMPION OLDER HORSE

FULL BROTHER TO FRANKEL

LANE'S END

extraordinary, unprecedented times and fortunately we are the ones that have the horses for that". Those horses allowed him to go for the jugular time and again in 2016 but the Mullins brand of training and placing was as central to success as their innate ability.

Who else would have substituted Annie Power with Vroum Vroum Mag in the Punchestown Champion Hurdle? Who would have stepped Yorkhill up in trip to tackle the mighty Yanworth in the Neptune Novices' Hurdle? And who in their right mind would have let a horse who was outclassed in the Fighting Fifth Hurdle at Newcastle take on Ascot Gold Cup hero Order Of St George in the Irish St Leger?

Mullins sees things no-one else can. To most eyes Wicklow Brave was little better than a decent handicap hurdler. He was a moderate 11th to Quick Jack in the 2015 Galway Hurdle and his only Flat wins had come earlier that year in minor events at Gowran Park and Listowel. Yet the seven-year-old caused one of the upsets of the Flat season as he and Frankie Dettori fended off the late surge of 1-7 favourite Order Of St George to give Mullins a first Irish Classic.

"Willie gave me free rein and said 'do your stuff'. It's a surprise but a Classic win is always great. Willie is a top man. His horses are always in good nick. We tried something different and it worked out," Dettori said.

Most things Mullins tried in 2016 worked out but whether they will work again in 2017 without the Gigginstown contingent remains to be seen. Clondaw Warrior's late surge in the Guinness Galway Hurdle, Ireland's richest jumps race in 2016, saw Mullins scurry into an early lead in the Irish trainers' championship but Elliott did not allow him to get too far ahead. After Tiger Roll's 20-1 surprise win in the Munster National, Elliott had this to say about the title race: "I doubt I'll be champion trainer. Willie Mullins is the man. I know that and everyone else knows that."

If Mullins manages to be crowned Irish champion again without any Gigginstown glories to help him along the way, he really will be the man.

THE SPECIAL ONE

If there is one horse above all others Willie Mullins would not want to lose, surely it has to be Douvan. Fortunately, as he wears the colours of Rich Ricci's wife Susannah, Douvan will be firmly in the Closutton camp for a campaign where everyone will be fascinated to see how high he can go in the senior chasing ranks and how his trainer copes without the Gigginstown House Stud contingent.

Mullins has never made any secret of his high regard for the French-bred, unbeaten in ten starts – seven in Grade 1s – since joining the Irish champion trainer. After Douvan had won the Herald Champion Novice Hurdle at the 2015 Punchestown festival, Mullins proclaimed: "He's an amazing athlete for a horse of his size and I'd say he's as good as I've ever had."

As good as he has ever had? Hurricane Fly wasn't too bad, Faugheen is no mug either and didn't Florida Pearl win four Hennessy Gold Cups? For Mullins to make such an audacious statement about a five-year-old was completely out of character. It is simply not his style.

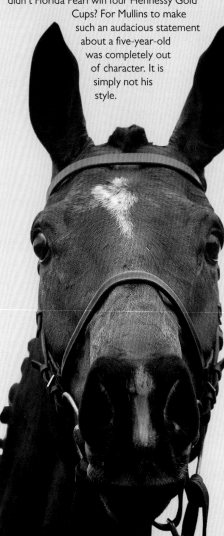

Yet the evidence has stacked up in support of Mullins' opinion. After a four-race winning streak in novice hurdles, culminating in victory at the Cheltenham and Punchestown festivals, Douvan continued on his merry way as a novice chaser in the 2015-16 season, winning six out of six. This time winning at two festivals was not enough; he also added victory at Aintree.

In his ten starts for Mullins his winning distances add up to 102 and a quarter lengths, an average of just over ten lengths per race. While he is not yet the best Mullins has had on Racing Post Ratings, he is within touching distance after reaching 176 at Aintree – the same figure achieved by Sprinter Sacre in his equally dominant novice days.

Those who had the privilege of riding Douvan last season share Mullins' high regard for him. "That's one of the best thrills I've ever had. He was magnificent," said Willie's son Patrick, who was called from the subs bench to replace the injured Paul Townend for the Racing Post Novice Chase at Leopardstown last Christmas. That race was won by 18 lengths, Douvan's biggest margin of victory.

Ruby Walsh knows he is special too. "He's brilliant and has a brilliant mentality. He's just so clever to jump. He makes fences feel as though you're jumping hurdles. He doesn't waste any time in the air. He just has a huge amount of natural ability." Those words came after he won the Racing Post Arkle at Cheltenham by seven lengths.

Townend joined the chorus after landing the Doom Bar Maghull Novices' Chase at Aintree by 14 lengths. "That was some experience," he said. "I was doing a half-speed everywhere. He had a little look between the last two fences, I gave him a squeeze and I've never felt anything pick up like it. I had so much horse underneath me."

Another flawless campaign was completed in the Ryanair Novice Chase at Punchestown but it left Mullins with a dilemma. "The question is do we try and take on Sprinter Sacre next year?" he pondered after the 11-length romp at Punchestown. "The Champion Chase looks the obvious one but he could be a Gold Cup horse."

In that respect, Douvan promises to develop like Desert Orchid and Kauto Star – a dominant chaser with the speed for two miles and the potential to last the Gold Cup trip. He is some horse to have on your side. And, if he does go on to end the Mullins hoodoo in the Gold Cup, Ireland's champion trainer will have had the last laugh.

DISCOVER GREATNESS
with REDOUTE'S CHOICE & SONs

"It is impossible not to be staggered by the sheer scale of what **REDOUTE'S CHOICE** *has achieved at stud.*

But it is his potency as a **sire of sires** *that will cement his immortality as a stallion..."*

–James Thomas,
Racing Post

Sensational
Sire Sons include

SNITZEL
Australia's Current
Leading Active Sire

NOT A SINGLE DOUBT
Australia's Leading
Active Sire 2015/16

SCISSOR KICK
New for 2016
Shuttling to
Haras d'Etreham
in France

THE POWER AND THE GLORY

Injury to Faugheen allowed Annie Power to take centre stage and she played a starring role with two commanding performances

By Lewis Porteous

ANNIE POWER and her rider Ruby Walsh had been here before. Clear of their rivals and hurtling towards the last hurdle with a cherished Cheltenham Festival prize at their mercy. All she had to do was put in a clean jump and her place in history as only the fourth mare to win the Champion Hurdle would be secured. This time she did not disappoint.

But as she sped off the final bend, leaving the rest of the field looking pedestrian in her wake, whether you were Annie Power's usually serene trainer Willie Mullins, her nervous owner Rich Ricci or merely a face among the Cheltenham fanatics, it was hard not to relive the near-identical scenario from 12 months earlier.

On that occasion, with the Grade 1 Mares' Hurdle already grasped by the scruff of the neck, Annie Power prematurely took flight at the final hurdle, clattered the top bar and came slithering to an ugly halt. "To see her fall was an awful moment," Mullins said.

Many of the crowd had choked on their cheers that day, but 12 months on there was a euphoric response as Walsh spotted a stride heading to the wings of the final flight in the Stan James Champion Hurdle and asked Annie Power up and out of his hands. Fearless, she answered his call, clearing her former nemesis with ease before devouring the final climb to the line.

"She's put in a brilliant performance," Walsh, rarely seen so

▸▸ *Continues page 50*

GIRL POWER

THE RPR VIEW

Annie Power registered an identical Racing Post Rating in Champion Hurdle victory as the one she achieved when runner-up in the 2014 World Hurdle.

With her 7lb mares' allowance factored in, Annie Power's 164-rated performance was at least on a par with the bulk of recent Champion Hurdle winners and, after setting solid fractions, she completed the course slightly quicker than the well-above-average Supreme Novices' Hurdle winner Altior on the same day.

She took her form to another level three weeks later when handing My Tent Or Yours, a four-and-a-half-length runner-up at Cheltenham, an 18-length drubbing over arguably her optimum trip of two and a half miles in the Grade 1 Aintree Hurdle.

That wide-margin victory earned her an RPR of 170 with her allowance factored in, a rating unrivalled among jumps mares in the history of RPRs and achieved without her rider having to ask for any kind of serious effort.

TOP TEN JUMPS MARES

Horse	Rating
Annie Power	170
Lady Rebecca	169
Bannkipour	166
Asian Maze	165
Apple's Jade	164
Flakey Dove	164
Ma Filleule	164
Function Dream	163
J'y Vole	163
Lady Cricket	163

Best figures in the history of RPRs

animated as he crossed the line with his arm pumping like a pneumatic drill, said in the winner's enclosure. "We always thought she had the pace to win a Champion Hurdle. She's a cracking mare."

****

RARELY is any race at the festival won so convincingly from the front, least of all one of the week's championship contests, but what made Annie Power's course-record performance more compelling was that she had been unconsidered and absent from the original Mullins teamsheet for the race.

To win so authoritatively is usually the result of meticulous planning and an uninterrupted preparation, but nothing could have been further from the truth here.

While it is true Mullins, Walsh and Ricci had been focused on Champion Hurdle success since the previous summer, their hopes rested with the horse nicknamed 'The Machine'. Faugheen, who 40 minutes before Annie Power's 2015 nightmare had impressively stamped his name on the Champion Hurdle roll of honour from the front, progressed so smoothly towards his title defence through the winter that he was a best-priced 4-11 on the morning of February 17.

▶All smiles: Annie Power and winning connections after her Champion Hurdle success; (below) owner Rich Ricci (left) is congratulated by JP McManus; (previous page) work rider Sonny Carey riding the mare on the Cheltenham gallops two days before her date with destiny

That day's edition of the Racing Post carried the headline 'Annie Power is back with World Hurdle on the cards' on a preview of her seasonal reappearance in the Punchestown.com Mares Hurdle over two and a half miles. She had not run since winning at Punchestown the previous May, having suffered what connections would describe only as a "niggly problem" in the autumn, and this was far from a championship-calibre comeback at odds of 1-20 against two vastly inferior rivals.

There was never any public indication that Annie Power might miss the festival but, in the run-up to her comeback, talk inevitably turned to which festival race might be her target. Ricci had suggested that without a prior run a shot at redemption in the Mares' Hurdle would be favourite, but that squeezing in a prep race would increase the chance of a second crack at the World Hurdle, in which she had been a narrow runner-up in 2014. Mention of the Champion Hurdle there was not.

****

FEBRUARY 17 proved a game-changer for the Champion Hurdle. Hours before the wraps were finally taken off Annie Power for her eagerly anticipated return to action, Mullins dropped a bombshell. "Unfortunately, we've
▶ *Continues page 52*

GO RACING
IN IRELAND 2017

Wherever you are in Ireland, you're never far from a race meeting and if you want to understand one of our country's great passions, choose from over 300 race meetings at any of the 26 racecourses around the country. Play the odds, raise a glass and enjoy good times with friends – you'll have a day out you'll always remember. So what are you waiting for?

It's time to go racing... because nothing else feels like this.

2017 RACING FESTIVALS

CORK
Easter Festival
15th - 17th April

FAIRYHOUSE
Easter Festival
16th - 18th April

PUNCHESTOWN
National Hunt Festival
25th - 29th April

KILLARNEY
Spring Festival
14th - 16th May

CURRAGH
Guineas Festival
27th - 28th May

DOWN ROYAL
Ulster Derby
23rd - 24th June

CURRAGH
Irish Derby Festival
30th June - 2nd July

BELLEWSTOWN
Summer Festival
6th - 8th July

CURRAGH
Irish Oaks Weekend
15th - 16th July

KILLARNEY
July Festival
17th - 20th July

GALWAY
Summer Festival
31st July - 6th August

TRAMORE
August Festival
17th - 20th August

KILLARNEY
August Festival
23rd - 26th August

LAYTOWN
September Festival
5th September

LEOPARDSTOWN & CURRAGH Longines Irish Champions Weekend
9th - 10th September

LISTOWEL
Harvest Festival
10th - 16th September

DOWN ROYAL
Festival of Racing
3rd - 4th November

PUNCHESTOWN
November Winter Racing
18th - 19th November

FAIRYHOUSE
Winter Festival
2nd - 3rd December

LEOPARDSTOWN
Christmas Festival
26th - 29th December

LIMERICK
Christmas Festival
26th - 29th December

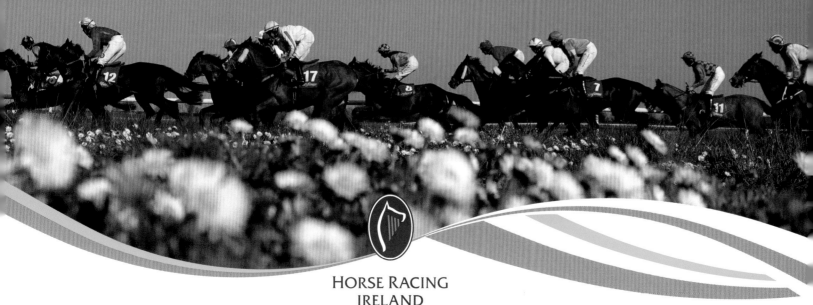

HORSE RACING IRELAND

To plan your day at the races or for a FREE racing information pack, please call the Marketing Team on **+353 45 455 455** or visit **www.goracing.ie**

 facebook.com/goracing   **twitter.com/@goracing**   **@horse_racing_ireland**

had a hold-up with Faugheen and he won't be going to Cheltenham," Mullins said at Punchestown. "We discovered he had a sore suspensory. It's come at a bad time and it means we've had to abandon plans to run him in the Champion Hurdle."

After steering Annie Power to a bloodless success, Walsh described Faugheen's loss to his Cheltenham hand as akin to someone "whipping the ace out of the pack". Trainer and jockey were downcast but, with the reigning champ floored, the door was ajar for a new challenger.

"We could get her added," Mullins said of the possibility of supplementing Annie Power for the Champion. "It's certainly something that could be on the cards."

The next day's Racing Post front page had an altogether different headline about Annie Power's Cheltenham target. 'FAUGHEEN OUT, ANNIE POWER IN', it said, the capitalisation emphasising the dramatic change to the Champion Hurdle picture. It did not end there, as just five days later Mullins suffered a fresh blow when another of his contenders, the 2015 runner-up Arctic Fire, chipped a sesamoid bone during a routine workout.

That was heartbreaking for Arctic Fire's connections but Annie Power, the mare with just one run in the past nine months and a mere three since her success at the 2014 Punchestown festival, was looking ever more likely to step into the breach. After a tumultuous few days, she was 7-4 favourite for the Champion Hurdle.

****

WHICHEVER festival target Mullins ultimately chose, Annie Power would have the chance to settle a score of some description. She had an obvious wrong to right in the mares' race plus a defeat in the World Hurdle to reverse, but there was also a sense of unfinished business about the Champion.

Had it not have been for dual Champion Hurdle winner Hurricane Fly, Annie Power would probably have lined up for the two-mile championship in 2014, when instead she was rerouted to the staying

championship and beaten by More Of That.

Annie Power went down all guns blazing but, with Hurricane Fly failing in his bid to add a third title, the decision to sacrifice the mare over three miles in the World Hurdle was questioned. Two years on, some of those questions were set to be answered, as the week before Cheltenham she was supplemented for the Champion at a cost of £20,000.

Despite having not even been considered for the race a month earlier, Annie Power topped the Champion Hurdle market and there was confidence behind her bid from those at her side.

"The history of the race shows plenty of winners who were proven over longer trips," Mullins said. "It looked the obvious year to give her a chance of winning it. She isn't short of pace and has the 7lb mares' allowance, so it would be fantastic if she could make it third time lucky at the festival."

Walsh concurred. "She has bags of stamina having gone close in a World Hurdle, but it's just getting her to settle well enough to bring that out of her. Dropping her back in trip, you would not have that problem."

'Willie asked me a few days before what I was going to do and I said I was going to ride her like she was Dawn Run'

Among the three mares to have won the race was the greatest of them all, Dawn Run, winner of the Champion in 1984, who secured immortality by becoming the only horse – male or female – to complete the Champion Hurdle-Gold Cup double two years later.

Mullins, the son of Dawn Run's trainer Paddy, needed no reminding of those achievements for inspiration but they certainly helped Walsh as he took his own trip down memory lane before Annie Power's date with destiny.

"Willie asked me a few days before what I was going to do and I'd looked up Dawn Run the other night and I said I was going to ride her like she was Dawn Run," Walsh revealed. "If they catch me, they catch me." As in 1984, they never did.

Setting a brisk tempo but one that was always in Annie Power's comfort zone, Walsh spoke volumes with his

▶▶ Queen of the track: (clockwise from top left) Ruby Walsh embraces owner Rich Ricci in the Cheltenham winner's enclosure; Annie Power surges up the hill to land the Champion Hurdle; Walsh acknowledges the cheers of the crowd as the bookies prepare to pay out; the mare en route to an easy victory in the Doom Bar Aintree Hurdle

body language through the race; he was always in control. Keeping his promise not to look behind him, Walsh dictated the contest and, under less restraint than the norm, Annie Power jumped more slickly than ever.

Even with Barry Geraghty and My Tent Or Yours travelling menacingly in the leader's shadow, Walsh resisted the temptation to twitch until the tight left-hander for home, at which point his rein slackened and his legs began to squeeze. Annie Power moved explosively through the gears in response, putting her rivals to the sword in a matter of strides before soaring over 'that' last hurdle.

Even in the absence of Faugheen, the Ricci colours had triumphed again and Annie Power's victory brought Rich Ricci's emotions flooding to the surface. Fighting back the tears, he said: "No horse deserves to win here – but she does really. Sport offers such a chance for redemption and it's fantastic to see." Mullins said he had never seen Ricci – or Walsh for that matter – so delighted with a victory.

It was third time lucky for Annie Power, whose only two defeats had come at the Cheltenham Festival, and she was in her pomp now. Three weeks later, in the Grade 1 Doom Bar

Aintree Hurdle, the first four from the Champion Hurdle lined up again and she was utterly dominant. My Tent Or Yours was runner-up again but Annie Power's margin of victory went from four and a half lengths at Cheltenham to a commanding 18 lengths.

The Aintree Hurdle was over two and a half miles and it is interesting to note that Annie Power has not run over the same trip twice in succession since her novice hurdling days in 2013. Mullins had been asked at Cheltenham about his policy of moving Annie Power up and down in trip and had this answer: "A good horse with the right temperament can race over a range of trips, and I'm not afraid to do it. We don't have the same opportunities in Ireland to pick races at certain trips – we just pick a race with the right prize-money, regardless of trip."

First at Cheltenham and then at Aintree, Annie Power proved both her class and versatility by bringing home prize-money of £361,000, more than doubling her career earnings in the space of 24 days. From supersub to superstar, she had proved there is more than one hurdling machine in the Mullins ranks.

NEW DAWN

Willie Mullins bought Annie Power because of her likeness to Dawn Run, the mare trained by his father Paddy to become the only horse to do the Champion Hurdle-Gold Cup double at Cheltenham, and he has always seen her as the type who could take high rank over fences as well as hurdles.

"When I saw her I said 'this is the nearest thing to Dawn Run (below) I've ever seen'," Mullins said. "I rang up Jim Bolger and it took me a while to do a deal with him. She's a different colour [to Dawn Run] but physically she's a big, strong mare with speed and stamina."

Annie Power became only the fourth mare to win the Champion Hurdle, joining African Sister (1939), Dawn Run (1984) and Flakey Dove (1994), and her victory came two days after the 30th anniversary of Dawn Run's epic triumph in the 1986 Cheltenham Gold Cup.

On that occasion Mullins had walked behind Dawn Run, arms outstretched in some effort at crowd control, amid the tumult that greeted her victory.

Even as he basked in Champion Hurdle glory, he could not resist dreaming of a similar occasion with Annie Power. "We bought her with the intention of going over fences, like Dawn Run. I would love her to have a go at [the Gold Cup] but her owner has other good horses too."

THE DARK DESTROYER

Don Cossack quashed all doubts as he took the Cheltenham Gold Cup by storm to emerge on top of a talented group of chasers

By Tom Kerr

AT THE dawning of the 2015-16 jumps season racing fans could glory in a view they had not seen for some years past: a team of senior staying chasers who carried with them the unmistakable aura of quality, perhaps even greatness.

Not since the exit of Kauto Star and Denman had the season crested the horizon with such a panoply of talent poised to compete in the campaign's biggest races, culminating, all being well, in a truly epic Gold Cup at the Cheltenham Festival.

Come March, the crowds watching at Cheltenham and beyond were not disappointed. Although the absence of Coneygree and Vautour cost the race some of its lustre, the belief of the previous autumn that this was a special group of senior horses was vindicated in a race that lived up to its star billing.

To the roar of a festival crowd brought to fever pitch over four days of euphoric bookie bashing, 9-4 favourite Don Cossack thundered up the hill to victory and recorded an RPR of 182, the best in the race since Imperial Commander's win in 2010 during the last golden era for staying chasers.

It was an explosive and emphatic confirmation of connections' high hopes for Don Cossack, as well as a thrilling riposte to those who had spent the past 12 months doubting his credentials for jump racing's most illustrious race.

****

AT THE start of the season there were two good reasons to question whether Don Cossack could win the Gold Cup. The first was simply that arrayed against him was one of the most impressive group of staying chasers in many a year.

Among this line-up of stars was reigning champion Coneygree, the first novice to win the Gold Cup since Captain Christy in 1974, a bold front-runner who had responded to being pitched in at the deep end the previous March with an irresistible performance at Cheltenham.

Willie Mullins, all-conquering yet remarkably still searching for his first Gold Cup winner, had half a barn of genuine candidates, spearheaded by the previous season's runner-up Djakadam and RSA Chase winner Don Poli, proven performers whose known ability at the trip contrasted with the unknowable potential of the yard's extravagant superstar Vautour, then untested beyond two and a half miles.

The second reason to question whether Don Cossack could win the Gold Cup was simply whether he had the ability to do it in any year, never mind a vintage one like this was shaping up to be.

Don Cossack had concluded the previous season as the highest-

▸▸ Continues page 56

rated chaser in Britain and Ireland and had defeated both the Gold Cup second and third by further than Coneygree, yet there was one big black mark on his record: blunders had twice cost him victory at Cheltenham.

****

A DARK powerhouse of a horse with a frightening engine, Don Cossack had caught the eye of his trainer early in his career. He was heralded the best Elliott had trained after a trio of bumper wins in the 2011-12 season, a bullish assessment that went down like a lead balloon with the youngster's owner, airline magnate Michael O'Leary of Gigginstown House Stud. "Michael gave out hell to me, so I don't say it about any horse any more," Elliott would later joke.

Don Cossack topped the chasing charts in 2014-15 despite failing, for the second season in a row, to get on the scoresheet at the Cheltenham Festival. A year after falling in the RSA Chase, Don Cossack was sent off the heavily supported favourite for the Ryanair Chase – the race sponsored by his owner – but his chance was compromised by an error at the penultimate fence and an encouraging rally to claim third place was only bittersweet.

What came next, however, offered connections concrete belief Don Cossack would live up to his lofty billing: first a 26-length demolition of Cue Card and Champagne Fever at Aintree, then a seven-length defeat of Gold Cup second and third Djakadam and Road To Riches in a Punchestown Gold Cup run at a fierce clip.

Don Cossack therefore entered the 2015-16 season as a proven champion even though he had failed chasing's key championship test. He had been officially rated the best in Britain and Ireland, had proved at Punchestown he stayed beyond three miles and handed out a handsome defeat to the Gold Cup placed horses. Yet questions still dogged his candidacy for the festival.

The 2015-16 season began in flawless fashion with a bloodless victory at Punchestown and an eight-length romp in Down Royal's

GOLDEN YEAR FOR ELLIOTT

Gordon Elliott won the Grand National with Silver Birch in 2007, his first season with a licence, and that triumph set the tone for a meteoric training career.

Last season Elliott's County Meath stable burst through the century barrier in Ireland for the first time, recording 123 winners, plus another 28 in Britain. Don Cossack's Gold Cup was one of three successes at the Cheltenham Festival, along with Diamond King in the Coral Cup and Cause Of Causes in the Fulke Walwyn Kim Muir Handicap Chase. That was his best haul yet, taking him to eight overall.

Since first establishing himself as the second force in Ireland behind Willie Mullins in the 2012-13 season, Elliott, 38, has more than doubled his prize-money, which stood at €2.57 million last year. That was more than €1m greater than the previous campaign's tally, although still almost €2m less than Mullins accrued.

Elliott's growing stature in the game wasn't just marked by a first Gold Cup. He also joined the ranks of jumps trainers to have won at Royal Ascot when Commissioned won the Queen Alexandra Stakes, although he missed the occasion as he was on holiday.

▸▸ Grand opening: Gordon Elliott with his National winner Silver Birch

Champion Chase. Inevitably, thoughts swiftly turned to March.

"I can't see an issue with Cheltenham," said Bryan Cooper, the Gigginstown stable jockey. "I got shuffled back a bit last year in the Ryanair and it wasn't ideal, but he finished out the race and flew home. People will have those question marks but there's only one way to find out and that's to get him back there in March."

Cooper himself may have fuelled some of the questions when he partnered Road To Riches instead of Don Cossack in the Punchestown Gold Cup, but now he seemed firmly committed to Elliott's star and the first chance to address whether they would have the beating of major Gold Cup contenders would come in the King George VI Chase at Kempton on Boxing Day.

Coneygree missed the race, laid low with a hock injury that would ultimately prevent him from defending his Gold Cup crown, but the brilliant Vautour and a rejuvenated Cue Card, transformed by an operation for a trapped epiglottis, lined up with Don Cossack in the mid-season championship.

'At the time he fell the only horse I was worried about was Vautour. I'm not saying we would have won, but I certainly don't think we were beaten, that's for sure'

Don Cossack, sent off the 15-8 favourite, ended up playing a peripheral role after making an untimely exit in the closing stages. Although he was bang in contention when falling at the second-last, thoughts of that ill-timed tumble were almost instantly swept aside amid a furious finish fought out between Vautour and Cue Card, with the latter just edging the duel to the line by a head.

Later, once heart rates had returned to safer levels, cooler contemplation suggested Don Cossack's performance was better than it first appeared. He had never looked entirely comfortable at Kempton, yet as he fell he was responding to pressure. "I felt I had Cue Card covered coming down to the second-last," Cooper reflected. "At the time he fell the only horse I was worried about was Vautour. I'm not saying we would have won, but I certainly don't think we were beaten, that's for sure."

Was the King George, like the previous year's Ryanair, actually a testament to Don Cossack's teak toughness? Or was the fall evidence of a deep-set vulnerability under pressure

▸▸ *Continues page 58*

ROA

TOP-NOTCH BENEFITS FOR OWNERS

ROA membership is the equivalent of just 63p* a day but the benefits are immense

- **SIS sponsorship (worth an average of £4,000 against ownership costs alone – annually per horse)**

- **Free racecourse admission and priority car parking (worth over £200 a year)**

- **Automatic third-party insurance (worth £290 a year)**

- **BHA 20% fee discounts (worth £55 on average)**

- **Thoroughbred Owner & Breeder magazine (worth £55 for 12 issues)**

Plus much more

Join over 7,600 owners today. Call 020 7152 0200 or visit **roa.co.uk**

*£230/365 days - £0.63

Terms and conditions may apply to benefits

that would be exposed in Cheltenham's boiling cauldron?

Perhaps mindful that Don Cossack had been undone twice by jumping errors at Cheltenham, Elliott sent him to Thurles for a minor race barely a fortnight after Kempton. A lazy performance on unsuitable ground sent bookmakers scrambling to see who could issue the biggest Gold Cup price, but the unglamorous outing had done its job – Don Cossack would head to Cheltenham off the back of a safe round and a win.

Elliott, meanwhile, was busy dismissing the idea his star had any problem with the Gold Cup track. "If you look back at the videos of his two trips to Cheltenham you'll see he has never travelled sweeter in a race than he did before he fell in the RSA in 2014," he argued, "and everything was going fine until the second ditch in the Ryanair last year. Nothing went right after that. We've had no luck at Cheltenham over the last few years and I just hope that changes this time."

This time it would.

****

THREE key things went Don Cossack's way in the run-up to his date with destiny. First, the rain stayed away and his preferred sounder surface was available. Second, Cooper brought his Don dilemma to a close when he opted for Cossack over Poli. Finally, Vautour was sent for the Ryanair instead, in which he secured a masterful six-length victory and prompted a thousand pub conversations about what might have been.

Those strokes of good fortune might have counted for naught if Don Cossack had not delivered the performance of his career when the moment came in the Gold Cup. Kept wide by Cooper, he was one of three with chances at the crest of the hill, along with Cue Card and a stock-still Ruby Walsh aboard Djakadam. Then, three out and to the accompaniment of a vast groan from the grandstands, Cue Card crashed to the floor, leaving Djakadam and Don Cossack to fight it out up the hill.

It was a one-sided fight. Shaken up by Cooper, Don Cossack responded

willingly and steamed up the hill, defeating Djakadam by an easy four and a half lengths. The previous year, Coneygree's margin of victory over Djakadam had been a length and a half.

"I can't believe we've won another Gold Cup," said O'Leary, who had first lifted the trophy in 2006 with War Of Attrition. "I'm so happy I could cry. We buy chasers specifically to win Gold Cups. We're not that interested in hurdlers. The Gold Cup

▶▶ Perfect answer: Bryan Cooper and Don Cossack silence the doubters with victory in the Timico Cheltenham Gold Cup

is the pinnacle, the ultimate ambition. We were fortunate to win one ten years ago. To win another is incredible. I never thought it would happen."

Elliott, having beaten his great Irish rival Willie Mullins to the Gold Cup, was equally ecstatic. "I was so nervous watching the whole way round," he said. "I put myself under pressure today. This is something you dream about. I won the Grand National when I was very young but probably didn't appreciate it. I appreciate this, though. I'm so lucky."

Luck, sadly, ran out after Cheltenham, when a tendon injury prematurely ended Don Cossack's defining season and as another jumps season gathered steam his future on the track remained in question.

His towering ability, however, no longer attracts any doubt. In the end-of-season Anglo-Irish Classifications he was the champion chaser on a mark of 177, 1lb ahead of Cue Card and Vautour and 2lb better than Sprinter Sacre. He had improved 2lb from the previous season – and he had needed to – and was the first back-to-back champion since Kauto Star.

That in itself was some achievement. How he did it, laying the ghost of Cheltenham past, will live long in the memory.

LOST HERO

Gordon Elliott and Gigginstown House Stud may have won a Gold Cup but they also lost a leading hope from the next generation when No More Heroes, a dual Grade 1-winning novice chaser, suffered a fatal injury in the RSA Chase.

The seven-year-old won the Grade 1 Neville Hotels Novice Chase by nine lengths from subsequent Grand National winner Rule The World on his last start before Cheltenham and had been widely pegged as an exciting staying chaser in the making.

Having travelled well at Cheltenham, No More Heroes weakened rapidly after the last and jockey Bryan Cooper dismounted. He was found to have severed a tendon, an injury serious enough for vets to recommend putting him down.

"You never like losing any horse in that way, especially a very good one like him," Elliott said. "He won his two Grade 1 chases and had a big future, but unfortunately it was a very bad injury and nothing could be done to save him."

BABY BOOM

Adam Kirby became a father for the first time on the opening day of Royal Ascot and then proceeded to ride two Group 1 winners in a week he will never forget

By Lewis Porteous

F OR any sportsperson, from an elite competitor to a fun runner, the advice in the final 24 hours before an important event would be the same: relax, stick to a familiar routine, eat healthily, focus the mind and visualise success. Above all, get a good night's sleep in preparation.

With rides in two of the three Group 1 races on the opening day of Royal Ascot, including second

▶ *Continues page 62*

favourite Profitable in the King's Stand Stakes, an early night was certainly a prerequisite for Adam Kirby. Fate thought differently.

Kirby and partner Megan Evans, the daughter of astute Welsh trainer David Evans, had expected to be parents by the time Royal Ascot came into focus but their first-born decided he would keep them waiting. Two days before the biggest Flat meeting of the season, there was still no sign he was ready to face the world.

Inevitably, just as Kirby was getting his Ascot game face on, baby Charlie decided to make his move and on Monday morning, 24 hours before an already significant day for his dad, Megan's waters broke. "It was one of those things," Kirby remembers. "We said to each other if he's going to come it will be when Profitable is about to run."

Anticipating a long night, Kirby hit the hay at 8pm but three hours later Megan's discomfort had passed her threshold and the pair headed from their home on the outskirts of Newmarket to Rosie Hospital in Cambridge, a little over 20 miles away.

Megan was in too much pain to sleep but in the early hours of Tuesday her partner managed to make use of the hospital's facilities. "While Megan was walking the box I got another few hours on the bed she was meant to be on. It was quite selfish of me but I'll be honest, I didn't like any minute I was there. It's not very nice seeing someone in pain and knowing there's nothing you can do to help or ease that."

By the morning there was still no sign of Charlie but there was never any discussion about a change of game plan. Missing Ascot was not an option. "Megan knows how important Ascot is and, not only that, I had a live chance," Kirby says. "She understood how important it is."

Less understanding was one of the midwives on duty that morning, who had no issue with telling one of the stars of British Flat racing her views on his plans to leave.

"I remember lying there in that bed," he recalls. "It was about 8am, by which time Megan was in a lot of

discomfort. I remember the midwife coming in and saying, 'What are you doing for the day then, Dad? You're obviously staying for the birth.' I said, 'No, unfortunately I'm going to work.'

"She looked at me in disgust and said, 'You're going to go to work and miss the birth of your child?' I said, 'Unfortunately I have to.' I'll never forget that until the day I die as it made me feel really bad. Why she had to be quite so abrupt with me I'll never know."

▸▸ Standing tall: Adam Kirby outside the Brighton weighing room in May; (previous page) Kirby returns to the Ascot winner's enclosure after the victory of Profitable in the Group 1 King's Stand Stakes

At 9.30am Megan's mum arrived with Kirby's suit and shirt, ready to relieve him as her daughter's birth partner. He slipped into his clean clothes in the car park and set off for Ascot, not knowing when he might become a father.

"More or less as I arrived at the track at around 11.30am, I had a picture come through and she'd had him," Kirby says. "That was an unbelievable moment. I was just delighted they were both safe. The worst thing was she told me not to tell anyone as nobody else knew at that stage. I rang her dad to let him know and the next thing you know I've told Clive Cox as well."

****

WITH a weight lifted from his mind and safe in the knowledge mother and son were both well, Kirby could regain focus on the job in hand, which kicked off in the opening race of Royal Ascot at 2.30pm.

Riding Kodi Bear in the curtain-raising Group 1 Queen Anne Stakes, he led with two furlongs to run but ultimately faded out of contention behind impressive winner Tepin. Without a ride in the next race, the new father was able to speak to his partner for the first time since Charlie's birth before it was time for Profitable in the King's Stand.

Only Mecca's Angel was shorter in the market but, like the rest of Profitable's 16 rivals, she could not lay a glove on him that afternoon. Kirby looked to be travelling ominously well on the heels of the favourite in the early stages and past halfway his biggest problem appeared to be getting a lead for long enough.

Well over a furlong out he could wait no longer and asked Profitable to go and win his race. His partner responded in devastating fashion, unleashing a rapid turn of foot that gave him a decisive advantage, with Kirby punching the air as they passed the post a neck to the good over runner-up Cotai Glory.

The day might as well have been sponsored by Carlsberg as far as the winning rider was concerned, for win doubles don't come any better than
▸▸ *Continues page 64*

South Africa's Innovative Thoroughbred Sales Company

Cape Thoroughbred Sales

CTS Graduate
ILLUMINATOR
winner of the inaugural
CTS MILLION DOLLAR

CAPE PREMIER YEARLING SALE
21 - 22 JANUARY 2017

19 G1 winners since 2012

South Africa's Leading Yearling Sale starts 21st January 2017 - a week before "Met Day", the highlight of the Cape Summer Racing Season, featuring the following races at Kenilworth Racecourse:

R5 Million Sun Met G1,
Investec Cape Derby G1,
Klawervlei Majorca Stakes G1
and the CTS Million Dollar - comprising two races of US$500,000 each for CTS graduates of 2015.

THE CTS MILLION DOLLAR
$1 000 000

STALLIONS REPRESENTED AT CPYS 2017 INCLUDE:

Captain Al,
Dawn Approach,
Duke Of Marmalade,
Dynasty,
Elusive Quality,
Frankel,
Fort Wood,
Galileo's Night,
Gimmethegreenlight,
Keep The Faith,
Kitten's Joy,
Oratorio,
Pierro,
Rock Of Gibraltar,
Scat Daddy,
Silvano,
Speightstown,
Trippi,
Var, etc.

Contact **Adrian Todd (MD)** E: adrian@cthbs.com or **Amanda Carey (Sales Manager)** E: amanda@cthbs.com
T: +27 (0) 21 873 0734 M: +27 (0) 82 465 4020 W: www.capethoroughbredsales.com
European Representatives: **Hermione Fitzgerald** E: hermionefitzgerald@gmail.com M: +44 (0) 78 3349 8373
Mick Flanagan E: mick@townleyhallbloodstock.com M: +353 86 609 8119

عالم

مهرجان سُمو الشيخ منصور بن زايد آل نهيان
HH Sheikh Mansoor Bin Zayed Al Nahyan Festival

WORLD

One World, 6 Continents

 The Capital

سمو الشيخة فاطمة بنت مبارك
HH Sheikha Fatima Bint Mubarak
Darley Awards

جائزة دارلي
Darley Awards

HOLLYWOOD 2017

March 31st Dolby Theatre, Highland Boulevard, Hollywood

◻◻ DOLBY THEATRE
at hollywood & highland center

April 1st HH Sheikha Fatima Bint Mubarak Darley Awards Stake (Grade 1)
Santa Anita Park, LA , CA
April 2nd HH Sheikha Fatima Bint Mubarak Darley Awards & The US Darley Awards
Gala Dinner at the Beverly Hills Wilshire Rodeo Drive

Sustained by

هيئة أبوظبي للسياحة والثقافة
ABU DHABI TOURISM & CULTURE AUTHORITY

coordinated by

Abu Dhabi Sports Council
مجلس أبوظبي الرياضي

Associate Partner
National Feed & flour
Production & Marketing Co I.l.c
الوطنية لإنتاج وتسويق
الأعلاف والدقيق ذ.م.م

Strategic Partner

آيبيك
IPIC

Official Partner

NATIONAL ARCHIVES Ministry of Presidential Affairs

Official carriers

Emirates

in cooperation with
 ERA IFAHR

Sponsored By

AYADI
MANPOWER SUPPLY

Global United Veterinary Services LLC

bloom.

بترومال
PETROMAL

RISE
Rise General Trading L.L.C
A National Holding Company

حياتنا
Hayatna

Wathba Stallions

AL WATHBA CENTRE

MOHAMED BIN ZAYED
Falconry and Desert Physiognomy School

EMIRATES FALCONERS' CLUB

Ladies Sports Academy

Motherhood & Childhood

Dr. Nader Saab
SWITZERLAND

DOLBY THEATRE

SANTA ANITA PARK

YAS

sports

ABU DHABI 2016
INTERNATIONAL HUNTING & EQUESTRIAN EXHIBITION

Al Awani

ADNEC

Kabale

PARIS-TURF
RACING POST

OMEIR TRAVEL AGENCY LLC

Viola
Communications

FADIA KARAM

JANNAH
HOTELS & RESORTS

EASTERN MANGROVES HOTEL & SPA, ABU DHABI

first-time fatherhood and Group 1 success. The usually level-headed 28-year-old jockey was in tears after the race as the emotion of the day flooded out.

"What got me, and upset me, was that unfortunately I lost my father four years ago and all he ever wanted was to see me win a Group 1," Kirby says. "When I mentioned that on TV and mentioned the baby, it got to me. That was my third Group 1 and it can't be explained the feeling that goes through your body when you win these Group 1s. Especially at Royal Ascot with that crowd; it's a big buzz."

He hailed Profitable the fastest he had ever sat on, having been amazed at having to restrain a horse for so long in a top-level five-furlong sprint. "Last year he was a boy but now he's filled out and he's big and strong. His neck's developed, his shoulders have developed, he's got a big backside on him and now he's a proper sprinter."

Kirby had time to compose himself before riding Wolfcatcher to finish tenth in the Ascot Stakes at 5pm, then he hot-footed it to the hospital to meet the newest member of his family at around 7.30pm.

"Although I'd already seen him on the photo I can't explain the moment I saw him in person. I can't put it into words. I was in great form from the afternoon and then to go and see him, with my own eyes, was a fairytale."

****

THE three of them slept "very well" that night, meaning it was a more conventional start to day two of Royal Ascot, where Kirby was in Group 1 action again, this time on unheralded 16-1 chance My Dream Boat in the Prince of Wales's Stakes.

He faced stiff opposition, headed by the horse rated the best on the planet at the time in Japan's A Shin Hikari, not to mention Breeders' Cup heroine Found and Group 1 winners The Grey Gatsby and Tryster. This was a high-class field but My Dream Boat was the beneficiary of a high-class and tactically astute ride.

"Ascot is a place you have to go and be positive. You have to believe in your horse and I did with My Dream Boat," says the rider.

Kirby's mount had looked

pedestrian when beaten more than 14 lengths behind A Shin Hikari in France on their previous starts and, with the Japanese star turning into Ascot's home straight in front, My Dream Boat had plenty of ground to make up once more. However, Kirby was winding his partner up for a sustained challenge down the outer and, as A Shin Hikari started to falter, My Dream Boat went into overdrive.

Challenging away from his rivals, My Dream Boat was now in pursuit of Found, who had bounded into a clear lead. Despite drifting further away from the leader, who had the inner rail for assistance, My Dream Boat was closing swiftly under Kirby's distinctive drive style. Split by almost half the track's width from the leader, he drew level only strides before the post and the pair lunged for the line almost as one.

Having had no idea of the result, Kirby's reaction was priceless as the photo revealed My Dream Boat had prevailed by a neck. The announcement started "First, number two . . .", which prompted Kirby to glance down at his saddlecloth before frantically wagging his finger in a state of euphoria when he realised he was the winner.

"When his number was called it was

▶▶ Dream catcher: My Dream Boat (right) comes wide and late under Adam Kirby to beat Found (left) in the Prince of Wales's Stakes, a second Group 1 winner on the first two days of Royal Ascot for the jockey

another unbelievable moment. If the race is run to suit and if he gets his ground he's quite a tool. Realistically we were taking on a very good filly in Found but I definitely thought we'd be in the shake-up."

After a second Group 1 winner in two days, only Frankie Dettori finished day two of Royal Ascot in front of Kirby in the race to be the meeting's top jockey, with eventual winner Ryan Moore third at that stage. He was in the best company but not out of place.

****

AT 5ft 11in, Kirby is among the tallest riders in the weighing room. When he has to do 'light' he is referring to riding at 9st, which is the lowest weight – including saddle and kit – he can manage. Typically one of the first to arrive at the track on raceday, he usually makes the racecourse sauna his first stop and he will revisit later in the day if needed. While he would never say it himself, his dedication is unwavering and he makes huge sacrifices to chase his dream.

"I have to put my mind to it every day and work hard at it," he admits, "but I don't really know any different, so it doesn't really bother me. You go

'HE'S A VERY SERIOUS JUDGE OF A HORSE'

All four of Adam Kirby's Group 1 wins have been for Lambourn trainer Clive Cox *(below, with Kirby)*, an equally formidable grafter whose association with the jockey goes back more than ten years.

Cox, like the rider, has made steady but sure progress up the ranks and 2016 has been his best year in terms of prize-money, thanks mainly to that Group 1 double at Royal Ascot with Profitable and My Dream Boat. That eclipsed his only previous £1m-plus season in 2013 when Lethal Force's wins under Kirby in the Diamond Jubilee Stakes and July Cup put both trainer and jockey in the big time.

Kirby rode his first winners for the stable as a 7lb claimer in 2005 and Cox recalled: "Adam rode Out After Dark to win the Gosforth Park Cup for me that year and he did nothing but impress me, even at that early stage, with his horsemanship and his ability.

"He's also a very serious judge of a horse, both at home and on the track. He's had a couple of very good retainers but throughout that time he continued to keep a close eye on our horses and help us as much as possible and I'm pleased he's more able to do so now.

"I trust him 100 per cent. He was always a very good rider, he's got more experience now and I'm proud he's done as well as he has. On top of all those good qualities as a jockey he's a top man, a really nice guy to deal with on a daily basis."

The feeling is mutual. "Clive Cox is the top man. He's an excellent trainer and great to ride for," Kirby said at Royal Ascot. "I'm a very lucky boy to ride these horses and I'd like to thank Clive as he's been very good to me. I have to be thankful to the horses as well – they do all the work."

there, get on with it and do your best on the track."

Regarding his weight, he says "when you start to rock it, it won't stop rocking". As a result he rides all year round to keep an even keel and is a regular on the all-weather tracks through the winter, clocking up more than 1,000 rides in recent seasons as demand for his services has grown. Habitually he goes well past 150 winners nowadays, with 192 his best score in 2014.

Unfairly, and probably down to his consistent success on an artificial surface, he has faced the misguided perception from some that he is foremost an all-weather jockey. While excellent on Polytrack, the truth is that Kirby is equally adept anywhere and on any surface. Considering he has had relatively few chances in Group 1 races, it is testament to his skill that he has already bagged four of the sport's top prizes.

Supremely strong, he rides the percentages in races, and in a driving finish he is a rider you want on your side. There are shades of Lester Piggott, not only in his height but also his technique, as his bum kisses the saddle time and again as he drives forward in a finish. In full cry, he is unmistakeable in a finish.

****

'GOOD horses make good jockeys' goes the maxim, and to have moved into the big league without always having those good horses at his disposal is perhaps the best indication of how highly Kirby should be rated among his peers.

With the help of longtime supporter Clive Cox, trainer of Profitable and My Dream Boat, those good horses were more frequently available to him in 2016 and helped cement his position in the top tier. The rider's dream week in June was capped when Commissioned, trained by Cheltenham Gold Cup-winning trainer Gordon Elliott, stayed on strongly from mid-division to win the Queen Alexandra Stakes, the last race of Royal Ascot.

"What do you say?" Kirby mused, trying to fathom a remarkable end to a remarkable week. "I didn't expect this sort of outcome – it's what it's all about. It's important to thank family and friends for their support as it might have been very different without them and I'm very grateful."

It was certainly a week to tell Charlie about in years to come. He will scarcely believe it, no doubt. As his dad says, it was the stuff of fairytales.

GIFT HORSE

Dartmouth's Royal Ascot triumph was the perfect 90th birthday present for the Queen in a year that reaffirmed the royal racing revival

By Julian Muscat

A REGULAR flow of gifts arrived at Buckingham Palace in 2016 as the Queen celebrated her 90th birthday, but for a perfect present there is no question Her Majesty would have put Royal Ascot success high on her wish list. She had to wait until the final day of the meeting, but then came that treasured victory as Dartmouth repelled Highland Reel to land the Hardwicke Stakes by a thrilling, hard-fought head.

The Queen delivered a gentle fist-pump in the royal box as Dartmouth reached the winning post in front and, although there was a stewards' inquiry into slight interference by the royal runner, the result was never going to be overturned. Exactly one week earlier there had been the formality of her official birthday, but this was celebration of a different order.

"It means a lot and the Queen got such a thrill from seeing him stick his head out," said John Warren, her bloodstock and racing adviser. "Halfway through the race, the Queen said, 'Hmm, things are going well', which is indicative of the outcome very often.

"You can't stage-manage this racecourse to have a winner, no matter how hard you try. For the Queen to have one in her 90th year is so special. She's so passionate about it but she never expects anything. She's so grateful for whatever comes her way." To put the icing on the cake, the Queen was presented with the Hardwicke Stakes trophy by her granddaughter, Princess Beatrice.

That Dartmouth prevailed on day five enhanced the sense of excitement. The best of the Queen's horses had been dispatched to Ascot, but on the first four days there was precious little to show for it. Thursday had closed on a particular low note after Guy Fawkes stumbled and fell with fatal consequences two furlongs into the King George V Handicap.

By Saturday, the best that six

Continues page 68

Rising to the occasion: Dartmouth (right) beats Highland Reel

royal runners had managed was Diploma's fifth place in the Sandringham Handicap. But all that changed when Sir Michael Stoute saddled Dartmouth for a Group 2 contest the Queen had won twice previously with Aureole (1954) and Hopeful Venture (1968).

The close finish heightened the sense of drama as Dartmouth and Highland Reel duelled hard throughout the final furlong. It looked as though the royal runner was set for a decisive victory when crack French rider Olivier Peslier brought him through with a smooth run to lead approaching the final furlong. But Seamie Heffernan aboard Highland Reel had other ideas.

Indeed, the photo-finish might have gone the other way had Heffernan not dropped his whip in the closing stages. Dartmouth veered off a true line as he strained for the winning post, encroaching on Highland Reel, but the Ascot stewards averted a public outcry when they rightly allowed the result to stand. "The last furlong seemed like a long one," Warren said, "and the stewards' inquiry added to the anticipation. He's a really tough, genuine horse."

After his Hardwicke heroics Dartmouth, who was bred by Sheikh Mohammed's Darley outfit, was supplemented into the race named after the Queen's parents, the King George VI and Queen Elizabeth Stakes, back at Ascot in July. It was an ambitious entry but the colt warranted his place.

Dartmouth was bidding to follow in the hoofprints of Aureole, who landed the 1954 King George after winning that year's Hardwicke Stakes. The Stoute runner couldn't quite manage it but ran with great credit to finish third behind the more enterprisingly ridden Highland Reel.

On a broader note, considerable speculation has surrounded royal participation in British racing in generations beyond the Queen. Those who run the sport have been concerned there is no obvious heir apparent to take the royal silks forward, but Warren said the canvas, previously blank, now had some definition.

"Prince Charles is now so interested

in racing," he said at Royal Ascot. "He has really been excited this week; he has had two runners and they haven't won, but they are participating and participation is what it is all about.

"The Prince of Wales is trying to really learn about the industry. About 30 years ago he told me racehorse ownership was probably like gardening. Until you owned your own garden, you could never quite understand what it was all about. But when you have your own garden, you have to look after it and concentrate. He said coming into Ascot this week, the anticipation of owning a horse was so enormous. I think he has got the bug, which is so important for British racing. Both he and the Duchess of Cornwall are absolutely smitten."

Warren's words will have had a soothing effect on the Ascot Authority, which runs the royal racecourse. The Queen has been a permanent fixture there since her inaugural ▸ Continues page 70

STOUTE MATCHES CECIL

Dartmouth's victory in the Hardwicke Stakes gave Sir Michael Stoute his 75th Royal Ascot winner, equalling the late Sir Henry Cecil's record at the meeting.

"It's a big thrill to equal Sir Henry's record. It's very poignant," Stoute said. "Seventy-five Royal Ascot winners is a great mark to reach and I hope it doesn't stop there."

Ten times the champion trainer in Britain, Stoute, 71, seems sure to claim the record outright before too long. He posted his first winner at the royal meeting when Etienne Gerard landed the Jersey Stakes in 1977, five years after he started training, and quickly followed up when he saddled Finite to win the Britannia Handicap two days later.

The Newmarket trainer has made the Hardwicke Stakes his own in recent years. Dartmouth was winning the race for Stoute for the seventh time in the last 11 renewals, and his ten victories overall is a record for the race.

Apart from the recently instituted Commonwealth Cup, Stoute has won every other Royal Ascot race that carries Group 1 status today. He has won the Coronation Stakes four times, the Queen Anne Stakes three times, the Gold Cup and Prince of Wales's Stakes twice and the St James's Palace Stakes, King's Stand Stakes and Diamond Jubilee Stakes once each. He has been leading trainer at the meeting five times.

▸ Special occasion: Sir Michael Stoute with the Queen after winning the Hardwicke Stakes with Dartmouth (above)

visit, aged 19, in 1945. The meeting would undoubtedly lose some of its lustre without daily royal patronage, since many in the galleries go to see the Queen ahead of the horses.

Her Majesty's love of all horses was manifest in celebrations commemorating her 90th birthday. The official celebratory party saw 7,000 people entertained by a filmed montage of her 90 years that featured 900 horses. Racing, too, paid its own tributes.

The Gold Cup, the Royal Ascot highlight won in 2016 by Order Of St George, was renamed The Gold Cup In Honour Of The Queen's 90th Birthday, while the Coronation Cup, run on Derby day, was restyled The Queen Elizabeth II Coronation Cup. And for the first time since she acceded to the throne, the Queen presented the winning trophy to connections of the Derby winner – on this occasion the Aga Khan, whose Harzand held off US Army Ranger.

It was no coincidence that official 90th birthday celebrations started on Derby day. In this, it mirrored the timetable scripted for the Diamond Jubilee celebrations four years earlier, when Her Majesty also savoured a Royal Ascot winner courtesy of Estimate's triumph in the Queen's Vase.

Dartmouth's Hardwicke Stakes victory offered further evidence that the Queen has much to anticipate on the racing front in her tenth decade. Carlton House's victory in the 2011 Dante Stakes was the first in a run of ten Pattern-race victories by royal horses – prior to that, the Queen had won just one Group race in the preceding 11 years, and that was in Germany, where Banknote won the Badener Mile in 2007.

It has been a similar story at Royal Ascot, where the royal colours have graced three winners in the last five years. Before that, there had been just one since 1999.

The revival in Her Majesty's racing fortunes runs right across the board. She won more prize-money in 2016 than in any year since the halcyon days of the 1970s, when she won Classics with Highclere and Dunfermline, and the season might have been even more rewarding but

ROYAL ROSTER

Dartmouth became the Queen's 23rd winner at Royal Ascot when he won the Hardwicke Stakes, a race the monarch had landed twice before with Aureole (1954) – who ranks as the best of her Royal Ascot scorers – and Hopeful Venture (1968).

The Hardwicke Stakes thus joined the Royal Hunt Cup and Ribblesdale Stakes as the Royal Ascot races the owner has won most often.

The Queen gained her first Royal Ascot victory only 15 days after her Coronation, when Choir Boy landed the Royal Hunt Cup in 1953. The 1950s was by far the most productive decade numerically: the Queen toasted 11 Royal Ascot winners in all and had at least one winner for seven consecutive years. Royal Ascot doubles in 1954 and 1957 helped her become champion owner in both years.

The Queen's only dual winner at the meeting has been Estimate, who ran away with the Queen's Vase in her Diamond Jubilee year, 2012, and scored a supremely popular triumph in the Gold Cup the following year. But in ratings terms she was a stone inferior to Aureole.

Estimate's Gold Cup remains the Queen's only Group 1 victory at the meeting. She won the St James's Palace Stakes with Above Suspicion (1959) and the Coronation Stakes with Aiming High (1961) but neither race had Group 1 status until 1988.

THE QUEEN'S ROYAL ASCOT WINNERS

Year	Horse	Race
1953	Choir Boy	Royal Hunt Cup
1954	Landau	Rous Memorial
	Aureole	Hardwicke
1955	Jardiniere	King George VI Handicap
1956	Alexander	Royal Hunt Cup
1957	Almeria	Ribblesdale
	Pall Mall	New Stakes
1958	Restoration	King Edward VII
	Snow Cat	Rous Memorial
1959	Above Suspicion	St James's Palace
	Pindari	King Edward VII
1961	Aiming High	Coronation
1968	Hopeful Venture	Hardwicke
1970	Magna Carta	Ascot Handicap
1979	Expansive	Ribblesdale
	Buttress	Queen's Vase
1992	Colour Sergeant	Royal Hunt Cup
1995	Phantom Gold	Ribblesdale
1999	Blueprint	Duke of Edinburgh
2008	Free Agent	Chesham
2012	Estimate	Queen's Vase
2013	Estimate	Gold Cup
2016	Dartmouth	Hardwicke

▶▶ Golden moment: The Queen with her dual Royal Ascot winner Estimate, after victory in the 2013 Gold Cup

for an injury sustained by Recorder, a highly promising two-year-old in 2015. Trained by William Haggas, Recorder won the Group 3 Acomb Stakes in impressive style before being sidelined.

Such a rosy picture is a far cry from royal fortunes over the previous three decades. The transformation is largely down to a gradual and discreet overhaul of the Royal Studs, which has incorporated several new strains of blood into the broodmare band. There are slightly more than 30 mares in residence and the covering sires used on them are increasingly distinguished. Among the 2016 yearlings to enter training were sons of Frankel and Sea The Stars; there were fillies by Dubawi and Shamardal.

The theme is ongoing. In 2016, five royal mares were sent to Dubawi and one each to the likes of Australia, Dansili, Frankel, Galileo, Golden Horn, Kingman, New Approach and Oasis Dream.

In this era of super-wealthy Turf patrons, any season in which the royal silks are carried to victory at Royal Ascot must go down as memorable and Dartmouth's success was perfectly timed in the year of the Queen's 90th birthday.

Unlike in previous decades, however, the quality of horse now populating the Royal Studs allows Her Majesty to anticipate the annual five-day gathering with a degree of optimism. The same is true for all who follow the fortunes of the royal silks.

MAXIOS

MAXimum **QUALITY** first foals and yearlings by the son of the great **MONSUN**

Top first Sales results at ARQANA, Goffs, BBAG and Tattersalls :

**€ 240,000 · € 220,000 · gns 180,000 ·
€ 150,000 · € 130,000 · gns 125,000 ·
€ 100,000 · gns 80,000 · € 80,000 [2x] ·
€ 70,000 € [2x] · gns 60,000 · € 60,000 ·
gns 55,000 · gns 45,000 · € 49,000 ...**

Averaging:

€ 60,125

6 x his Nomination Fee

FÄHRHOF

Luke Lillingston
Tel: +353 - 87 - 919 57 80
luke@kernlillingston.com

Daniel Krüger
Mobile: +49 162 733 2 339
krueger@faehrhof.de

www.faehrhof.de
www.maxios.de

For MAXimum **SUCCESS**

TRANSPORT ALLOWANCE!

THE
BIGGER
PICTURE

Fashion on the first day of Royal Ascot reflects
the burning question in the world beyond
racing: Leave or Remain in the EU? Brexit was
the verdict in the referendum, held five days
after the royal meeting drew to a close

EDWARD WHITAKER (RACINGPOST.COM/PHOTOS)

By Nicholas Godfrey

The brilliant US mare played by British rules and scored a highly significant victory in the Queen Anne

TERRIFIC TEPIN

ALTHOUGH Mark Casse and his family thoroughly enjoyed their visit to Royal Ascot, the US trainer remains slightly disappointed that he never met the Queen. But perhaps Casse should not have worried, because he brought the Queen of the Turf with him in the shape of mighty mare Tepin, who thwarted her European counterparts with a gutsy display to win the Queen Anne Stakes.

"There were so many things against her that I'm still trying to figure out whether it was a dream," says Casse, reflecting a few months later on a famous transatlantic triumph. "It was definitely one of the highlights of my career, that's for sure. I've been asked many times what it meant to me and I put it right up there. It would be tough for me to separate our Breeders' Cup wins, and when we won the Queen's Plate [Canada's senior Classic] it was a big deal, but Royal Ascot might very well be number one. If somebody said to me, 'look, you've got to give me your number one,' that would have to be it."

Compared to her long-haul predecessor Black Caviar, the exalted racemare who sparked a media frenzy four years earlier, Tepin was greeted more with a degree of respect than outright awe.

Like the Australian sprint sensation, however, Tepin arrived in England as a star attraction, blessed – or maybe burdened – with a big reputation on the back of a long winning streak. Otherwise, though, the similarities were less obvious: the Black Caviar team came more in expectation than hope before her unforeseeably dramatic victory in the Diamond Jubilee, whereas Tepin's connections readily admitted they knew the magnitude of the task facing North America's finest in the Queen Anne.

Black Caviar, after all, was the world's best by some measure in a sprint division habitually dominated by her compatriots; Tepin, on the other hand, was a miler, a category in which European turf horses reign supreme, and here she was competing with them on their home patch, without the anti-bleeding medication

▶ *Continues page 76*

Lasix and minus her customary nasal strip, applied to aid her breathing at home but outlawed in Britain. Moreover, Tepin was running on an undulating straight course, the like of which she had never seen before, on ground softened by days of rain.

"I have a lot of faith in her but I had a lot of questions, and probably handling the track was the biggest concern because it's so different from here," recalls Casse, 55. Indiana-born and Florida-raised, Casse has held a training licence for 38 years, right back to when he was 17. Now with more than 2,000 winners to his name, he heads a family operation with barns in Toronto, Kentucky, New York and Florida.

"I was okay without the Lasix," he says. "I didn't really think it was gonna be a huge factor, and if she'd been a bad bleeder, we wouldn't have brought her. Anyway, we had tested all those things – but the one thing we couldn't test was how she would handle the track."

On the other hand, Tepin had a potent weapon in her armoury: an immense talent, as a near-perfect record over the two seasons before Royal Ascot demonstrated. An Eclipse Award winner after her memorable Breeders' Cup Mile success at Keeneland, Tepin had won nine of her previous 11 starts; indeed, but for a nose and a head, she would have gone unbeaten in seven in 2015, and she had not been extended in winning four more in 2016.

Tepin's owner Bob Masterson started considering Royal Ascot as soon as the daughter of Bernstein had won at the Breeders' Cup. "She didn't just beat the boys, she destroyed them," Casse says. "Then, when Mr Masterson decided he wanted to keep her in training another year, Royal Ascot was one of the goals, alongside the Woodbine Mile and the Breeders' Cup again at Santa Anita. She had pretty much done everything she can do in the US – she'd beaten colts, won the Breeders' Cup. She's owned by a true sportsman and he wanted to explore other avenues; it's not about the money for him."

Despite her imposing record, Tepin was still sent off an 11-2 chance in a double-figure field

for the Queen Anne, reflective of scepticism in Britain over her chances. Although Tepin had never needed fast ground – indeed, she'd won on an 'off' track in the States – overnight rain can hardly have been welcomed by her connections, which led to jockeys describing the ground as anything from 'soft' to 'very heavy' (although as the latter came from Cristian Demuro, it is possible something was lost in translation, as it didn't seem that bad). "The day itself was nerve-wracking," Casse recalls. "We all thought Royal Ascot was just magnificent – my wife said it was like the Kentucky Derby on steroids – though if you could've told us before that we were going to win, I would've enjoyed it more."

In the event, Casse's mare handled both track and conditions as well as anybody could have hoped. Shortly after breaking from the gate, the Queen Anne field split

▸▸ American express: Tepin takes the Queen Anne from Belardo and jockey Julien Leparoux salutes the crowd as he is led back in; (below) owner Bob Masterson with Leparoux

in two, nine on the far side of the course and the remainder, including Tepin, racing nearer the stands. Julien Leparoux's mount stalked the pace throughout, well within range, until her Eclipse Award-winning jockey began asking for a serious effort about a quarter of a mile out.

She hit the front at the furlong marker and continued to respond to her rider's urgings. Although the winning margin was only half a length, Tepin stuck on gamely and never really looked likely to succumb to the late challenge of the Roger Varian-trained Belardo in the Godolphin blue.

"She had a lot to prove, because we know she's a champion in America, but she had work to do coming here," said Kentucky-based Frenchman Leparoux, who described riding at Royal Ascot as the veritable "dream come true". He added: "We knew we came here with a good chance, but Tepin overcame a lot of things today. She's a champion and proved it today. She had to work for it. The last 100 metres was a long way to go and I'm glad we got it done." Tepin's owner was exultant. "The mare is

▸▸ Continues page 78

مهرجان سُمُو الشيخ منصور بن زايد آل نهيان
HH Sheikh Mansoor Bin Zayed Al Nahyan Festival

WORLD

One World, 6 Continents

AbuDhabi **The Capital**

المؤتمر العالمي لخيول السباق العربية
WORLD ARABIAN HORSE RACING CONFERENCE

MOROCCO **2017**

National Feed & flour
Production & Marketing Co l.l.c

الوطنية لإنتاج وتسويق
الأعلاف والدقيق ذ.م.م

World Arabian Horse Racing Conference
Morocco - May 8 - 14, 2017

Sustained by

هيئة أبوظبي للسياحة والثقافة
ABU DHABI TOURISM & CULTURE AUTHORITY

coordinated by

Associate Partner

Strategic Partner

Official Partner

Official carriers

in cooperation with

Sponsored By

the best thing in the world – she's fantastic and she did a fantastic job today," Masterson said, before considering the thorny question of US racing's reliance on raceday medication – notably the Lasix that Tepin had done without. "It's a great message to send back home. People say Americans have to have drugs in their horses but she had no drugs, no nasal strip and nothing that everybody was worried about in the paper."

Tepin's performance could prove highly significant in terms of persuading other US trainers that it can be done at Royal Ascot. "Tepin's victory was hugely important, as in the light of high-profile defeats for Animal Kingdom and Able Friend in the Queen Anne, it showed the best from outside Europe could compete in that race," says Nick Smith, Ascot's director of racing and communications.

"On the wider stage, it sent out a real message in that Tepin won without Lasix and her nasal strip. That has to resonate in many ways and will hopefully open doors for others to come now that the concern over the straight course and the medication restrictions have been overcome."

Casse cannot help but smile at the memory. "There were a lot of things stacked against us but in the end her greatness prevailed," he says. "Julien hit her a couple of times, which he usually doesn't have to, so I was just waiting for the wire to come, but she's a remarkable horse and it's nice that the world knows it."

For the record, Tepin became only the second older American-trained horse to win at Royal Ascot, following the Wesley Ward-trained Undrafted in the 2015 Diamond Jubilee. Apart from Ward, Casse is the only US trainer ever to win a race at Britain's most prestigious meeting – a fact of which he is quietly proud.

"It's an entirely different type of world over there and it's something that sets us apart from other North American trainers," he says. "Only Wesley has gone and done it, so it puts us in a different category. It was a magnificent experience, just unbelievable. But I'm still very upset I didn't get to meet the Queen!"

'LADY AURELIA IS A FREAK'

For Wesley Ward to have a winner at Royal Ascot might be considered business as usual. Nothing else about Lady Aurelia's astonishing victory in the Queen Mary Stakes could be regarded as remotely standard fare.

The second US success of the royal meeting after Tepin was a long way out of the ordinary. When Ryan Moore won the Queen Mary in 2015 for Ward on Acapulco, he described the winner as an aeroplane; after a scarcely credible display from Lady Aurelia, Frankie Dettori said it was like sitting on a rocket.

Ward had expected nothing less of a filly for whom he could not entertain the prospect of defeat, despite the rain that ensured ground conditions were softer than ideal. "I mean, she will run an amazing race and it will take a would-be champion to beat her," he said a few days before the race. "She is just awesome."

The trainer wasn't wrong. The daughter of Scat Daddy was sent off 2-1 favourite and those odds soon looked generous as she scorched the Berkshire turf in an explosive performance that must surely rank as the

most staggering seen at the meeting since Frankel. Never headed in a dazzling display of raw power, Lady Aurelia had the prize in safe keeping before halfway.

Even though Dettori was saluting the crowd half a furlong out, she stopped the clock at 60.14sec – a sensational mark on ground described officially as 'soft' (probably good to soft in reality) and more than two and a half seconds faster than Profitable had clocked in the previous afternoon's King's Stand. It was seven lengths back to Al Johrah in second place.

"To win a sprint race over five furlongs by seven lengths on the bridle is madness really," Dettori said. "It's unheard of and we didn't think she'd like the ground, but Wesley Ward is a master. I thought there was no way she could keep that pace up but surprisingly she quickened off it. I've never felt anything like it in my life. It was stunning."

The job of a handicapper is to provide a lucid, cold, figures-based assessment. Usually, that is. Here, like the rest of us, Racing Post Ratings expert Sam Walker was astounded. "Lady Aurelia is a freak," he said. "There is no other explanation for that ludicrously impressive seven-length win. To win by such a huge margin in conditions softer than ideal and against 16 rivals spread right across the track suggests something was wildly out of kilter from normality. The performance was worth a huge RPR of 123, which would have been good enough to secure her the title of European champion juvenile in four of the last five seasons. It was quite simply a massive performance."

That she never repeated the performance in two further starts matters not a jot, though she hardly disgraced herself in winning the Group 1 Prix Morny before bleeding in the Cheveley Park. Lady Aurelia's place in Royal Ascot history was already assured.

FAST-TRACK DELIVERY

Dougie Costello's decision to move from jumps to Flat paid instant dividends on dual Group 1-winning sprinter Quiet Reflection

By James Burn

PROS and cons are often attached to any job offer but when Karl Burke approached jump jockey Dougie Costello with the idea of becoming attached to his Middleham stable, a promising bay filly was the overriding factor in the decision to switch codes.

In Quiet Reflection, Costello found more than perhaps he could have bargained for in his first full season on the Flat, but she was right at the front of his mind when Burke suggested linking up in October 2015.

"I knew she was a bit special when I watched her win the Cornwallis as a two-year-old," he says. "When Karl offered me the job I started thinking about her and got a bit excited. I asked Karl, 'Would that mean I get my leg over the mare?' She's every jockey's dream."

The dream came true in the most wonderful fashion at Royal Ascot when Quiet Reflection gave Costello an emotional Group 1 victory in the Commonwealth Cup. The 33-year-old jockey's tearful interviews, both immediately after the race and following the prize presentation, made clear how much the triumph – only his 39th Flat winner in Britain – meant to him.

"It took 25 years of graft to get here," he said at Royal Ascot. "Any sportsperson will tell you that to get to a top level, you have

to sacrifice so much. I was a big lad in my teens. I had to suffer. There were nights when I was sitting in while my friends were out partying. I missed my best friend's wedding, stuff like that."

Costello was more composed, though no less thankful, after Quiet Reflection followed a fine third in the July Cup with another Group 1 success in the 32Red Sprint Cup at Haydock in September. "It's unbelievable. I come in on my first year, get on a filly like this. I'm still dreaming."

****

COSTELLO, rooted in hunting and jump racing and with a Cheltenham Festival winner on his CV, found his mind wandering to the Flat a few years ago after riding out for William Muir and a summer dipping down to Deauville in 2015 opened his eyes to the riches on offer.

"When I saw the prize-money in three months it was like the prize-money of six months over jumps. I thought, 'Wow'. I wasn't getting any younger and didn't have a base over jumps, but at the same time AP McCoy had retired," he says, recalling how he was torn between staying over jumps for a 15th season or taking his chances on the Flat. "Then Karl, who I was riding out for, offered me a job and it was too good to turn down."

The father of one had no problems with his weight and, thanks to a McCoy-like dedication to his trade, made a smooth transition, although there have been challenges.

"Two-year-olds are like young kids in that they change

very quickly. I remember Paul Nicholls won two Gold Cups with Kauto Star and said, 'We're just learning about him'. He'd trained him for six or seven years and that's the best jumps trainer in the country, so on the Flat the jockeys and trainers have to pick things up very quickly."

Quiet Reflection has been one of the more straightforward rides for Costello, as well as the best. She impressed him when digging deep for a Group 3 success at Chantilly in April and followed up by landing Haydock's Group 2 Sandy Lane Stakes to become favourite for the Commonwealth Cup at Royal Ascot – the jockey's new Cheltenham.

"She was a better filly at Haydock than in France and was only in second gear when she won the Sandy Lane," he says. "She wants to win and has natural ability and those two things are hard to find in a horse."

If the pressure was building as Ascot approached, Costello wasn't feeling it. "I loved that. I was lucky enough when I was riding over jumps for John Quinn that I was riding fancied horses in big handicaps and I relished it – that's why you're in the game. It's nicer having that pressure because you're on good horses.

"I've been to Cheltenham Festivals and Grand National meetings and you get interviewed and you say you really fancy your horse, when in the back of your mind you're thinking, 'If this runs fourth it will have run well'. But honestly I couldn't see Quiet Reflection being beaten at Ascot."

Costello, thoughtful and articulate, had not suddenly become a flash, brash Flat jockey; he was just full of confidence in his horse of a lifetime.

"I went through the Commonwealth Cup in my head the night before and tried to think 'this could beat us, that could beat us', but before I went to bed I thought, 'No, they can't beat us'. By the time I woke up I was 100 per cent confident, if everything went right."

He may have been a newcomer to this level on the Flat, but as he said afterwards it was just a case of getting down to basics. "If you strip out the stands and the crowd, it's a green field and you start at A and end at B. You keep it as simple as that, and I've been doing it since I was ten, when I was racing ponies round a field."

Costello was touched by the reaction of colleagues old and new to the triumph. "John Ferguson came up to me walking back and said, 'This is better than Market Rasen'," he recalls. "I was thinking of the sacrifices I'd made, like every other lad in the weighing room. The emotion takes over. I've not watched the interviews I did after the race and I don't want to because I'm a bit embarrassed."

****

HAVING had time for quiet reflection of his own, Costello is still pinching himself. "She's given me a Group 3, a Group 2 and two Group 1s – and my goal was just to keep Karl Burke happy. I couldn't have any regrets about the decision. I didn't pack up jumping because my bottle was gone or because of injuries – and I'd still like to ride another Cheltenham winner and win the National. I packed up jumping because I was given a great opportunity."

With the help of a speedy bay filly, Costello seized that opportunity with both hands.

▸ Emotional release: Dougie Costello in tears after his Royal Ascot success (left)

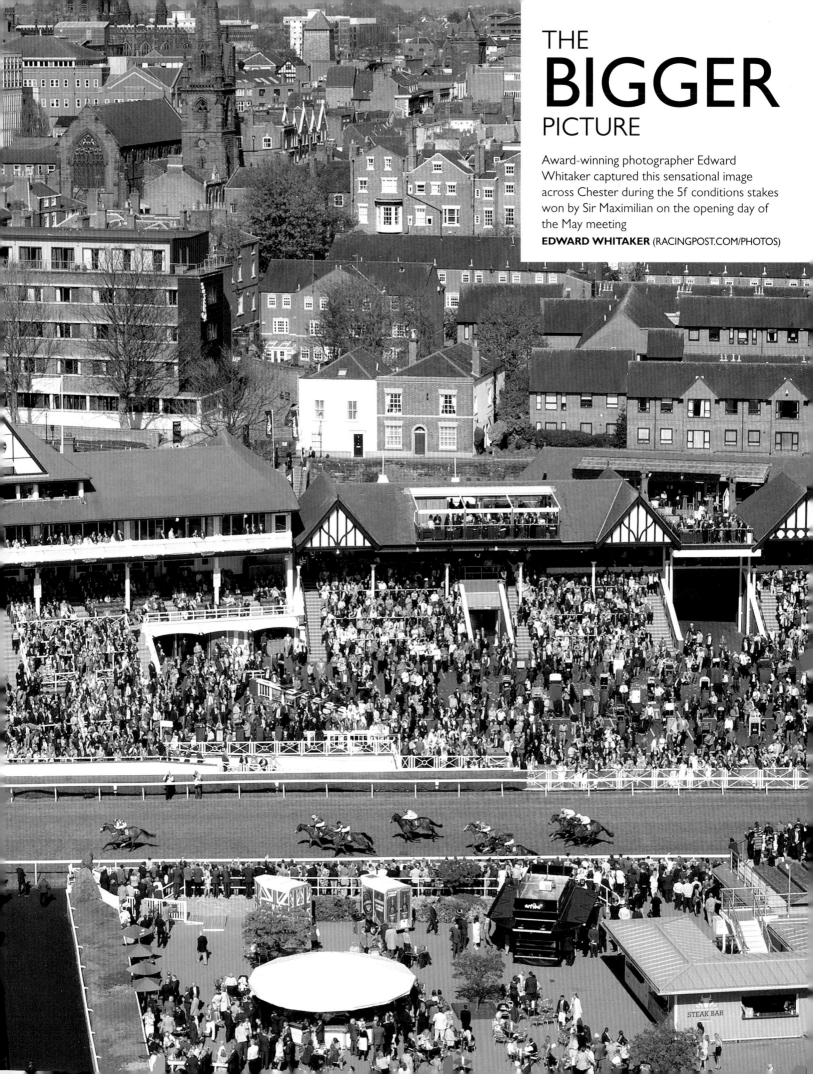

THE
BIGGER
PICTURE

Award-winning photographer Edward Whitaker captured this sensational image across Chester during the 5f conditions stakes won by Sir Maximilian on the opening day of the May meeting

EDWARD WHITAKER (RACINGPOST.COM/PHOTOS)

STEAK BAR

'We've had help from somewhere. Tiff must have been looking down on me'

Mouse Morris had twin moments of glory in the Grand Nationals at Aintree and Fairyhouse but there was agony amid the ecstasy

By Lee Mottershead

FOR most of us, sport is an enjoyable distraction from the real world. For those who earn their living from sport it is rather more than that. It is about towering highs and plummeting lows. It requires dedication, persistence and commitment. Yet even for those whose lives are submerged in sport on a daily basis, it can sometimes be as much of a distraction for them as it is for us. Other stuff can be, and often is, of vastly greater importance.

One thing must always be placed in context with another. In the moments after the 2015 Irish Grand National, Mouse Morris was dejected and it was easy to see why. One of Ireland's truly great jumps trainers had sent out three runners in the nation's most valuable steeplechase. Rogue Angel got no further than the ninth fence, but making the turn for home Morris could surely visualise a second win in the race he had captured with Hear The Echo seven years earlier and won as a jockey in 1977. It was not to be.

Band Of Blood, a 50-1 shot belonging to Gigginstown House Stud, had made much of the running. He approached the third-last fence
▸▸ *Continues page 86*

still in the lead and with another Michael O'Leary-owned stablemate, Rule The World, as his nearest pursuer. A bad mistake two out hampered the progress of Rule The World, but by the final fence he had nonetheless managed to draw level with Band Of Blood. So, too, had a further Gigginstown contender, the Sandra Hughes-trained Thunder And Roses. He won. Morris did not, with Rule The World in second and Band Of Blood an exhausted fourth.

It was a blow to Morris. Far worse was to come in June that year when his son Christopher, known throughout racing as Tiffer, died while abroad. Soon after, on the Wednesday of Royal Ascot, the Irish contingent was down in numbers with many attending the funeral of a lost son, brother and friend.

It is frequently said, but plainly true, that the suffering of a parent forced to bury a child is immeasurable and unthinkable. It is a trauma from which complete recovery is impossible. How, placed against such wretched misery, can sport possibly matter? For Morris and Tiffer's brother, Jamie, it immediately mattered less. Perhaps, though, in some ways, it also started to matter more.

"The only way to get through it was to work hard," the 2006 Cheltenham Gold Cup-winning trainer said later in the year. "The harder you work, the easier it is." So he worked, not so much seeking reward as temporary release. At the Galway festival reward and release seemed destined to come together. Rule The World jumped the penultimate fence travelling like the winner. Then, on the famously short run to the final jump, he somehow managed to slip up and part company with Davy Russell.

Two days later, Rogue Angel put a smile on the face of Morris when winning a significantly less valuable Ballybrit handicap chase. Even better was to come at Listowel's September jamboree. On the opening Sunday, Rogue Angel finished second in a two-and-a-half-mile handicap chase. Three days later he won the Kerry National by a short head under 3lb claimer Ger Fox. Back in third, ridden by another conditional

'It is a trauma from which complete recovery is impossible. How, placed against such wretched misery, can sport possibly matter?'

jockey, David Mullins, was Rule The World.

Thereafter the two stayers were trained towards Grand National glory by a man famed not only for looking a little dishevelled and smoking copious quantities of Majors cigarettes, but also for being just about the best target trainer in the business. Both made it to their chosen targets. First up was Rogue Angel back at Fairyhouse.

He had been beaten in three starts after Listowel but was an obvious contender to win the BoyleSports-backed Irish Grand National at 16-1. Also in the field, this time priced up at 20-1, was a second Morris candidate, and yet another member of the Gigginstown chasing battalions, Folsom Blue.

As Morris was about to leave his yard in Fethard, County Tipperary, he made a point of looking at a photo of Tiffer. "I need a little help here," he said, once again meeting his son eye to eye. Help came.

Rogue Angel did what Band Of Blood had tried to do 12 months earlier. There were a few moments when he was not in front but not many. Running down to the final fence he seemed destined to be denied. Ruby Walsh had persuaded

the quirky Bless The Wings to launch a challenge on the bridle. He only had to convert a little of what appeared to be in his tank to triumph, but at the end of a marathon he flattered only to deceive. If there was a real rogue in this race it was the horse who ended up in second, a short head behind the horse who left Morris in bits.

Interviewed live on television, he broke down. He had asked Tiffer to assist. He believed Tiffer had done just that. "This is for him," he said, while speaking later, he reflected: "It was virtually a year to the week since I'd last seen him when Rogue Angel won, so I was up front about it, and the horse having Angel in his name . . .

"I'm not a religious fellow. I don't believe. But Tiffer was definitely helping, I've no doubt."

****

WHEN it comes to the most famous of all horseraces, doubts will always dominate. In a 40-runner handicap over more than four and a quarter miles with 30 fences to be jumped, it can be no other way. At Aintree, 12 days after Fairyhouse, Morris had two Grand National runners. Gigginstown's retained rider, Bryan Cooper, planned to partner Rule The World until changing his mind on the morning of declarations. Instead he preferred Morris's popular veteran First Lieutenant. The old lad fell at the second fence.

Jumping never looked likely to be a problem for Rule The World. This, though, was a horse whose career had been littered with much bigger problems. There had been two fractured pelvises, but for which Morris is adamant the son of Sulamani would have proved better than Gold Cup hero War Of Attrition. He had managed to avoid serious injury since making his chasing debut in November 2014 but had never won a chase. When facing the Aintree starting tapes under Mullins, nephew of champion trainer Willie Mullins, he was, astonishingly, a maiden chaser of long standing. Thirteen outings over fences had yielded 13 losses. No novice had won the sport's signature contest since Mr What in 1958.

▸ Continues page 88

Christopher 'Tiffer' Morris, one of Mouse Morris's two sons, was only 30 when he was killed by carbon monoxide poisoning in Argentina in June 2015.

Tiffer had worked as a chef in London for several years and was exploring Argentina, looking for fresh food and recipe ideas with a view to opening a restaurant back home in Ireland.

He was also a talented musician and had performed as drummer in a band the night before he and fellow group member Munra Borghi lost their lives in the apartment they shared. A carbon monoxide leak from a water heater, combined with a lack of ventilation, proved fatal to both men.

Following Tiffer's death his family have been involved in a campaign to encourage people to purchase portable carbon monoxide alarms.

Talking about his brother after Rule The World's Grand National triumph, Jamie Morris – whose childhood difficulty in pronouncing his sibling's real name led to Christopher becoming Tiffer – said: "We were much the same – a bit of a Jack the lad. We loved our music and enjoyed a party."

▸▸ On top of the world: David Mullins, having his first ride in the Grand National, takes the glory on Rule The World in front of the vast Aintree crowd

This was a tough task for the horse but also for a young jockey known to his friends as 'Stud'. Mullins had never even seen the big green fences close up until walking the course on the morning of the race. After finishing the walk he felt dazed, in part due to having to ride at a light weight in the first race. He would again feel dazed later in the day.

Aside from making a terrible blunder four fences out, Rule The World ran the perfect race. The eye was regularly drawn to the blue cap of Mullins, whose 33-1 mount ambled through a Grand National staged on ground turned gruelling and sodden by heavy raceday rain.

Defending champion Many Clouds took the lead on the second run to Becher's Brook, but the testing conditions and his weight burden had begun to take their toll by the time the Melling Road was crossed for the second time. Jumping the final fence 8-1 joint-favourite The Last Samuri and 13-year-old pensioner Vics Canvas, eventual second and third, were already engaged in a mighty duel. Just after the Elbow, Rule The World swept past on their outer and it was all over. The victory margin was six lengths.

What we saw soon after was beautiful. It was a shot of Morris and son Jamie, now his sole remaining child, embracing, both in a state of shocked ecstasy.

"The whole idea was to stand beside Dad and watch the race with him," Jamie recalls. "I actually led down Rule The World with one of the other stable lads. By the time I got back up the chute Dad had gone into the middle of the track and I got stuck stands' side.

"The plan to watch the race together didn't pan out but when

RARE DOUBLE

The victory of Rule The World at Aintree placed trainer Mouse Morris in an extremely select club, just one month after Gordon Elliott had been the first to be inducted into that same club for just over four decades.

Both men are now among four Irish-based trainers who have sent out at least one winner of the Cheltenham Gold Cup and Grand National.

First to achieve the feat, not surprisingly, was the legendary Vincent O'Brien, who dominated jump racing before dominating Flat racing. He was responsible for Cottage Rake's hat-trick of Gold Cup wins between 1948 and 1950, and he won the race again with Knock Hard in 1953. In the same season he tasted Grand National glory for the first time, courtesy of Early Mist, and then remarkably with another two different horses, Royal Tan and Quare Times, in 1954 and 1955.

Dan Moore completed the double with one horse, L'Escargot, who supplemented his Gold Cup wins in 1970 and 1971 with victory in the 1975 Grand National.

Of the famous quartet Elliott is the only one who won the Grand National before the Gold Cup. Silver Birch sprang a 33-1 shock in 2007, nine years before the trainer's Don Cossack scored at Cheltenham.

Morris preceded his Grand National victory by ten years, having orchestrated War Of Attrition's Gold Cup victory in 2006.

All to play for: Rule The World clears the final fence in third as he goes in pursuit of The Last Samuri and Vics Canvas; (below) Mouse Morris, jockey David Mullins and owner Michael O'Leary with Rule The World

the horse won I managed to get across the track and we had an emotional meeting that the cameras managed to capture. We didn't do much talking. Dad was completely out of breath after smoking all those Majors. We were in a daze. There were no words, just a lot of hugging, shouting and cheering. I think it will be April next year, and I'm watching the 2017 race, that it finally sinks in."

****

IN more ways than one this was a momentous Grand National, once again thankfully free of equine casualties. O'Leary, uncharacteristically reduced to tears, had won the Gold Cup with Don Cossack prior to Rogue Angel's success at Fairyhouse. This was some spring for the Ryanair boss.

"It doesn't get any better than the Gold Cup and two Grand Nationals," said O'Leary, whose thoughts then turned to Morris. "It's amazing. What a training performance. I think it's wonderful for Mouse."

Indeed it was, but Mouse, generally a man of few words, found words even harder than usual to locate. "It's

▶▶ Continues page 90

Feel happy. Feel informed. Feel healthy.

#FeelTheExcitement

Randox Health gives you the full understanding
of your body's condition, arming you with
the information for sustained well-being.

Discover more:

Search Randox Health

Disneyland, fairytale stuff," he said. "We've had some help from somewhere. Tiff must have been looking down on me."

If so, he would have liked what he saw. He would have liked the events of the following day as well when Rule The World, pensioned off to enjoy retirement after one last outing at Punchestown, was paraded by Morris, first in Mullingar, then Fethard.

"Rule The World is the best I've trained," Morris said during the first parade. He was also heard to say something else. "Jamie, Jamie," shouted father to son. "Where are my fags?"

Providing the fags on that memorable day was a vital job. Jamie Morris, however, has done more that. The pair have worked together since Tiffer's death. As Morris mourns a son, Jamie mourns a brother. They have been there for each other.

"I was going back home anyway to babysit the old man," Jamie says. "Someone needs to keep an eye on him. He's a very grumpy man to babysit, a creature of habit, but we get on very well and we've had a bit of success together."

The most important success of all continued the Grand National's remarkable tradition of yielding results that tug on the heartstrings. It was, however, just a horserace.

"It doesn't do much to change anything, to be honest," Jamie says. "What did make a big difference was the support we received from everyone, especially in the racing community. That was overwhelming. Without those people it would have been a lot tougher."

On the day of the parades those people made their feelings clear. They could not have been happier for a man so deserving of happiness himself.

"Since he died I see things completely differently," said Morris, by then a Grand National-winning trainer. "It was definitely a lift," Jamie says. "This isn't something we'll ever come to terms with, but the Grand National was a welcome distraction."

Given what they had been through, and given what they had achieved, countless others joined them in welcoming that glorious distraction.

Grand occasions: Ger Fox embraces Mouse Morris after winning the Irish Grand National on Rogue Angel (top); a huge turnout in Mullingar as Rule The World arrives home (left); Morris's two National winners parade at Tipperary

IN THE PICTURE

Walsh performs miracle to score on gutsy Killultagh Vic

The race appeared all but over as Killultagh Vic approached the final fence with a three-length advantage in the somewhat appropriately named Grade 2 "Money Back On Fallers" at Coral.ie Novice Chase at Leopardstown in January. Little did we know the drama that was about to unfold.

Killultagh Vic, the 2-7 favourite ridden by Ruby Walsh, overjumped the fence and pitched on landing before sliding on all fours through the soft turf. Many jockeys would have been catapulted out of the saddle but Walsh managed to hold on to his mount and miraculously regained control, despite losing an iron.

That was all very well but in the meantime Blair Perrone and Lord Scoundrel had gone past the floundering favourite and seemed certain to fight out the finish. In-running layers certainly thought it was all over with more than €1,000 matched at 999-1 on Killultagh Vic on Betfair.

Walsh, however, refused to give up and he had a willing partner in Killultagh Vic. Having got up off the ground, the son of Old Vic stuck his neck out under Walsh's urging and chased down the leaders to win by three-quarters of a length from Blair Perrone, with subsequent Galway Plate winner Lord Scoundrel another length and three-quarters back in third.

"It was a good performance to get back up and win, wasn't it?" said Walsh with more than a little understatement. "He's got some turn of foot and that's with me flapping up and down on him. I was nearly off him [at the last]. He just pinged it and pitched."

Willie Mullins, Killultagh Vic's trainer, paid tribute to his stable jockey. "I thought he was gone and a lot of riders would have pulled up after what happened, but not Ruby. What happened was unbelievable, quite extraordinary, and full marks to horse and rider. The two horses he caught and beat are no slouches, and to beat them having made the running and then having to give them several lengths after the last fence was staggering."

Killultagh Vic was cut to 7-2 favourite for the JLT Novices' Chase at the Cheltenham Festival following his extraordinary performance. Unfortunately, three weeks later the seven-year-old picked up a suspensory injury that ended his season.

As we saw on Killultagh Vic, there was no stopping Walsh, who enjoyed another triumphant season. He took top jockey honours at the Cheltenham Festival for the tenth time, with seven winners taking his overall score to 52, and was Irish champion jump jockey for the 11th time.

Pictures: ALAIN BARR (RACINGPOST.COM/PHOTOS)

By Katherine Fidler

AMONG the newcomers to the Cheltenham Festival of 2016, there was one racegoers couldn't fail to notice.

One that stood head and shoulders above the rest, demanding attention, drawing admiration, taking the breath away. Below the gleaming new Princess Royal Stand – 19 months in the making for its festival debut – there was no disputing that the most impressive festival first-timer out on the hallowed turf was Thistlecrack.

Over the course of a stunning season, Colin Tizzard's emerging star had risen to the top of the staying hurdle ranks with a winning run that cemented him as one of the bankers of the festival. Yet even his evident quality – and Tizzard's unequivocal confidence – did not prepare the Cheltenham crowds for one of the most extraordinary performances of recent times.

Thistlecrack simply ran away with the Ryanair World Hurdle, powering seven lengths clear in a breathtaking show of class. This was a performance that, like the Princess Royal Stand, will be a monument for years to come, a mighty demonstration of what can be achieved at Britain's premier jumps track.

"Thistlecrack puts rivals to sword in blistering display," was emblazoned across the top of the World Hurdle report in the next day's Racing Post and he earned "the highest hurdle mark at the festival in the past 30 years" with 178 on Racing Post Ratings.

Reaction from those involved in the race was just as forthright in appreciation. Mouse Morris, trainer of runner-up Alpha Des Obeaux, described Thistlecrack as "a hell of a machine", while winning jockey Tom Scudamore said: "If you're enjoying watching him, just think what it's like riding him. I've spent my whole life running around in these races and now I finally have a horse like this. It's unbelievable."

Here, truly, was a hurdler for the ages.

****

WHEN Thistlecrack walked out on to the track with his 11 rivals for the World Hurdle, Cheltenham's new stand towered above him. But looming even larger was the shadow of Big Buck's, for so long the poster boy of staying hurdlers with his record

▶▶ *Continues page 96*

CRACK SHOT

Thistlecrack rose to superstar status with a series of brilliant performances in staying hurdles and now sights are set on a new challenge

four consecutive World Hurdle victories. This was the benchmark by which Thistlecrack, if he won, would be measured.

So far Thistlecrack, a €43,000 purchase for John and Heather Snook, had done everything right. His form figures of 111 denoted victories in the Long Distance Hurdle, Long Walk Hurdle and Cleeve Hurdle by a combined distance of 26 lengths, but now came the acid test on his first visit to the festival. Could he overturn last year's winner Cole Harden and a slew of talented contenders to add the World Hurdle?

He already had beaten Cole Harden first time out when springing something of a shock at Newbury, described as "the new kid on the block" after 6-4 favourite Whisper and Cole Harden finished last and third respectively behind Tizzard's then seven-year-old, who had been a Grade 1-winning novice at Aintree the previous spring.

"He was actually a bit behind on fitness at Newbury," says the Dorset-based trainer, who admits it wasn't until last season that he knew quite how special Thistlecrack was. "He'd had mixed performances until he went to Aintree [winning the Grade 1 Sefton Novices' Hurdle] but he got better for racing. His second run looked brilliant."

In that second run Thistlecrack firmly threw his hat in the ring for young upstart status when putting the kibosh on Reve De Sivola's bid for a fourth Long Walk Hurdle. The fans' favourite had been cruising along until the market favourite Thistlecrack brushed past him with little regard for his standing. Reve De Sivola the seasoned defender, Thistlecrack the impetuous new striker.

"He felt as impressive as he looked," said Scudamore, who would have missed out but for overturning a ban two days before. "To be in a Grade 1 like

that and not have a moment's worry was a great thrill. It was a mighty performance."

A mighty performance indeed, but one that had not simply been pulled out of a hat. For Tizzard and his team, the star emerging in front of them was the result of years of patience and careful management.

"He was the opposite of straightforward," Tizzard says. "He couldn't take the training when he first arrived and we had to back off him a few times – more than a few times. He went into pre-training and was late coming back because he couldn't take being trained.

"For two or three days he'd be fine, but if you worked him he'd be stiff, we'd have to back off and start again, back off and start again, but

▸▸ Easy does it: Thistlecrack makes light work of winning (clockwise from top) the Long Walk, Long Distance and Cleeve Hurdles for his delighted connections (below)

he developed into the horse he is now – a very, very good horse."

Two from two, Thistlecrack enjoyed a Christmas break before a festival test run in the Cleeve Hurdle. A first visit to the track had not gone well when, 12 months earlier, 61 lengths had separated Thistlecrack and Ordo Ab Chao, winner of the Grade 2 Classic Novices' Hurdle.

Tizzard was buoyed by his last two outings – as were the punters who backed him into odds-on favouritism – and was defiant. "I don't know why [he ran so badly] but I have absolutely no concerns about Cheltenham," he said. "There must have been something wrong that day but I don't know what it was, nothing came to light. This is another big race and we want to win it. It's a proper prize and there will be no excuses afterwards. We're not going there to put him right for March – we're going to try to win."

'Try'. A word that generally denotes some effort or exertion, yet those who watched that day

▸▸ Continues page 98

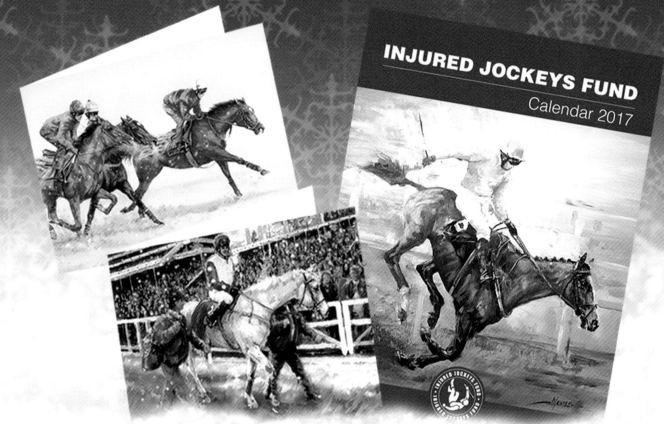

will recall how Thistlecrack floated up the hill, completely unchallenged and with the only question being his margin of victory. The answer: 12 lengths, from subsequent French Champion Hurdle winner Ptit Zig.

****

NOW the World Hurdle was surely just a formality, wasn't it? It would be easy to presume so, but there were new rivals to factor in. He had faced 15 different opponents in his three wins, but here he would tackle other, more experienced contenders. The market was not so sure he would carry on winning – he was still sent off favourite, but at evens. Big Buck's had been odds-on for three of his four victories. Would – could – Thistlecrack live up to the hype and announce himself successor to the stayers' throne?

Oh ye layers of little faith. Evens proved a remarkable bargain for backers as Scudamore and Thistlecrack again glided across the verdant stage, gradually easing their way up to challenge the leader and reigning champion Cole Harden. The point at which the pair chose to break their rivals' hearts can be pinpointed to an exact moment – mid-air over the penultimate hurdle. Thistlecrack, Cole Harden and Alpha Des Obeaux took off as one, but only one literally took flight, landing with two lengths in hand and streaking away.

Alpha Des Obeaux put up a noble fight but was seven lengths adrift of the Snooks' now bona fide hero at the line – a distance just a length and a half shy of the combined total by which Big Buck's won his four renewals, such was his habit for doing just enough up the Cheltenham hill.

Thistlecrack is evidently not in the business of giving his supporters – nor his jockey – cause for concern.

"I never thought it would be so easy," Scudamore said. "I was always very confident in my fella. He's the best I've sat on – I can say that in public now."

Thistlecrack's public welcomed him back into the winner's enclosure with the adulation such a performance deserves – and yet he was not done dazzling his growing legion of fans.

A little over three weeks later

Tizzard's staying star made his longest trip since arriving at Venn Farm from Ireland when lining up at Aintree for the Liverpool Stayers' Hurdle. Four years earlier Big Buck's had completed the same seasonal five-timer with a nine-length victory over Crack Away Jack. A somewhat depleted field of five turned up to take on the champion-elect, his 2-7 favouritism proving bookies wouldn't make the same mistake again – even if Thistlecrack made his first when hitting the penultimate flight. It was a brief moment of concern forgotten about quickly as he eased away to score by seven lengths.

▶▶Demolition job: Thistlecrack powers home under Tom Scudamore to land a breathtaking victory in the World Hurdle; (below) trainer Colin Tizzard with his star hurdler and King George winner Cue Card (left)

The Aintree victory confirmed him as a hurdler of rare standing, a match for Big Buck's with that epic five-timer and his RPR of 178 – identical to the best achieved by his predecessor. The chief difference was that, whereas Thistlecrack had reached that mark at Cheltenham, Big Buck's did it at Aintree.

With a new season came the adventurous project to see if Thistlecrack could succeed where Big Buck's didn't: over fences. Within 24 hours of his Cheltenham romp a chasing campaign had been confirmed – a bold one, with Timico Gold Cup dreams.

"Going chasing we need him in the same form as last season – there are a lot of things we've got to get right before he's a brilliant horse again," says Tizzard, who knows there are many unknowns in this new field.

"There's any number of good novices coming through who might go chasing – and no-one was talking about Thistlecrack this time last year."

But they are now, as Tizzard's star sets out to shine in a new sphere.

DOWN TO EARTH

Colin Tizzard had a shot at more festival glory when Cue Card lined up as 5-2 second favourite for the Timico Cheltenham Gold Cup, just 24 hours after Thistlecrack's World Hurdle, but those hopes were dashed by a crashing fall at the third-last.

As well as the glory of the race, there was a £1m bonus on offer if Cue Card could complete the chasing triple crown after his victories in the Betfair Chase and King George VI Chase. In a red-hot contest, the ten-year-old – for so long the Tizzard flagbearer – had just taken the lead when he fell.

"That's championship racing for you, isn't it?" said a disappointed but philosophical Tizzard. "Two seconds before he fell I thought 'here we go' but he just put down, hit the top of the fence and over he went. It's the first time he's fallen in four years of chasing. Thank God he got up."

Cue Card bounced back to win the Grade 1 Betfred Bowl at Aintree less than three weeks later but was below par when beaten at odds-on in the Punchestown Gold Cup in late April.

Just as much as Thistlecrack, Cue Card played a starring role in Tizzard's greatest season. Even if Gold, and all the associated riches, eluded him at Cheltenham.

THE BIGGER PICTURE

Some of Sandra Hughes's string exercise at the Curragh on a frosty morning in February when the temperature dipped to -5C. The following day Hughes beat the freeze with a Grade 2 win for Acapella Bourgeois, her leading novice hurdler of the season
PATRICK McCANN (RACINGPOST.COM/PHOTOS)

The trainers and jockeys who got on the scoreboard for the first time at the 2016 Cheltenham Festival tell their stories

DAN SKELTON AND HARRY SKELTON

Superb Story, Vincent O'Brien County Handicap Hurdle

IN A golden year for the Skelton family, brothers Dan and Harry combined to break their Cheltenham Festival ducks as their increasingly successful trainer-jockey partnership reached new heights.

While father Nick claimed Olympic gold at the age of 58 in the individual showjumping at the summer Games in Rio, the brothers reached the top step of the podium at jump racing's 'Olympics' in a season that saw both of them break the century barrier for the first time.

Dan Skelton, 31, who spent nine years learning from ten-time champion trainer Paul Nicholls in the glory days with Kauto Star,

Denman and Master Minded, has been quick to take high rank in his own right since starting his training career in 2013, but he was still searching for his first festival winner as Cheltenham 2016 entered its final day.

The stable's festival runners had been performing with great credit – promising novices Its'afreebee and Three Musketeers as well as lovable veteran Al Ferof all ran blinders without getting home in

front – but it was left to Superb Story in the perennially competitive County Hurdle to break the duck.

After Superb Story's fine second in the StanJames.com Greatwood Hurdle at the track in November, Skelton had taken the brave decision to avoid running the five-year-old during the winter and keep him fresh for the toughest assignment of his career.

Stable confidence was as high as

THAT WINNING FEELING

it can be for a race of this nature and it was more than justified as the 8-1 shot scored impressively by two and a half lengths, with Harry riding an assured race as he joined his brother in landing that all-important festival first.

To complete the family celebrations, father Nick was there to witness the landmark triumph.

The winning trainer says: "It was great to experience the many top days during my time with Paul and I'll always cherish those memories, but to do it yourself for the first time at the festival is priceless and it was great to have Harry on board the first winner.

"Every emotion you can imagine was going through my mind as he crossed the line in front, though it was mainly sheer elation that we'd done it.

"It proved we'd made the right decision to hold back with him for the race after his fantastic run in the Greatwood and to be vindicated like that was a great feeling. It was magic – a dream come true."

By the end of the season, the Skelton stable in Alcester, Warwickshire, had notched 104 winners – up from 73 in the previous campaign – and finished sixth in the trainers' table.

Harry, 27, had 101 in the jockeys' standings – nearly double his previous best of 55 – and matched his brother with sixth place.

"I'm indebted to my whole team as it's down to them for getting us to where we are today," Dan says. "We're now keen to kick on and achieve more success on the big days.

"Once you get a taste of success on the big stage, you strive for more."

▶▶ Continues page 104

HARRY FRY
Unowhatimeanharry,
Albert Bartlett
Novices' Hurdle

DAN SKELTON was not the only former Paul Nicholls assistant to land his first festival winner in his own name at Cheltenham 2016. Harry Fry, who oversaw the preparation of 2012 Champion Hurdle winner Rock On Ruby from Nicholls' Seaborough satellite yard, followed hot on Skelton's heels by landing the Grade 1 Albert Bartlett Novices' Hurdle with Unowhatimeanharry – just 40 minutes after Skelton had struck with Superb Story.

Fry, 29, who had his first runner in October 2012, is one of the brightest young talents in the jumps game and a masterful campaign with Unowhatimeanharry was high-profile evidence of his skills.

Without a win after 11 starts over hurdles, Unowhatimeanharry seemed far from a Cheltenham winner in waiting when he joined Fry for the 2015-16 season. But in the space of a few months he went from a 123-rated handicapper to a Grade 1 winner with an official mark 26lb higher.

"At the start of the season the aim was just to win a race," the trainer admits. "To win five on the bounce and end up in the winner's enclosure after a Grade 1 was fantastic. Having a winner at the Cheltenham Festival is enormous."

Fry can rely on the support of some of the sport's most high-profile owners and he was 14th in the championship last season with a career-best 54 winners and more than £700,000 in prize-money. But, at a time when triumphs for the little man seem to happen less frequently than in bygone eras, it was heartwarming his first festival triumph should come with the 40-strong Harry Fry Racing Club.

"At no point did anyone expect it [festival victory] and that added to the joy and fun of it all," Fry says. "There was a good gang at Cheltenham on the day – you probably noticed the celebrations in the winner's enclosure."

Unowhatimeanharry's rise from obscurity to a starring role on the big stage was well worth celebrating.

JACK SHERWOOD
Ibis Du Rheu, Martin Pipe
Conditional Jockeys'
Handicap Hurdle

THE 2015-16 campaign was a tough one for Jack Sherwood but months of torment were blown away in five magical minutes at Cheltenham in March.

Having ridden 14 winners the season before, Sherwood struggled to hit the same heights after injury caused his opportunities to dry up. That was until the 24-year-old conditional jockey got the leg up on Ibis Du Rheu for his boss Paul Nicholls in the Martin Pipe

▶▶ Kings of the hill: (top) Noel Fehily celebrates on Unowhatimeanharry as he lands the Albert Bartlett Novices' Hurdle for Harry Fry; (inset) Fry greets his winner; (bottom) Jack Sherwood drives Ibis Du Rheu (right) to victory in the Martin Pipe Conditional Jockeys' Handicap Hurdle

Handicap Hurdle on the final day of the festival.

"I had an absolute nightmare of a season," says Sherwood, who went so far as to consider a change of career. "I broke my arm at the end of October after a quiet summer and wasn't back until Boxing Day, when Paul wasn't sending out many runners due to the soft ground. It's really hard to get going again when you've been out for a while and not riding winners, especially with so many good lads at Paul's. I wasn't in a very good place, it was a dark time."

Not for the first time in its storied history, the unpredictable magic of the
▶▶ Continues page 106

PALACE HOUSE
NEWMARKET

Frankie Dettori meets Our Vic

The King's Yard

The Rothschild Yard

Much More Than a Museum

A unique attraction on a five acre site in the heart of Newmarket,
all in the royal settings of Charles II's sporting palace and stables.

National Horseracing Museum

A much expanded Museum where the latest audio visual technology charts the history of the sport from its origins to the global sport it is today.

Fred Packard Galleries

The National Gallery of British Sporting Art with loans from Tate Britain and the V&A featuring artists as diverse as Stubbs to Blake and Munnings to Wallinger.

Rothschild Yard

The opportunity to meet racing's equine heroes, for the first time former racehorses can be seen seven days a week with daily demonstrations in the Peter O'Sullevan Arena.

King's Yard

Enjoy a relaxing meal in The Tack Room Restaurant and take home unique gifts from the Palace House Shop.

For more information T: 01638 667 314, E: info@palacehousenewmarket.co.uk
Daily opening times 10am -5pm.

National Heritage Centre, Palace House, Palace Street, Newmarket, Suffolk, CB8 8EP

palacehousenewmarket.co.uk

festival sprinkled a touch of its restorative power upon Sherwood and lifted him from the gloom.

"I went there not really expecting anything," says Sherwood, whose father Simon rode Desert Orchid to Cheltenham Gold Cup glory in 1989 and is now clerk of the course at Ludlow. "Nick Scholfield is a good friend of mine and he fancied Ibis Du Rheu a bit more. In the race I had a good position at the start and got where I wanted to be, around seventh or eighth. It all just stemmed from there and went very well.

"Any winner is amazing but that moment when I knew I'd won was surreal. I still have to pinch myself really. The crowd was brilliant and coming back down the horsewalk was an amazing feeling. It was just crazy."

PAT KELLY
Mall Dini, Pertemps Network Final

IRELAND has become accustomed to banking on the Willie Mullins battalions, but one of the most popular winners at Cheltenham 2016 came from the other end of the training spectrum when Mall Dini – one of seven horses in Pat Kelly's Galway stable – provided a memorable festival first on St Patrick's Day.

After returning to the hallowed winner's enclosure on the 14-1 winner, jockey Davy Russell diverted praise to the veteran trainer, a stalwart of the Irish jumping scene. "All credit goes to Pat Kelly, what a man. People might not know who he is but he's a very shrewd man from Galway. He's a genius and had him spot-on."

Mall Dini was the first runner in Britain for Kelly since the 2008-09 season and for his last winner outside Ireland the record books had to be scoured all the way back to November 1991 and a handicap hurdle victory at Ayr with Kilian My Boy.

Of course there had not been too many runners in the intervening years, although Mall Dini was not the first to represent Kelly at the festival, as he recalled in the winner's enclosure.

"It's very exciting as I've been here before twice but haven't had much luck. In 1990 I had a nice horse [Art

Trail, who broke a leg] in the Supreme Novices' and then I had one in the National Hunt Chase that Willie Mullins rode [Take The Town in 1994] but unfortunately he was unseated. So this is the first bit of luck I've had."

Not that Kelly was hoping for any change in his set-up and he scoffed at the idea of more owners sending horses in his direction. "I prefer to be small," was his understated reaction.

In contrast, winning owner Philip Reynolds was irrepressible as he celebrated his own festival first after chasing the dream for 30 years.

▶ Green for go: (top) Mall Dini (green) and Davy Russell win the Pertemps Network Final for Pat Kelly; (bottom) Ian Williams (right) in the winner's enclosure with Ballyalton, winning owner John Westwood (left), jockey Brian Hughes (green colours) and top golfer Lee Westwood (third left), John's son

"It's a dream come true. I've wanted to do this all my life," the son of the late Taoiseach, Albert Reynolds, told the Irish Times. "This is a small man's day. To come to Cheltenham and take on the big guys. Pat brings one horse and has one winner – 100 per cent, what about that?"

IAN WILLIAMS
Ballyalton, Close Brothers Novices' Handicap Chase

IAN WILLIAMS had resigned himself to the familiar sinking sensation of missing out on the Cheltenham party when Ballyalton
▶ Continues page 108

was headed after the last in the final race of the opening day, but any despair quickly turned to delight as a long-held dream was realised.

"I remember watching him travel well at the top of the hill and seeing him still going well at the second-last, but after that it was all a blur," he says.

"I remember thinking 'not second again at the festival' and then he picked up and got his head in front. I was very happy and quite emotional."

Williams, 48, has trained Grade 1 winners over jumps and won lucrative Group races on the Flat from his Worcestershire yard, but he yearned for festival success, an aspiration only intensified by a raft of near-misses including a particularly galling 2005 festival that brought second places with Bambi De L'Orme (Grand Annual) and At Your Request (Fred Winter) and Brewster's close third in the Brit Insurance Novices' Hurdle (now the Albert Bartlett).

"There had been plenty of close calls at Cheltenham and after Ballyalton won it was the wonderful feeling you get when you win any race, multiplied enormously," says Williams, whose quiet family celebrations were different to those of golfer Lee Westwood.

"The horse was a Christmas present from Lee to his dad John and the next day he texted me asking if it was real – I think he'd had a long evening."

Ballyalton, who had been another festival runner-up for Williams when he followed Faugheen home in the 2014 Neptune Investment Management Novices' Hurdle, had suffered a crashing fall on his previous start at Ascot and, while discussions took place about the possibility of switching to hurdles for the Martin Pipe race, Williams stuck to his instincts.

"The horse has always had ability but there was still the apprehension as to whether he would cope with the fences and Cheltenham," he says. "It was other people's concerns and I knew in my own mind there would be no issue."

Reporting by Jack Haynes, Tony McFadden, Mark Scully, Jack McCarron and Andrew Dietz

THE ONE THAT GOT AWAY

For local trainer Martin Keighley there is no place like Cheltenham and he was delighted when Any Currency ended his long wait for a festival winner with victory in the Glenfarclas Cross Country Chase. Or so he thought.

The veteran chaser had been runner-up in the previous two years, but finally came home in front at the grand age of 13.

"It's a dream come true. I had him in great form, better than he was last year," said Keighley, 42, who was once on Cheltenham's groundstaff and now trains at the late David Nicholson's former base at Condicote in the Cotswolds. "I've had so many horses go close here. We've had plenty of winners at Cheltenham, but not at the festival, so it's absolutely great."

The dream turned sour, however, when the BHA told Keighley in April that Any Currency had tested positive for triamcinolone acetonide, a corticosteroid that can be used legally to treat horses but must have cleared their system by raceday.

After the positive test became public knowledge in June, Keighley said Any Currency had undergone the same preparation prior to running second in the race 12 months earlier.

"Given that he has mild arthritis in his hocks, our team agreed he should have a routine cortisone injection. The BHA guidelines state that this treatment should be made no later than 14 days before a race, to allow enough time for the traces of the injection to leave the horse's system," he said.

"Any Currency received the treatment 42 days before the festival, three times longer than the advised timing, similar to what we did in 2015. Despite that, it appears that somehow there was still a trace of the treatment in the horse's system on the day of his amazing, emotional and almost universally popular win at Cheltenham."

There was a great deal of sympathy for Keighley, not least from Enda Bolger, whose Josies Orders was awarded the race in August on the disqualification of Any Currency.

"It's heartbreaking for the Keighleys and my heart goes out to them," Bolger said. "The rules are the rules but you never want to win a race like this."

▶▶ High price to pay: Any Currency, a winner in March but a loser in August

THE BIGGER PICTURE

Horses cool down after work as the sun rises on a glorious August morning in Deauville. As well as the traditional midsummer races and sales, the Normandy venue also hosted the French 1,000 and 2,000 Guineas in 2016 during Longchamp's redevelopment

PATRICK McCANN (RACINGPOST.COM/PHOTOS)

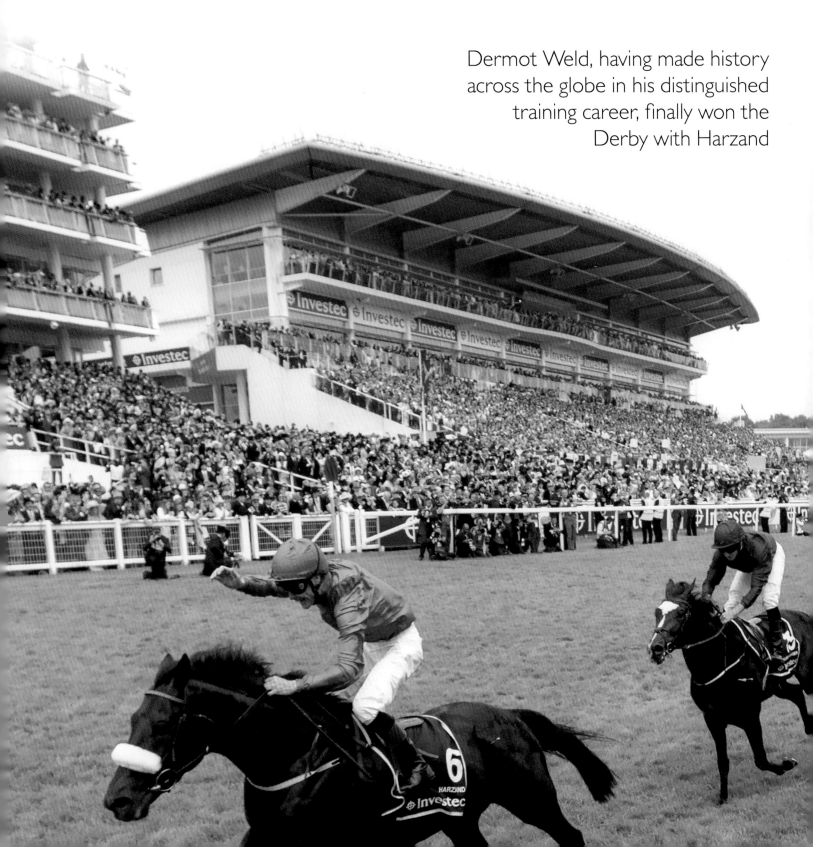

'It had to be done. It was important to me'

Dermot Weld, having made history across the globe in his distinguished training career, finally won the Derby with Harzand

By Alan Sweetman

THE story of Harzand, winner of the Investec Derby and the Dubai Duty Free Irish Derby, encapsulates an essential dilemma of how we assess an individual horse differently in terms of merit and significance.

Harzand is clearly a highly significant performer. However, the question of merit is blurred by the evidence of the final two starts of his 2016 campaign and by the suspicion that he sprang from a largely unexceptional three-year-old middle-distance cohort. On the positive side, he stamped himself as a tough and talented colt in completing the Epsom and Curragh double. Besides, he had a legitimate excuse when failing to feature in the Qipco Irish Champion Stakes.

In the wider picture, Harzand will be remembered as one of the most important horses in the remarkable career of Dermot Weld. Failure to achieve a single coveted goal is a recurring theme of sporting debate, ranging from the greatest golfer who never won a major to the best tennis player who never won Wimbledon or the best athlete who never won Olympic gold. Until Harzand's

Epsom victory, Weld was perhaps the greatest living European trainer never to have won the Derby.

Weld, 68, long admired as a pioneer in international racing and a record-breaker on the domestic scene, has now achieved a defining accolade of his sport and he acknowledged its significance. "It had to be done. It was important to me," he said in a moment of reflection on the day after Epsom.

The trainer's laconic summary was in stark contrast to the drama that prefaced Harzand's defeat of US Army Ranger and Idaho in an Irish-dominated battle. The son of Sea The Stars spread a plate on the morning of the Derby, drawing blood, and required urgent remedial attention before getting the go-ahead to run. Weld's great ally, Irish champion jockey Pat Smullen, after achieving the most important victory of his career, recounted how his final instruction was to withdraw the horse at the start if he had any concern about his soundness.

Harzand was a fifth Derby winner for the Aga Khan and had echoes of Sinndar's triumph for John Oxx 16 years earlier, an outcome tracing to the owner's decision to remove his horses from training in Britain in the wake of

Aliysa's Oaks disqualification in 1989. If that state of affairs was dictated by principle, it was for strategic reasons that the owner pointed to the ending of a long association with Oxx by sending yearlings to Weld at Rosewell House in 2013.

Weld's attention to detail, a factor in the meticulous planning of audacious successful raids on races such as the Belmont Stakes and the Melbourne Cup, is legendary. He is highly intelligent, reflective and observant. One can easily imagine how those qualities came into play during the years he watched on the Curragh gallops as the Oxx horses went through their paces. Informed by a keen sense of racing history, he would have looked at the Aga Khan's horses with professional interest, musing over some of the stoutest middle-distance pedigrees in the book, and perhaps wondering how he would manage such raw material if the chance arose.

He did not have long to wait for a good one after succeeding Oxx as the owner's principal Irish trainer. Among the two-year-old intake of 2015 was Harzand, a March 6 foal with a pedigree heavily shaped by Oxx, by the brilliant Sea The Stars out of Hazariya. Weld may have

recalled how Hazariya beat a filly of his called Mermaid Island to win a Listed race at Gowran Park ten years previously. Harzand was her fifth foal. All four previous offspring had won for Weld's near-neighbour.

****

WELD introduced Harzand in a mile maiden at Gowran Park in September of his juvenile season. Sent off second favourite in a field of 16, he betrayed his inexperience before making late headway into fifth. That was it for the season, but his showing was sufficiently promising to ensure he started 4-9 favourite when returning in a maiden over a mile and a quarter at Cork in March.

On a day when the ground was bottomless, several horses won with considerable ease, including Jet Setting, who would go on capture the Irish 1,000 Guineas. The subsequent Ebor winner Heartbreak City recorded a 12-length margin in a handicap. Harzand put him in the shade, winning by 16 lengths from Street Fighter, who later took the Queen's Vase and the Curragh Cup.

A fortnight later Harzand stepped up in class against six rivals, including three trained by

▶▶ *Continues page 114*

Aidan O'Brien and two by Jim Bolger, in the Ballysax Stakes, the Group 3 Leopardstown event that provided a stepping-stone for O'Brien's first two Derby winners, Galileo in 2001 and High Chaparral in 2002.

Weld enthused about Harzand's defeat of O'Brien's Idaho in a race run at a decent gallop on heavy ground. "I love the way he switches off," he said, although he warned the colt was still very green and had plenty to learn. Smullen was impressed too, but did not yet have the Derby at the forefront of his mind. "I think he's too big and heavy to go around Epsom. He could be an Irish Derby horse, but personally I think he could be a St Leger horse."

Just under a month later, with the going now good at Leopardstown, the make-up of the Irish challenge for the Derby was left unclear when Idaho could manage only third behind Bolger's Ballysax also-ran Midnight Magic in the Derrinstown Stud Derby Trial.

In the weeks leading up to Epsom, as Ballydoyle's Derby ambitions focused more specifically on the twice-raced US Army Ranger, an unconvincing winner of the Chester Vase, Weld was satisfied with Harzand's progress. Despite Smullen's initial misgivings, Epsom was now the target. It was just a question of whether the ground would come right for him. While confident the colt did not need the heavy ground he had raced on in Ireland, Weld wanted some ease for him.

The rain came in time, with the ground officially described as good to soft on Derby day. Despite racing a bit wide, Harzand travelled well within himself out of Tattenham Corner and took the lead from his Ballysax victim Idaho just over a furlong out. He then found another response inside the last half-furlong as US Army Ranger, hanging to the left, delivered a late challenge that was not fully sustained.

Weld, having won every Irish Classic at least once along with the Oaks with Blue Wind in 1981 and the 2,000 Guineas with Refuse To Bend in 2003, had his Derby at last. "It's very special to win this race," he said. "I think I've had 23 Classic

winners in Europe. Blue Wind was my first when she won the Oaks many years ago. I suppose not winning the Derby has been nagging away at me for a bit. It's a race I've always wanted to win. Quite often, though, you don't have a horse good enough to run in the race, let alone win it. You have to make the opportunity count when you do."

Smullen, 39, Weld's stable jockey since 1999, also had his first Derby. "It's what you dream of," he said. "I'm so privileged to be in the position to ride these horses. For the boss to win this race is more fitting and I'm delighted to have won for him. He's the world's greatest trainer."

****

CONCERN that Harzand had been through a hard race at Epsom evaporated sufficiently to make him 4-6 favourite when lining up against eight opponents, including Idaho and Epsom sixth Red Verdon, in the Irish Derby three weeks later. An exciting duel with Idaho developed before Harzand got on top in the closing stages for a half-length win. No real fireworks, but an efficient and resolute display.

Weld's initial reaction was that it was "a better race than Epsom", that the two protagonists had improved. "They didn't just quicken once, they quickened twice," he said. Idaho's victory in the Great Voltigeur would

LATE DRAMA

Dermot Weld revealed after the Derby just how close Harzand had come to being unable to take part. As a qualified vet and a trainer with more than 40 years' experience, Weld's knowledge – and that of his team – was vital.

"This morning, when he came over [from Ireland], he just stood on himself. Racing plates are very light and unfortunately he pulled one off. By doing this, he drew blood as well, so his foot was very sore.

"I've got excellent staff and immediately old-fashioned treatment came in. We poulticed him and then, when he got to Epsom this morning, he was very sore. So we treated him again and I was happy then that we'd drawn anything we had wanted to out of the foot. We then put him in ice for four hours.

"He hadn't damaged the plate – it was clean and hadn't buckled at all. Jim Reilly, Jim Bolger's farrier, was able to tack that back on. Jim is a very gifted man and we were lucky to have him here. He tacked the plate back on so delicately and then we put the foot in ice again.

"The track veterinary was there watching him all the time and we both agreed that he had to pass three tests. We took him out then as His Highness [the Aga Khan] was due to leave at 2.20pm to come to Epsom. The shoe was tacked on at 1.55pm and I was happy when he jogged with the track vet and he was perfectly sound. I called His Highness and away he came.

"We put his foot back in a bucket of ice for the next couple of hours and I stayed with him. We came down and saddled him later, which was the next test, and he jogged out perfectly sound. The track vet was also happy. We did it again to be sure and he was fine. The final test was Pat's call. I told him that if he wasn't happy with him at the start then he should just pull him out. I watched him go down on the big screen with Pat and he trotted down sound. So here we are – such is life!"

THREE OTHER IMPORTANT WINNERS FOR WELD BEFORE HARZAND

Blue Wind *1981 Oaks*
In Shergar's Derby year Bertram Firestone's Blue Wind proved almost as dominant in the Oaks three days later for Lester Piggott, cantering to a seven-length victory that provided Weld with a breakthrough Classic success. Blue Wind went on to confirm her superiority under Wally Swinburn in the Irish Oaks the following month.

Go And Go *1990 Belmont Stakes*
Weld first discovered Moyglare Stud's son of Be My Guest had an aptitude for dirt the previous October, when the Grade 2 Laurel Futurity was switched from turf owing to a rainstorm. At Belmont Mick Kinane was always travelling easily on the inside of runners and Go And Go surged to an eight-length success, becoming the first – and so far only – European-trained winner of a leg in the US Triple Crown series. "Today was the day," Weld told legendary ABC presenter Jim McKay during the post-race presentation ceremony.

Vintage Crop
1993 Melbourne Cup
No European horse had won the Melbourne Cup before Vintage Crop *(below)* and for Weld to do so with a horse who had run in the Champion Hurdle at Cheltenham eight months earlier was even more remarkable. Ridden by Mick Kinane for owner Michael Smurfit, Vintage Crop came with a powerful run in the straight to claim a great win. Other Europeans have matched that, including Weld with Media Puzzle in 2002, but it was Vintage Crop's success that opened the door. "Vintage Crop more than anything moved the Cup to where it deserves to be, a major world race," Weld said.

---

later give substance to the form and O'Brien's colt might have further consolidated his reputation but for stumbling and unseating his rider in the straight when odds-on for the St Leger.

On the same afternoon as the St Leger, Harzand participated in what was billed as one of the best races ever staged in Ireland, the 12-runner Qipco Irish Champion Stakes. Despite the absence of Harzand's stablemate Fascinating Rock and the late defection of the 2014 winner The Grey Gatsby, it was a star-studded contest.

Harzand, the 2-1 favourite, was never seriously involved, looking one-paced in eighth as the Prix du Jockey Club winner Almanzor mastered the Ballydoyle-trained fillies Found and Minding. It soon transpired Weld's colt had been struck into early in the race.

The dual Derby winner recovered quickly and was given the green light for the Prix de l'Arc de Triomphe at Chantilly just over three weeks later. This time there was no apparent excuse as he failed to pick up in mid-division. He finished an anonymous ninth of 16 runners, scant consolation provided by the fact that he was second-best of a six-strong three-year-old contingent, one place behind the long-priced Savoir Vivre.

Whatever Harzand's ultimate ranking, he has played a part in an evolving narrative of Irish racing that took root almost 60 years ago when Mickey Rogers saddled Hard Ridden to win the Derby in 1958. By the time Rogers won the race again, with Santa Claus in 1964, Vincent O'Brien had recorded the first of his six wins. Ireland's Flat trainers were beginning to be taken seriously, a state of affairs enhanced when Paddy Prendergast, whose one great regret in a glorious career was his failure to win the Derby, captured the British trainers' championship three years in a row during the 1960s. After David O'Brien foiled his father's bid for a record-equalling seventh Epsom victory in 1984, when Secreto beat El Gran Senor, there was no Irish-trained winner of the race until Sinndar in 2000. That barren period has been firmly consigned to history, Weld's colt being the ninth Irish-trained victor in the last 17 editions.

For Weld, who took over the training licence in his early twenties following the death of his father Charlie in 1972, the Derby represented one of the last frontiers. "At the beginning of the year the two things I set out to achieve were to win the Epsom Derby and train my 4,000th winner. I achieved both in the month of June," he said later in the year.

In Harzand he had the horse to win the Derby, and Weld is not the type of trainer to let opportunity slip.

▶▶ Landmark horse: (from left) Pat Smullen punches the air as he passes the post at Epsom on Harzand, a first Derby winner for him as well as for Dermot Weld; the Aga Khan's colt follows up in the Irish Derby; Weld and Smullen celebrate at the Curragh

MONGAN'S LAW

Laura Mongan's small Epsom stable hit the jackpot with Harbour Law's triumph in a dramatic St Leger

By Peter Thomas

WHEN it comes to the St Leger, there are certain immutable laws that have stood the test of time. The first rule is that female trainers don't win the St Leger; the second is that Epsom trainers don't win the St Leger; and the third is that trainers like Laura Mongan don't win the St Leger.

Before 2016, no woman had won the oldest Classic; Epsom hadn't won any Classic since John Sutcliffe's Right Tack landed the 1969 2,000 Guineas; and a 20-box trainer who fits in the morning gallops around the school run and feeding a seven-month-old baby was long odds against ever scaling such heights.

Mongan, however, is no respecter of rules that threaten to thwart her ambition. "I want to be an answer on a Trivial Pursuit card," she said after rewriting the history books with Harbour Law, and few would deny her that modest ambition.

More pressing matters than mere board games are on the horizon for Mongan and her loyal assistant and husband Ian. Aside from parenting seven-year-old Daisy and hungry Max, and sharing morning duties on Epsom Downs, the couple now have the welcome responsibility of plotting a path through some unfamiliar reaches of the programme book with their new stable star.

Where their normal itinerary involves low-grade handicaps at nearby Lingfield, with occasional jaunts to exotic Kempton and the odd day at the seaside in Brighton, from early next season they'll be forced to reset the GPS for forays to Grade 1 tracks around the country and, if the couple have their way, much further afield.

Where once their training highlight was achieved barely seven miles across Surrey at Sandown – with First Avenue in the 2013 Imperial Cup – by next autumn they may be looking around the M25 to Heathrow and 10,000 miles beyond.

"Yes, I'd love to end up in Australia for the Melbourne Cup," says Mongan, typically unfazed by ▸ Continues page 118

▸ History maker: Harbour Law wins the St Leger from Ventura Storm (right) and Housesofparliament (centre); (left) Laura Mongan with her Classic hero

the thought of unfamiliar territory, "and I'm sure it's at the back of the owners' minds. The Australians even tried to buy him at one point and I'm sure plenty of others did too – when he was a bit cheaper.

"Before that, though, he'll improve for a winter break and realistically there's no reason why we shouldn't have the Sagaro Stakes as a starting point, and again no reason why he can't be a proper Cup horse. We'll sit and discuss it with the owners, but why not? He's a Classic winner, after all."

These are heady times for the local girl made good. Where Ian had a sizeable taste of the big time in his days as a key player at Sir Henry Cecil's yard – earning himself a Group 1 success on Twice Over in the 2011 Juddmonte International before quitting with weight problems two years later – Laura flew rather closer to the ground.

She made her way through Pony Club, worked for Epsom trainer Brooke Sanders from the age of 14, rode five winners as an amateur (as Ms L Sheen) and started training as a permit holder, preparing a few jumpers for her parents Mervyn and Penny, before things at Condover Stables began to evolve.

Mum and dad are still key figures – not least as owners of the yard and half the horses, as well as being key child-minders – and the core of the business remains the same, but when Harbour Law arrived in the spring from the recently sold stables of trainer Jo Crowley, the world slowly turned upside down.

The son of Lawman came with a decent reputation after finishing second on his debut over a mile and a half at Lingfield as a big, burly three-year-old, and although his early work for the Mongans wasn't always spellbinding, they soon discovered he was a different beast once unleashed on the track.

"I remember working him on the grass with a slow horse of ours who was rated 100 over hurdles and I couldn't get by him," Ian says, "but a week later he did another bit on the grass and it was unreal, amazing. That's just him. Three weeks before the Leger he did an awful bit of work

at home and I started to worry. Then we took him to Kempton for a racecourse gallop and he kicked First Avenue out of the way and we were back in business."

Maiden and handicap wins at Salisbury and Sandown under regular partner George Baker were followed by close-up placed efforts behind the Aidan O'Brien-trained Sword Fighter and Housesofparliament, both of whom would head to the Leger. Harbour Law grew and strengthened and the confidence behind him followed suit, even though he was sent off a 22-1 shot for his biggest test on Town Moor.

"From the moment I saw him come into the pre-parade, I really thought he stood out," Laura recalls, "and it was only because he had my name next to him that he was such a big price. It's quite sad that the market went with the fashion rather than the horse's CV, but that's the way it is every time, so you can't let it dishearten you."

Owners Jackie and Nick Cornwell had turned down some substantial offers for their young pretender and wouldn't have been human had they not been tempted either to sell him or move him on to a trainer with more of a Group 1 pedigree, but they kept

'From the moment he came into the pre-parade I really thought he stood out. It was only because he had my name next to him that he was such a big price'

the faith and were rewarded by an exemplary preparation and a masterful ride from Baker.

The 2016 St Leger, of course, will be long remembered as the renewal in which O'Brien's hot favourite Idaho stumbled and unseated his rider approaching the three-furlong pole, but the late charge that put Ballydoyle challenger Housesofparliament in his place and saw off runner-up Ventura Storm was enough to convince Harbour Law's connections that they had a deserved winner on their hands and not a horse who had been gifted a Classic.

"There were no true stayers in the race – I don't think Idaho would have stayed – and that's what we had," Laura reflects. "If he'd been a 100-1 no-hoper we wouldn't have gone there – we're not that sort of yard – and, although I'm not saying we ever let ourselves dream he'd win it, the more I looked at his form, the more I knew it was right for him to be there.

"I'm sure the owners had plenty of opportunities to sell him before the Leger and I'm sure sometimes the offers became very appealing, and I'm sure there have been other trainers offering their services, but they let us get on with it. I didn't feel the pressure because I don't doubt myself, I don't

George Baker suffered the anguish of narrow defeat on the eve of the St Leger but that pain was soon washed away on a tide of Group 1 glory.

In the Doncaster Cup, the highlight on the Friday of the St Leger meeting, Baker and Quest For More led everywhere but on the line as they lost out by a nose to Sheikhzayedroad. It was an agonising defeat but Baker dusted himself down and, most importantly, trusted in his own instincts.

The next day he refused to follow the strong pace in the St Leger before bringing Harbour Law with a relentless run down the outside to score by three-quarters of a length.

It was a first Classic success for the 34-year-old rider, who is very tall for a Flat jockey at 6ft and maintains his weight using good diet, long runs and hot baths. "I had a hard day yesterday but I normally pick myself up pretty quick and I played golf after racing and cleared my head," he said. "As we turned in I was trying to be confident and do things in a nice rhythm and it worked out great."

At the Arc meeting the following month it worked out great again – and this time on Quest For More – as Baker arrived late to take the Group 1 Prix du Cadran by a short neck.

"I haven't really come down from cloud nine since the St Leger. It's still sinking in and I'm going to enjoy it all," Baker said as he celebrated a second top-level success in the space of three weeks.

For this popular and extremely capable rider, those moments of triumph were richly deserved.

doubt us and I never doubted we were doing the right thing."

Ian was rather less measured in his reaction to the success, crying on national TV and not regretting a second of it. The emotions of the Brighton-raised ex-pat Scot, although they might not have found favour with his hard-nosed mentor Gary Moore, were heartwarming evidence of the impact of Harbour Law's win in a yard not used to the big time, and what a plan well executed meant to a hard-grafting couple with "just one bullet" in a race where O'Brien started with 16 on the original entry list.

"They went far too quick," Ian remembers, "but that showed what a good rider George is. He could have kicked him in the belly and gone up there with them, but I'm glad he didn't. After a furlong I was thinking 'aagh', but when I saw Muntahaa take hold of the bridle and we were a quarter of a length down on Idaho, I was happy. I think if there's pace, he just needs a target to aim at.

"Then two out, when those three quickened clear, and I saw George put his stick down and pull him out, brilliant, and then he went. I lost my voice, I was screaming, I choked Olly [Jago, Harbour Law's lad], nearly

broke his shoulder, and I was blubbing away afterwards. That was how much it meant to us all, not just the day, but everything since we got him, all the getting up in the middle of the night to check on him.

"It was a relief to know that Laura and I and the team had done everything we were hired to do by the owners. They'd have had a lot of people in their ears telling them to send him to a big trainer, but I've been in a lot of big yards and I know what it takes – it's just that every trainer does something different to achieve the same goal. On the day he did what he should have done because we did our job properly."

When John Sutcliffe and Lady Jane Cecil texted to congratulate them on a job well done, it completed a circle that had taken 47 years to turn. Epsom was back on the map, a woman had won the Leger and the Mongans were very much the type of people who might have a Classic winner.

Next year there are plenty more rules to break with a horse who is set to take on the world.

▸ Treasured moments: (from left) Laura Mongan with husband Ian, daughter Daisy, baby Max and dog Ronnie at Condover Stables in Epsom; Harbour Law (left) wins the St Leger; Olly Jago and Harbour Law on Epsom Downs; (below) the trainer and jockey George Baker with the St Leger trophy

By Nick Pulford
and Richard Lowther

HUGO PALMER felt sick with nerves for most of April, but on the last day of the month all that tension turned to elation in the space of 96 thrilling seconds as Galileo Gold raced to Qipco 2,000 Guineas glory. Winter favourite Air Force Blue had been downed and Palmer had his first British Classic winner – just as he had hoped and dreamed in the build-up.

"I've never believed in a horse quite like I believe in this one," the ever-rising Newmarket trainer said in the winner's enclosure. "I've felt so ill for the last three weeks waiting for today but it's been a wonderful story."

The story was only just beginning, not simply for Galileo Gold but also in a three-year-old colts' miling division where the balance of power kept on swinging through a series of top-level battles across Europe.

Palmer's colt was first to stake a claim. While Air Force Blue ran a listless race at Newmarket and trailed home in 12th, Galileo Gold beat Massaat by a length and a half – and it would have been further had he not edged over to the stands rail when in front. Palmer had his Classic, to go with Covert Love's win in the 2015 Irish Oaks, while for jockey Frankie Dettori, at 45 ten years Palmer's senior, it was a first 2,000 Guineas since 1999.

Looking back a few days later, Palmer said he had agonised over whether to swerve Air Force Blue and go instead for the French Guineas but concluded: "There is only one Guineas. The Irish Oaks was very special, but not as special as winning a 2,000 Guineas on home turf. I'd rather win one Guineas than a million other races."

****

FRANCE was the next stop on the Classic miling circuit – at Deauville rather than the usual venue of Longchamp, which was being redeveloped – and this time Aidan O'Brien, having suffered disappointment with Air Force Blue, was victorious.

The Gurkha hadn't raced at two and indeed was "lucky to be alive",

GAME OF THRONES

The three-year-old miling colts produced a series of thrilling duels across Europe in the battle for the ultimate crown

according to O'Brien, after two colic surgeries. As the season opened he was just one of a phalanx of well-bred dark horses lurking among the ranks at Ballydoyle and had contested only a couple of maidens before being hoisted in grade for his Classic assignment. The son of Galileo proved a revelation in the French 2,000 Guineas, storming clear to win by five and a half lengths with the promise of better to come.

The question was whether O'Brien would seek to realise that potential in the Derby – a 'will he?

won't he?' issue that had already been settled for Galileo Gold with the decision to stay at a mile, but would linger a while yet with The Gurkha.

****

SIX days later and another contender emerged from the pack. The Tattersalls Irish 2,000 Guineas was billed as a rematch between Newmarket hero Galileo Gold and villain Air Force Blue, but Chris Hayes had other ideas. "We feel we have a colt with a big chance and I'm as

confident going into a Guineas as I've ever been," said the jockey of Awtaad, who would go off 9-2 third favourite behind the big two.

Hayes had won only one Classic – the 2013 Irish St Leger on Voleuse De Coeurs – and it was

▶ *Continues page 122*

▶▶ Head to head: The Gurkha (centre) beats Galileo Gold (left) and Ribchester in the Sussex Stakes

difficult to know what his pre-race confidence amounted to, but we soon found out. On yielding ground that suited Awtaad, the 28-year-old jockey took the lead inside the final quarter-mile and held Galileo Gold at bay rather comfortably by two and a half lengths. Air Force Blue was beaten almost 20 lengths in seventh.

Kevin Prendergast, Awtaad's 84-year-old trainer, has a deeper well of Classic experience than Hayes and his own comparison bore great weight. "He has always looked like a good horse. He's definitely as good a horse as I've had, and I had Ardross," he said. Besides that dual Ascot Gold Cup winner, who started in the Prendergast stable before being sold and transferred to Henry Cecil, the veteran trainer had seven Irish Classic successes on his CV before Awtaad – as well as the 1977 2,000 Guineas with Nebbiolo – and this first Classic in almost two decades was cheered to the rafters at the Curragh.

Prendergast never really gave up hope another top-class horse would come along. "I suppose fellas do the lotto every week and always think they have a chance of winning, don't they? I always say, if you have a good horse it will get you out of bed."

****

WHILE Awtaad was getting Prendergast out of bed with a spring in his step, the boys at Ballydoyle had slept on The Gurkha's target and decided he would be a miler for now, while in Newmarket there was still plenty of confidence in Galileo Gold, who had not had a clear run at the Curragh.

The stage was set for a showdown between the three Guineas winners in the St James's Palace Stakes at Royal Ascot. Punters clearly believed French form would prevail and The Gurkha started at 4-5. Awtaad was 5-2, with Galileo Gold allowed to go off at a generous 6-1.

Once again Palmer was on edge – "he made me feel nervous just talking to him," said Dettori later – but this time there would be no mistake with Galileo Gold; instead it was the favourite who ran into problems. Dettori had Galileo Gold perfectly positioned in second and kicked for

home turning into the straight whereas Ryan Moore, in contrast to France, dropped his mount out with just one behind him. The Gurkha met trouble when trying to improve and, although he overhauled Awtaad for second late on, he was never going to catch Galileo Gold.

It was hardly vintage Moore, but Galileo Gold was back on top and that was where he belonged, according to Palmer. "I think it's fair to say he's proved himself to be the best three-year-old colt in Europe," the trainer said. The judgement would not quite survive the season, but for now Palmer's colt was indeed the gold standard.

****

AFTER Royal Ascot, The Gurkha tackled an extra quarter-mile in the Coral-Eclipse at Sandown but found Hawkbill half a length too

▶ Glory days: (clockwise from left) Frankie Dettori celebrates winning the 2,000 Guineas on Galileo Gold; Awtaad storms home at the Curragh; The Gurkha after the Sussex Stakes; (below) Chris Hayes on Awtaad

strong. O'Brien conceded that the colt might have found the trip too far, particularly on rain-softened ground. "We always viewed him as a miler and because he did so well after Ascot we thought we'd take in this race on our way to the Sussex," he said.

That was the cue for another battle with his old rivals in the Qatar Sussex Stakes. The Gurkha went off 11-8 favourite, with Galileo Gold 9-4 and Awtaad 13-2, and this time O'Brien's colt emerged on top. Galileo Gold went from the front at Goodwood, but The Gurkha got to him deep in the final furlong to win by a neck. Ribchester, third in the 2,000 Guineas before winning the Jersey Stakes at Royal Ascot, was only a short head back in third. It didn't happen for Awtaad, who finished only eighth.

▶ *Continues page 124*

Ladbrokes

ONLINE & MOBILE

BEST ODDS GUARANTEED *PLUS*

TAKE 8/1 SP 9/1 YOU GET 10/1*

Over £2.5m in extra winnings paid in 2016.

WHEN THE **FUN** STOPS **STOP**™ gamble**aware**.co.uk

"It's been tough on The Gurkha," O'Brien said. "I was worried because he's had such a big career crammed into a short space of time. He didn't race last year, but he's danced every dance since."

The dancing had stopped for The Gurkha, however, as the Sussex turned out to have been his last race. In August he underwent surgery for a displaced colon. Happily he pulled through, but the decision was taken to retire him to stud.

****

RACING POST RATINGS at this stage showed just how closely matched these crack milers were. The Gurkha's Sussex success earned him an RPR of 124, matching Galileo Gold's top figure from Ascot. Awtaad earned 122 at the Curragh (but only 112 in the Sussex) and right in the mix was Ribchester, with 123 at Goodwood.

Ribchester was next to strike a blow and add a Group 1 victory to his honours board when, two and a half weeks after the Sussex, he took on Galileo Gold again in the Prix Jacques Le Marois at Deauville. Palmer's colt ran a lifeless race, finishing eighth, but the Richard Fahey-trained Ribchester took his opportunity with a half-length success.

"He's got plenty of speed and class. He's the best horse we've ever had – he's got everything," Fahey said. The form backed up the trainer's view, with runner-up Vadamos going on to land the Prix du Moulin next time out, while third-placed Ervedya had won the 2015 Moulin.

****

NOW came a hiatus, filled only by Awtaad proving his wellbeing with a Group 2 victory at Leopardstown in early September. Galileo Gold and Ribchester were waiting for the Qipco Queen Elizabeth II Stakes, and now Awtaad was too.

When Champions Day arrived, the colts were faced by a new rival who had contested two Guineas in the spring – except that Minding's had been prefixed with '1,000'. Aidan O'Brien's filly had won at Newmarket and been second at the Curragh before going up in trip, but now she was coming back to a mile and, such

was her exalted reputation, she was 7-4 favourite.

The colts could not live with her as Ryan Moore made her superior stamina count by taking the lead two furlongs out and forcing the others to give chase. Awtaad and Galileo Gold never got near in fourth and fifth, while Ribchester closed to half a length in second place but without looking likely to catch the filly.

Tiredness at the end of a long season must have played a part but Minding was in the same position as the colts and produced her best

▸▸ Battle joined: (clockwise from top) Ribchester lands the Prix Jacques Le Marois for a delighted William Buick before finding Minding too good at Ascot

performance of the season after seven Group 1 races spread over five and a half months.

Ribchester also produced a career-best on Racing Post Ratings, moving up to join Galileo Gold and The Gurkha on 124. Remarkably, after all those battles, there was nothing between these three Classic miling colts.

As for Minding, she was rated 123 on RPR for her QEII win. In effect that put her top, as she would receive 3lb from the colts if they met again.

All hail the miling queen.

ROSSDALES
VETERINARY SURGEONS

ROSSDALES NEWMARKET
t: 01638 663150
e: practice@rossdales.com

ROSSDALES LAMBOURN
t: 07887 754766
e: robert.dallas@rossdales.com

www.rossdales.com

Thoroughbred Veterinary Services

Rossdales is renowned for providing the highest quality veterinary services to the Newmarket Thoroughbred community. Now, from January 2017, Partner Robert Dallas MRCVS will be offering those services to Thoroughbred owners in the Lambourn area.

Why choose Rossdales?

• Dedicated team of experienced racing yard vets.

• Expertise coupled with modern, portable diagnostic equipment.

• World-class equine hospital and diagnostic centre for specialist surgery, diagnostic or medical investigations.

• In-house laboratory, Rossdales Laboratories, which provides a comprehensive, reliable and cost-effective diagnostic service designed for and trusted by equine practitioners throughout the UK and abroad.

IN THE PICTURE

Newcastle changes northern landscape with Tapeta track

Newcastle unveiled its new Tapeta all-weather surface in May, just eight months after the controversial end to 133 years of Flat racing on turf at the Gosforth Park track.

Joey Haynes had the honour of riding the first all-weather winner at Newcastle when he partnered the Karl Burke-trained Tap The Honey to victory in a 1m2f maiden on May 17. "I couldn't fault the track. It was the first time I'd ridden on it and it was very fair," Haynes said.

His view was echoed by other professionals following the £11m redevelopment by Arena Racing Company, which runs Newcastle. The switch had divided opinion but Mark Johnston, who was among the critics, sent out Turbine to win a 7f handicap on the opening day and said: "I've always said it was the best turf course in the country, so it was a great pity they dug it up. However, it's now the best all-weather track in the country."

Former jockey Dale Gibson, representing the Professional Jockeys Association, said: "It's great to have an all-weather track in the north at last and it's amazing what they've achieved here in such a short space of time. It's a good, galloping course and looks fair for everyone."

The positive response was reflected in a high-class entry for the Northumberland Plate, the feature race of Newcastle's Flat season, which took place six weeks after the opening. Based on official ratings, the 20-runner field was the best in the past decade and the 2m½f handicap turned out to be a thriller.

Seamour stormed into a clear lead a furlong out but was caught close home by Antiquarium, ridden for Godolphin by visiting New Zealand jockey James McDonald. It was a heartbreaking outcome for Seamour's trainer Brian Ellison, who was born on Plate day in 1952 and thought he had finally achieved his dream of winning his local race. "Seamour was going too well," rued Ellison, tears in his eyes. "He looked the winner a furlong out and it's a shame he got caught."

The switch to all-weather was not completely smooth. Shortly after the opening meeting, concerns were raised about suspiciously fast race times for the advertised distances and Newcastle had to remeasure the track. In turn, that led to all British Flat courses being remeasured, following a campaign by the Horseracing Bettors Forum.

Newcastle, which continues to hold jump racing on turf, became Britain's first all-weather track north of the Trent and brought the total to six. Just over 20 per cent of British Flat fixtures now take place on all-weather surfaces.

A DAY AT THE RACES

Derby day 2016 and a disparate group of people, from trainers and jockeys to groundstaff and racegoers, swing into action to play their parts in the making of a race meeting. But this is not Epsom, this is Worcester – different course, different code, different vibe

By Steve Dennis

THE same day awaits them all. They will share it, take from it different things, their experiences will overlap and diverge, and at one point the parts they play on this hot and humid afternoon will bring them all within 50 yards of each other. It's a day at the races.

Today is June 4, a Saturday, and it is Derby day at Epsom, the focus of the entire racing world. It is not the only meeting in Britain today, of course. There are six other racecourses at work and one of them is Worcester, 140 miles north-west of Epsom and at once very different from and exactly the same as its more famous fellow. Not so many people will pay much attention to Worcester races today, but for a few it is all they can think about.

Worcester's day begins when Libby O'Flaherty's alarm clock shatters the silence at 3.40am, a time when the sheer wrongness of being awake is at its most acute. O'Flaherty, 28, is the new clerk of the course at the Arena Racing-owned track and is at the stage of her career when a 3.40am start is an opportunity to be grasped rather than a waking nightmare. Rise and shine.

"It's my first fixture. My fourth in all, but the first flying solo. It's my big day; I'm so excited," she says. "All week I've been watching the marquees going up, everything getting ready for a big crowd. You can feel the excitement."

Even at 3.40am. O'Flaherty arrives at Worcester an hour and a half later, takes strength from a mug of coffee, pulls on her boots and goes out to walk the course with the head groundsman and his assistant. It has been a dry week.

"I check the weather constantly, because Worcester seems to have its own little weather system separate from the rest of the country. It's either hot or it floods," she says. "We've been watering the track, yesterday we put 3mm on the straights and I'm very happy with the surface. The going is good."

She declares the state of the ground at 6.19am. At seven she'll send a text to all trainers with a runner at Worcester today, offering the same information in bespoke

style. By then, of course, like dawn breaking across the time-zones, the same day has begun for everyone.

Jenny Cheshire, executive director at Worcester, is up at 5am to see to her own horses before driving in. In Lambourn, the alarm clock belonging to Amy Deans is set to the slightly more civilised hour of 5.45am, so she can haul on work clothes and be at Oliver Sherwood's yard for ten past six to muck out, ride out, sort out novice chaser Salto Chisco for his date with destiny in the second race today. By the time she's got a yard-fork in her hand, on-course

bookmaker Gary Wiltshire is in his morning bath, still half-asleep after getting back from Bath races at well past midnight.

The ensemble cast assembles. Clerk of the scales Derrick Blake is 68 but still has a paper round, getting up at 6.30am to deliver newspapers to his street, putting the Racing Post on one side for himself. Before Blake's had a look at the front page, conditional jockey Ryan Hatch is out of bed, ready for the 15-minute drive to his boss Nigel Twiston-Davies's yard where first and second lot await. While Hatch is on the

gallops, Racing Post reporter Andrew King gets up, turns on his laptop and begins his daily forensic examination of the racecard. BHA veterinary officer David Freeman is already on the road, keen to be at Worcester his usual four hours before the first race, trying to beat the weekend traffic.

****

THE little country racecourse draws them in like a magnet. Cheshire has found its attraction unwavering over the last 16 years – she has worked her way up from the tea-urn and the constant jangle

of the telephone and is now the boss. She was here at 7.30am, had a happy ten minutes with the Racing Post and a bowl of Weetabix, cut a swathe through her email inbox, and now sits down, possibly for the last time all day.

"This is Worcester's biggest day of the year. It's ladies' day and we're expecting around 11,000 through the gates, and what happens on this one day informs our whole year," she says.

"If today goes well, the year goes well. We can make a third of our
»Continues page 130

profit for the whole year in one go – our next best day is about 5,000 racegoers, so today is critical from a commercial aspect.

"Today my role is about overseeing all areas, briefing all areas, catering, security – and I get very involved in hospitality and sponsorship. Repeat business works well here because I look after all the clients personally.

"We have a very strong team here. I've got 20 or 30 managers in all and they're set for a busy day managing a large crowd, a drinking crowd, on our only Saturday of the year. It's about managing their expectations, making sure they can find a toilet, can get a drink, can enjoy themselves – when you're a small course at absolute capacity things can get stretched.

"It's an adrenaline rush, really exciting, quite daunting, with a huge feeling of elation when it's all over and it's gone well."

****

HOW well will Salto Chisco's day go? At around half past eight Deans prepares the eight-year-old for the journey, bandages his forelegs and tail, walks him across the yard to the horsebox. He steps carefully up the ramp, the only traveller today, and the doors close quietly on him as Deans, 21, a five-year veteran of Sherwood's yard, hops into the cab alongside the driver. The box rolls away down the drive into the misty Lambourn morning. Salto Chisco is 7-2 paper favourite for the two-mile John Burke Memorial Novices' Handicap Chase, and Wiltshire is expecting him to be a popular choice for punters.

Wiltshire is a popular choice himself, a big man but still only half the man he used to be – "Fred Done paid for me to have a gastric operation, he saved my life" – still the 'belly from the telly' famous from the BBC's racing coverage. He pulls in to Worcester at 9.30am laden with equipment for his three pitches (his sons Charlie and Nicky are also standing up today) and gets to work setting them up.

"It feels a bit strange being here today – it's the first Derby I've missed in 20 years," he says. "I was told that business was good here last year and I have to go where the people are.

"There'll be plenty of atmosphere here today, plenty of girls, I think it'll be a good crowd, so all I have to do is get a few quid off them. It'll be a lot of small punters, two quid, two quid, two-quid each-way, five quid, that sort of thing. If I can take five grand, make ten per cent profit on that . . . at least it'll cover expenses. The game's not quite what it used to be, see."

As Wiltshire bolts his pitch together, Blake sits down at his desk in the antique wooden weighing room and begins a most meticulous checking process that never varies from one day to the next, one course to the next. He's been a clerk of the scales for 25 years, has already retired once but still does around 40 days a year on the circuit. "It's the best job in the world," he says.

"I'd rather be here two hours early than ten minutes late, and the first thing I do is proofread the racecard – it doesn't happen very often but sometimes a penalty or an allowance has been missed, and when I find that, that's what I get paid for.

"I check the jockeys' licences, check the colours, make sure there's a

▸▸ Early start: Salto Chisco is loaded on to the horsebox for the 70-mile journey from Oliver Sherwood's Lambourn stable to Worcester racecourse

'There'll be plenty of atmosphere here today, plenty of girls, I think it'll be a good crowd, so all I have to do is get a few quid off them'

different cap to use if an owner has two runners in one race. I've got to be sure that it's all right, because I have to sign a piece of paper saying that it's all right. I'm the safety net. I treat every day as though it were Derby day – although it really is today – because it's no good me going racing and thinking 'that'll do'.

"And then during the afternoon I'm weighing jockeys in and out. My job is all about making sure everything runs smoothly."

The journey runs smoothly for Salto Chisco – much smoother than it will for his trainer, who later bemoans the hour it took him to cover the final mile or two from the motorway – and Deans, who draw into the stable lorry park at 10.45am. He comes off the box calmly, looking benignly around, no sign of the highway blues, and Deans leads him into the stable yard past the ever-vigilant BHA integrity and welfare officers, who check his passport and scan his microchip.

"He travelled well, he's an absolute gentleman to deal with," says Deans, who had a long day's journey and a

▸▸ Continues page 132

Horse Racing Abroad prides itself as the UK's leading specialist tour operator focusing purely on horse racing holidays. This has resulted in the excellence of the racing tours provided. It is the service, staff and world-wide associations with Racing Authorities and industry professionals that has made Horse Racing Abroad such a well-established and integral part of the world of racing.

Horse Racing Abroad offer tours to most of the major race meetings worldwide:

- Breeders' Cup
- Melbourne Cup
- J&B Met – Cape Town
- Irish Guineas & Coolmore Stud
- The Dubai World Cup
- Qatar Prix de l'Arc de Triomphe

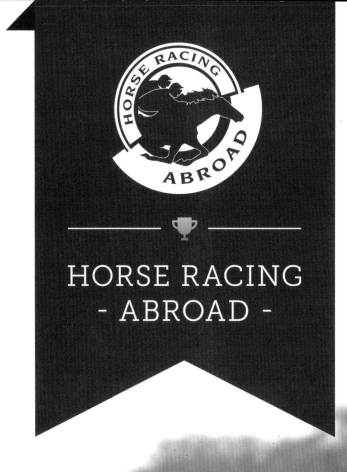

HORSE RACING
- ABROAD -

Call our Travel Specialists on **01244 355 498**
or visit **www.horseracingabroad.com**

late finish yesterday, all the way to Market Rasen and back, but made worthwhile by a winner.

"We stopped for a cup of tea on the way but I'd normally go to the canteen here. Now I'll walk over to the weighing room to declare him, come back and wash him down, plait his mane and tail, and wait for his race. I'm doing this today because Lisa [Kozak, travelling head girl] is on holiday, and I love this side of the job.

"This is what I want to do in racing, travel horses. You see the country, see different people, do different things every day."

Another for whom every day is different is Freeman, crossing the track at the same time as Deans, tracing the steps he'll retrace several times this afternoon, from the stable yard to the parade ring and back again. Few racegoers will be aware of the role played by the veterinary officer and his three-strong team, which is just how he likes it.

"I could have a very quiet day, I could have a very hectic day. I hope it's a quiet day," he says. "But you never know what to expect.

"I downloaded all the information for today's meeting from Weatherbys' database this morning. We check all the passports and microchips, and it's mandatory to do so for horses running for the first time, horses running for a new trainer for the first time.

"Then we make veterinary checks on a number of horses – those who were on the database for having post-race problems last time out, lameness, dehydration, that sort of thing. There are four on today's list, I've told the clerk and the vets to keep a particular eye on those.

"I'll look at any horses who haven't run for a long time – already done two today – and after racing starts it's more about checking tongue straps and other equipment, going back to the yard, going back to the parade ring, staying on top of things. I hope it's a quiet day."

O'Flaherty isn't having a quiet day. "There isn't really a relaxed moment," she smiles, constantly referring to her checklist, bee-busy in the final minutes before the gates open to the

public. "I'm making sure the course maps are up to date, all the signage is in place, checking that the valets are happy – and I've already had that weird hour when there's nothing much to do, accompanied by the horrible feeling of 'should I be doing something?'"

****

AT 11.30am, as the first phalanx of the ladies-day fashion crowd marches through the gates and begins looking for something to drink and somewhere to sit, all hats and handbags, O'Flaherty, armed with the traditional clerk's pointy stick, leads the way out on to the racecourse for a final check, accompanied by the chairman of the stewards, Peta Evetts. They complete a circuit, making sure all is as it should be, treading carefully around the takeoff and landing sides of the fences. Halfway down the back

▶▶ Pleasure and business: (clockwise from above) racegoers Helen and Tanya all dressed up for ladies' day; clerk of the course Libby O'Flaherty (left) and Peta Evetts, chair of the stewards, walk the track; Racing Post reporter Andrew King gets the quotes from winning trainer Robin Dickin after Myroundorurs' victory

straight they're overtaken by four jockeys in bobble hats and tracksuit bottoms, mobiles at their ears, sweating off a pound or two while seeing how the land lies, multi-tasking.

From his eyrie in the grandstand, King can watch their progress. It's two hours before the first race and the Racing Post man is tapping away at his laptop, sending early details to the office, non-runners, jockey changes, praying that the Wi-Fi holds up.

"The Wi-Fi at racecourses is the bane of a journalist's life, but these days there aren't too many problems at Worcester," he says. "I cover practically every Worcester meeting – I don't live far away – and it's a friendly track, the atmosphere is good, and the class of horse has improved a lot over the years.

"Most of the races today are competitive in their own way, no odds-on favourites, pretty open and interesting racing for what you'd say was not the most professional crowd of the year here.

"I try to keep a keen eye on the betting moves – even on Derby day there are market movers at Worcester

▶▶ Continues page 134

'It's a friendly track, the atmosphere is good, and the class of horse has improved a lot over the years'

DON'T LOOK A GIFT HORSE IN THE MOUTH

PUNCHESTOWN FESTIVAL
25TH - 29TH APRIL 2017

EARLY BIRD TICKET AND HOSPITALITY OFFERS AVAILABLE
FOR A LIMITED TIME ONLY

SITE: WWW.PUNCHESTOWN.COM | PHONE: +353 (0)45 897 704 | EMAIL: info@punchestown.com

– because as well as a written report I'm also producing copy for the 'live reporter' section on the website. The news desk wants 500 words by 5.30pm, earlier if possible because it's Derby day, so I'll aim to have everything written up by five. The last two races won't make the cut, unfortunately.

"I get on pretty well with all the jump trainers and jockeys – some of the Flat guys can be more difficult, though. But they all know I've got a job to do and most people are helpful and forthcoming."

****

AS the clock ticks towards the first race at 1.45 a well-dressed crowd swarms across the lawns, drinks in hand, racecards at the ready, revelling in the warmth. O'Flaherty has changed out of her jeans and boots, Wiltshire is dealing in two quid, two quid, two quid each-way, Cheshire is on patrol, Blake has weighed out the nine jockeys in the opener.

By the time The Tourard Man has got favourite backers off to a good start, Deans is bringing Salto Chisco across the course towards the saddling boxes and a waiting Sherwood.

"My travelling head girl is on holiday. My assistant's on holiday too – it's bad planning on my part!" he says, safe in the knowledge that he's the next one leaving on a jet plane, on an 11am flight tomorrow to Mustique.

"The owners are at Epsom. It's just me, Amy and the horse. And I'm a bit old-fashioned, I like proper winter racing, I'm not really a summer jumping man. I know it has its place but it's not really my thing. Good to see a big crowd, though."

He talks as he saddles Salto Chisco, as he pulls the girth tight. His mind is not altogether on today's race; his thoughts are on the beach with his wife Tarnya, or on the months ahead.

"This is a quiet time for us, there are hardly any horses in. Through the summer we'll be steam-cleaning the boxes, doing all the necessary maintenance, there's loads to be done to get everything ready for the start of the winter season. Touch wood the business can cope with a quiet few months over the summer, and by now I'm exhausted – a lot of it is mental fatigue."

He slaps Salto Chisco on the backside, sends him out to circle the parade ring with Deans. He's a warm favourite but today is not his day – he trails in last of the six to finish, scarlet splashes on his white feet, a burst blood vessel the cause of his lacklustre display. Deans leads him away, back across the course, back to the stable yard, one for Freeman to

▸▸Watching the horses: scenes from the paddock, a far cry from the hubbub of Epsom; The Tourard Man (below) gets favourite backers off to a good start in the opening race

look at, to make another note for the database. Behind them, the connections of Myroundorurs celebrate in the winner's enclosure. It'll be someone's round, anyway. For every race, a happy story for King to write down, type up.

And now the sun comes out properly, dappling off the surface of the Severn that peacefully girdles the racecourse in summer, often chokes it lifeless under a rising tide in the winter. There are famous photographs of canoeists paddling up the home straight, past the winning post, but today the boatmen are on the river, oars lifting lazily as they pass behind the grandstands.

Sharp Rise gives the punters another boost in the third race, after which Cheshire presents one of those oversized cardboard cheques – this one for £3,000 – to Tricia Cavell, fundraising director of the local St Richard's Hospice, the racecourse giving a little back to the community that supports it.

****

THE bookmakers give a little more back after the favourite Gustave Mahler wins the next, just an ordinary bumper, just £1,949 to the winner, but at this level you often find that it's not about the money. Ask winning owner Mervyn Jones. "I've a quarter-share with two

▸▸Continues page 136

friends, retired dairy farmer Richard Jones and his son James, a landscape gardener," says Jones, a point-to-point enthusiast, 30 years an owner.

"I've been coming here since I was a kid, so it's a dream to finally have a winner here. It means a hell of a lot – a lot of people we know are here too, so it's lovely. It's fantastic.

"I just love racing. When your horse comes to the last with a chance, the feeling is just unbelievable. If you could bottle it you'd make a fortune. I can't put it into words. How are we going to celebrate? We haven't got that far yet – I don't like to plan things because you can get disappointed by horses. Not this time, though."

The owners of the next winner, Castlemorris King, certainly have a plan. The race unearths an instance of the great serendipity of racing – five years ago to the hour Castlemorris King was running in the Derby, finishing 12th behind Pour Moi, and now on this Derby day he's here winning a two-and-a-half-mile handicap hurdle. King's report writes itself.

"David [Pipe, trainer] advised me to buy the horse out of a claimer when he won at this course about two weeks ago, and whatever he says I do," joint-owner Stuart Mercer tells him. "We've already had a lovely meal and a few drinks but I'm going to go the whole hog now and get plastered. Let's hope they've got enough champagne because here we come."

In the centre of the course it's more a beer and wine crowd, the grass turned into a vast picnic table, rugs strewn with plastic plates and plastic glasses, cans and bottles. The picknickers bask pinkly and peaceably in the sun, women with their shoes off, men with their shirts undone, watching the horses go by. Among them stumbles the ubiquitous stag-weekend man, looking slightly forlorn in the customary red-and-yellow-quartered jockey jacket stretched over his not-so-chiselled torso, already a little browbeaten by booze. Stag-weekend man always wears the same jockey jacket, hooped sleeves, quartered cap – the silks are registered at Weatherbys but you never see them on a real jockey.

****

A LONG gap between races provides the opportunity to concentrate on the Derby, with the on-course betting shop packed deep by punters staring at the television screens. It's the epicentre of the racing world, and the tremors are felt here, felt everywhere. Somewhere on the road home to Lambourn, Deans is in the cab of the horsebox listening to the Derby on the radio, a tired Salto Chisco in the back, not caring who wins. Harzand wins, shouted home by a few, and others look at the newspaper and the racecard, mouthing his name, trying it out for size.

"We all watched the Derby in the changing room," says Ryan Hatch, sitting in his green and black silks on the steps outside, waiting for his second ride of a typical summer Saturday.

"It's a quietish time of year. I rode out a couple of lots for the boss this morning, left about 11am to get here an hour and a half before my first ride, then ran round the track before racing, it was nice to have a bit of a blow because I'm not riding so much at the moment.

"Worcester's a fair track to ride, it's flat and very straightforward, doesn't

'I love racing. When your horse comes to the last with a chance, the feeling is unbelievable. If you could bottle it you'd make a fortune'

lend itself to a lot of excuses because it suits most horses – and they do a great job with the ground here.

"Two rides is an ordinary day in the summer – I did have three, but my one in the last is a non-runner – while I'd expect four or five on a winter's afternoon. Look, it's a nice day, I've got a couple of rides, I'm just happy to be here."

Hatch doesn't expect a great deal from 50-1 shot Silent Doctor and isn't mistaken, the hurdling debutant being pulled up before three out in a race won by favourite One More Go. As he returns with his saddle he outlines his schedule – out of here within half an hour, home by half past six, hoping to make a friend's birthday party this evening.

The party has been in full swing for some time for Helen and Tanya, who had their money on One More Go, have been doing well with the favourites today, are dressed in the elegance of Royal Ascot.

"A few of us had a champagne brunch at a friend's house, we all had our outfits ready to go," says Tanya (or was it Helen?). "I got the dress yesterday, but my fascinator was the last one in the shop, the display model, so I'm lucky the lady let me

buy it. I was frantic. There's always a last-minute panic, isn't there?"

Helen (or maybe Tanya) agrees. "We got here at a quarter past one, and I've never seen so many people in one place in Worcester. It's my first time at the races and I'd love to come again. It's great – nine out of ten for enjoyment, I wouldn't want it to be any hotter, but we found a spot by the river and it's just beautiful."

River Of Intrigue is an aptly named winner of the seventh race, drinking greedily from a bucket of water after his exertions, and Robert's Star makes all to justify favouritism in the last as the light begins to soften. It's been a good day for punters, which can mean only one thing. He's still smiling, though.

"Results have been terrible, but we'll still have lobster thermidor on the way home," says Wiltshire, sounding like a sitcom bookie, wide, but not as wide as he used to be. He'll be home by 9.30pm, a trip to Goodwood on the agenda for the morning.

****

SHERWOOD is already home, packing his suitcases for his slightly more glamorous destination. Salto Chisco is in his box, Deans having seen to his comfort before heading

home herself. Hatch is on the road already; King filed his copy three-quarters of an hour ago, drained his last cup of press-room tea, fancied his chances of beating most of the traffic. Blake, having weighed them all out and weighed them all in, is away by 6.30pm with no stewards' inquiry after the last to hamper his progress.

O'Flaherty, her first day safely behind her, will wait for the Bee Gees tribute band on stage in the middle of the course to take their bows before hitting the road – home by 8.30pm. Freeman had the quietish day he forecast – a couple of horses with heat exhaustion and, unfortunately, the death of the Caroline Bailey-trained Fearthedark, who broke down in the first race – and will be home by nine to update the records on the Weatherbys database.

The last of the stragglers trail out of the

▶▶ Party people: (clockwise from far left) punters near the approach to the finish; the stands on Worcester's biggest day of the year; the end is nigh; cameras at the ready as the action unfolds; (below) Worcester executive director Jenny Cheshire (left) presents a cheque for £3,000 to Tricia Cavell, fundraising director of the local St Richard's Hospice

racecourse, are quickly absorbed into Worcester nightlife alongside Helen and Tanya, who are at the after-party in Bolero wine bar, spending their winnings. Cheshire alone remains at her post as the sun goes down and the litter-pickers get to work.

"Everything has to be cleared up tonight because the racecourse is on common land, we can't leave any rubbish lying around. I'll also wait for accounts to count the money, because we have to have the results tonight. The attendance was 10,731, as good as we hoped for. It's been a good day for Worcester – for everyone, hopefully."

At 11.30pm Cheshire locks the gates, makes the ten-minute drive home, is in bed by midnight. The day is over.

Tomorrow, somewhere else, another day at the races will begin.

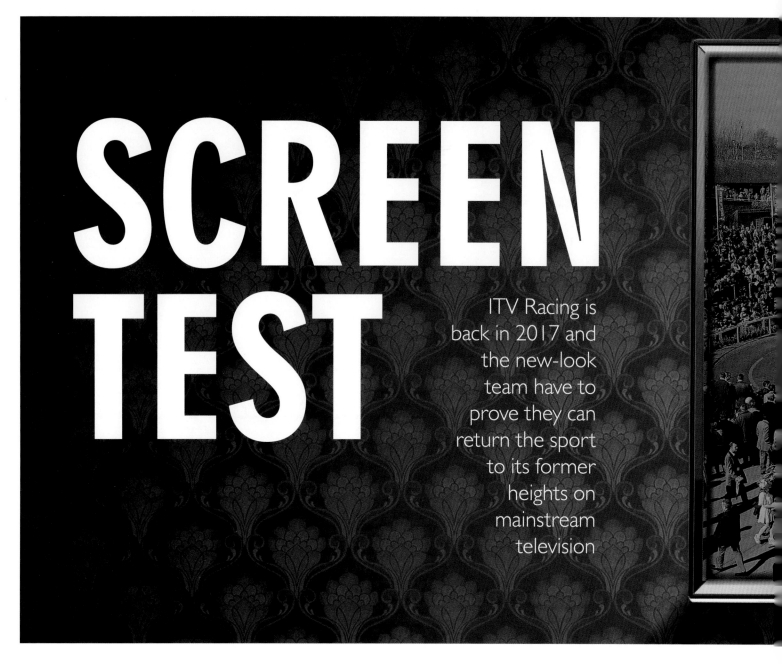

SCREEN TEST

ITV Racing is back in 2017 and the new-look team have to prove they can return the sport to its former heights on mainstream television

By Lee Mottershead

THERE has arguably never been such a seismic change to the way in which British horseracing is televised. It could prove to be an inspired move that revitalises the sport or one that will come to be deeply regretted. Only time will tell.

What is certain is that a decision taken at the end of 2015 put Channel 4 on a 12-month notice period. Taking its place is the broadcaster that, ironically, was responsible for Channel 4 forging what became a 33-year relationship with racing.

It was at Doncaster on Thursday, March 22, 1984 that Channel 4 first offered a platform to racing. It did so because ITV had decided to give up almost the entirety of its midweek coverage. For a year and a half exactly the same team worked simultaneously for ITV and Channel 4 until in October 1985 ITV also conceded all Saturday racing rights. Everything ITV once had then belonged to Channel 4.

From 1985 until the end of 2012 racing on the telly proper was the domain of the BBC and Channel 4. The BBC owned the majority of the crown jewels, one notable exception being the Cheltenham Festival, which it lost to Channel 4 from 1995. The Derby was regained by the BBC but gradually the corporation's interest faded to the point where it offered licence-fee payers only 13 days of British racing a year. The sport became frustrated. Channel 4 took advantage.

The decision to hand Channel 4 a four-year exclusivity deal from 2013 to 2016 had huge implications, given that so many of racing's most iconic moments were inextricably linked to the BBC, Britain's biggest and most watched broadcaster. For the rights holders, led by Racecourse Media Group, handing everything to Channel 4 was dangerous. For Channel 4 Racing it proved lethal. In achieving its greatest success, it also set in motion its own downfall.

Even before Channel 4 took over the Grand National and Royal Ascot, which had hitherto only ever belonged to the BBC, it had taken a radical decision. Long-time production company Highflyer was axed in favour of IMG.

Executive producer Andrew Franklin was replaced by former BBC racing editor Carl Hicks. Channel 4 stalwarts Alastair Down, John McCririck, Derek Thompson and Mike Cattermole were dropped, while John Francome refused to join the IMG squad. Clare Balding moved from presenting racing's biggest days on the BBC to doing so on

RACING P ST

Channel 4, while Nick Luck hosted almost everything else.

Although it is nigh on impossible for a television programme to receive universal praise, it was also impossible to pretend the new-look Channel 4 output was not regularly criticised. Some of those watching claimed the fun had been taken out of the bits between the races, while the decision to do much of the presentation from inside a studio truck did not please all. Nor did the touchscreen table that, at times, seemed to have come without an instruction manual.

Yet Channel 4 Racing's biggest problem was Channel 4 itself. When the BBC was dropped one

reason given was that Channel 4 would expand racing's audience. Exactly the opposite happened.

For practically everything apart from the Grand National, the ratings made for grim reading. The Derby's audience plummeted to a record low, while the numbers watching Royal Ascot were halved with frightening speed. Given the importance of Ascot to the media rights deal, that signalled huge trouble for Channel 4.

The rights holders spoke of the changing television landscape and how ratings were falling across all major sports, while glossing over those events whose ratings were solid or increasing. Publicly they put their heads in the sand.

Privately they must have shared the same concerns as everyone else because the principal motivation for the ITV switch was to produce "a substantial increase" in ratings. ITV's job, at least in terms of racing's public appeal, is to take the sport back to where it was before the BBC was axed, to undo the damage inflicted during the Channel 4 monopoly.

Had Sky emerged victorious it would likely have done so in partnership with the BBC. Indeed, Sky mounted a fierce bid to win the racing contract for exactly the same reason as ITV. Channel 4, which between 2005 and 2013 received £5.275 million in Levy Bord grant funding, won its own

exclusive deal having realised that, with the legalisation of bookmaker advertising, racing on television was suddenly a way of making good money. ITV's long-dormant interest in racing was reignited because of that money.

That, however, is not to say it will not do a fine job editorially. Certainly many of the early signs are promising. The number of broadcast days will increase to nearly 100, with Newmarket's Craven meeting given back a mainstream platform. The second-site meetings will have an ITV anchor, while there will be an underlining that racing is an outdoors sport by doing all the

▸▸ *Continues page 140*

presenting outdoors. The studio truck is to be a thing of the past.

Crucially ITV will want to give the programmes the sense of lightness they have lost. Racing on what used to be called terrestrial television has to look different to what is transmitted on the racing channels and ITV understands that. There will therefore be less punditry but no less emphasis on betting.

ITV's betting pundit Matt Chapman will be adept at adding humour and entertainment, while lead presenter Ed Chamberlin, a high-profile transfer from Sky's football department, is an impressive acquisition. Yet it would be foolish to believe viewers will not hanker after some of those they are losing. Clare Balding will no longer have an involvement in racing on TV, while Luck and commentator Simon Holt are going to be greatly missed. Chamberlin and Richard Hoiles will undoubtedly establish themselves as accomplished replacements, but it is hard to believe they will prove superior to those they are replacing.

In the end, though, just as the reason Channel 4 Racing ultimately failed was because of Channel 4 itself, ITV Racing's greatest asset is that it is on ITV.

Around 60 days of coverage have been scheduled for ITV4, on which ITV also shows the Tour de France, snooker and darts. Just as fewer people watched racing on More 4 than Channel 4, so it could follow that the ratings for racing on ITV4 could be smaller than for the equivalent days on Channel 4.

Ultimately, though, what matters most are the major showpiece afternoons. Channel 4 was kicked out of the sport because of the decimated audiences for Royal Ascot, the Derby, British Champions Day and other key fixtures. The major racecourses want to see viewing figures back to what they were before Channel 4 took over. ITV ought to be capable of realising that ambition, not least because of its far greater ability to cross-promote by advertising racing off the back of the likes of Coronation Street, Britain's Got Talent and This Morning.

The real danger for racing is what happens if ITV decides during its

▸▸ Past and future: The Channel 4 Racing team with the touchscreen table in their studio truck, a set-up that drew regular criticism; (previous page) Ed Chamberlin, lead presenter for ITV Racing, will be based outdoors as the new broadcaster seeks a fresh approach

four-year term that it would rather not go on beyond on 2020? Should the government choose to ban daytime bookmaker advertising, as was rumoured in the autumn of 2016, ITV would be highly unlikely to continue. As a fiercely commercial operator its greatest loyalty is to shareholders. For that reason it can be fickle with its favours. In 2004 it pulled off a coup by stealing the Boat Race from the BBC. In December 2008 it announced it would not renew the five-year deal because "it had invested significantly in securing a fantastic football portfolio". Most of that portfolio was subsequently lost. What happens to racing if it is won back?

That, however, is for the future. From the start of 2017 Channel 4 Racing is in the past. The sport now belongs to ITV, an unashamedly populist channel. ITV must now make racing more popular.

WAY BACK WHEN

For decades racing and ITV were inextricably linked. By stealing Sandown from the BBC in 1955, back when it was known as Independent Television, ITV sent out a message of intent. Soon enough it held all five British Classics and, although the BBC shared the rights to the Derby for a while, it was only on ITV that Shergar's iconic Epsom triumph in 1981 was shown.

John Rickman, Ken Butler and commentator Tony Cooke became popular ITV figures, later followed by Brough Scott (below right), John Oaksey, John Penney and Raleigh Gilbert. Midweek racing programmes were common, while every Saturday afternoon there was racing on ITV's Grandstand imitation, World of Sport, with the action packaged under the famous ITV Seven branding from the early 1970s. As the BBC dominated the jumps season, it was not unusual for Dickie Davies (below left) to link to a presenter at Fakenham, Catterick, Wolverhampton or Kelso during the winter months.

Eventually ITV lost interest in racing and, in effect, bowed out completely with three contests from Redcar in the final World of Sport on October 5, 1985. For a few years it continued to give up an hour to broadcast the Derby alongside Channel 4 but, in reality, racing on ITV was over. Until now.

✔ Improves forage palatability

✔ Is suitable for colic-prone and post-operative horses

**Clean hay means healthier horses –
that's pure horse sense.**

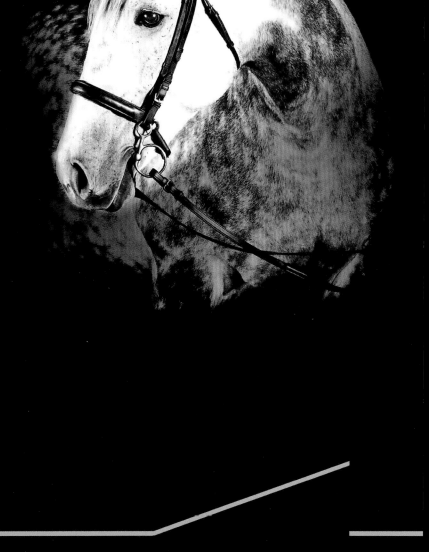

T : 0333 200 5233

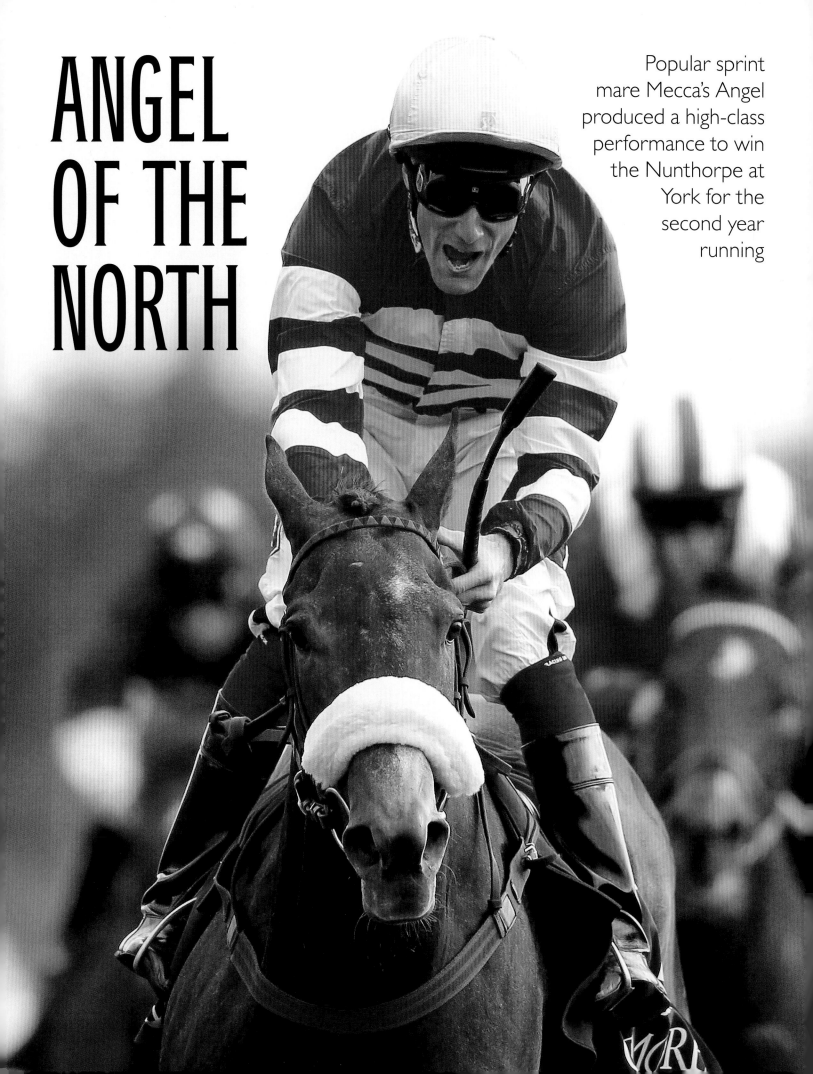

ANGEL OF THE NORTH

Popular sprint mare Mecca's Angel produced a high-class performance to win the Nunthorpe at York for the second year running

By Keith Melrose

THE best days are often preceded by the worst nights. A sense of dread cast itself over trainer Michael Dods after the second day of York's Ebor meeting when it was announced that, with rain forecast, no more water would be added to the course before day three.

Everything that Dods could control had for months been centred on August 19, the day his stable star Mecca's Angel would defend her title in the biggest sprint in the north, the Coolmore Nunthorpe Stakes. But he could not control the weather for his soft-ground-loving mare and, even in Yorkshire, the clouds do not come with the same certainty as a hosepipe.

Dods's Darlington stable is just over 50 miles from the Knavesmire; too far away reasonably to gauge the weather but close enough to feel like you can hazard a guess. He spent a sleepless night waiting in vain for the telltale tapping on his roof. Nothing. As the day brightened, Dods darkened. Each mile of the journey down the A1 that morning cut a little deeper, until the grey clouds finally did what they had long threatened.

"It started to rain when we got within half an hour of the track," Dods remembers. But still they were not in the clear; the official going was good to firm and Mecca's Angel had never won on anything faster than good. Dods, owner David Metcalfe and jockey Paul Mulrennan walked the track. After the first race enquiries were made with riders on the state of the ground. Andrea Atzeni, who rode winner Barsanti, summed up how close a call it was: "It's sort of getting in, but still firm underneath."

The three men walked the track again. The rain had got into the ground; finally, Dods had what he wanted. He told Metcalfe it would be suitable good ground by the time of the Nunthorpe, the fourth race on the card. The owner would admit afterwards that he was more

cautious "but that's what you pay the trainer for".

A short while later, the white smoke spread from the weighing room: Mecca's Angel would run.

The Dods-Mulrennan team got off to an inauspicious start with Glen Moss, who finished last of ten in the City of York Stakes, but before that race clerk of the course William Derby had enacted the trainer's prophecy, changing the official going from good to firm to good. This gentle encouragement was not enough for punters, who saw the hesitation over running Mecca's Angel as reason to get stuck into Limato. The July Cup winner was backed from 3-1 into 15-8, with the mare at 9-2.

Limato's trainer Henry Candy had been sat on the opposite end of the see-saw from Dods all morning. "The main hope we had was that the ground stayed fast and was unsuitable for her and in our favour," he said afterwards, adding, not entirely convincingly, "but you can't really think like that."

In racing, stalking is the sincerest form of flattery and it was immediately clear connections of Limato saw Mecca's Angel as their main threat. Harry Bentley broke from stall four and within half a

furlong had slipped in behind Mulrennan, who had come from three doors down. It is doubtful that Mulrennan ever saw him. His eyes did not stray from the winning line.

Dods's instructions beforehand had been "jump, travel, take a lead and when you're ready press on". Mecca's Angel had provided the first two, didn't need the third and just past halfway her rider executed the fourth. All the while, Bentley waited in behind. If Mulrennan had gone too early by any meaningful margin, he was sunk and everyone knew it – except that he knew differently. He could feel the power underneath him and the line remained his only target, a simplicity of approach that was not available to Bentley and Limato, who had to barge Goldream aside inside the two-furlong marker.

The favourite got back on Mecca's Angel's quarters briefly but no closer. The mare stretched away in the final furlong, picking up better than Limato, whose turn of pace had lit up the July Cup but here was made to look relatively pedestrian. He drew two lengths clear of the rest but was beaten by the same distance. Mecca's Angel had blown them all away.

"It was a lot easier this year," said Mulrennan, who had wept after Mecca's Angel's win in 2015 – his first Group 1 success – but this year was the coolest man on the Knavesmire as the 15,000 spectators enthusiastically greeted a top-class northern winner. "She's a very special filly, an aeroplane on her day," the jockey added. "She's the best and that's probably her best performance."

Racing Post Ratings agreed, going so far as to rate her win the best in the Nunthorpe since Oasis Dream 13 years earlier, and the winning time was just 0.08sec outside Dayjur's track record set on good to firm in the 1990 edition.

Mecca's Angel became the tenth dual winner of the Nunthorpe and the first mare to join the club. Metcalfe admitted afterwards there would be no bid for the hat-trick. "She's got to go to the paddocks at the end of the year. She's too valuable and I'd be stupid to keep her." There would be no fairytale ending, as she finished third in the Prix de l'Abbaye to Marsha, the three-year-old filly who is perhaps her heir apparent, and then a flat 12th in the British Champions Sprint.

Replacing Mecca's Angel, one of the most explosive and popular sprinters of recent times, may seem a daunting task, especially for a 70-box yard that has housed only one previous Group winner, but Dods struck a bright note in the York winner's enclosure, banishing all traces of the pessimism that had dogged him the previous evening. "In jump racing there is a north-south divide but in Flat racing I don't think there is. If you get the right horses I hope we have proved you can do it."

With polished skill, Dods controlled everything in his power to prepare Mecca's Angel for her big day at York. When the rain came, he was ready and so was his Angel of the North.

CANDY RUSH

Veteran trainer Henry Candy unleashed not one but two high-class sprinters in an exciting division

By Keith Melrose

SOMETIMES one of the most interesting stages of an invincible champion's career is what comes immediately after they retire. The vacancy for a top job draws in horses from all over and the threads soon tangle.

Such a situation presented itself when the sprint division was left wide open by the retirement of Muhaarar. In his wake, an undisputed champion over six furlongs did not materialise – the nature of sprints dictates that they rarely do – but unique in this instance was that two of the major players in the power struggle were housed in the same yard, and that one of them started off his season in the Lockinge Stakes.

Limato had been runner-up to Muhaarar in the Commonwealth Cup at Royal Ascot 2015 and was then sent down the seven-furlong route by trainer Henry Candy, finishing his three-year-old season with a fast-finishing second in the Prix de la Foret at Longchamp. That was exhibit A in the decision to try him over a mile in 2016.

"We've chosen the Lockinge as it's the earliest chance we'll get to try him on a flat, straight mile," explained Candy. "Once we've seen what he does at Newbury, we'll take it from there as to how we approach the rest of the season."

Limato finished fourth in the Lockinge, getting no luck in running but equally not rattling home like a mile Group 1 winner in waiting. It was back to the drawing board.

Meanwhile, Candy also had in his yard one of the likeliest successors to Muhaarar. Twilight Son won the only major six-furlong sprint in the second half of the 2015 season that the champion had ducked, Haydock's Sprint Cup, and had been second to him in his valedictory success on Champions Day. His route through the first half of the season trod a well-worn path: preparation, Diamond Jubilee, July Cup.

The chosen prep run was in the Duke of York Stakes at the Dante meeting, where Candy's pre-race fears ("He's done very well through the winter – probably too well") were realised. A rusty Twilight Son was only fifth behind Magical Memory, who added the win to his Abernant Stakes success the

previous month. All of a sudden, he looked just as likely to succeed Muhaarar and when they next met in the Diamond Jubilee he was 3-1 favourite ahead of The Tin Man (100-30) and Twilight Son (7-2).

Where Candy has been fortunate with his two star sprinters is that, while Limato is deemed to be in need of quicker ground, Twilight Son seems to do better when he gets his toe in. On the unseasonably soft conditions that prevailed during Royal Ascot week and with Ryan Moore in particularly determined mood on his back, Twilight Son won a thriller in the smallest Diamond Jubilee field for years, with five of the nine runners covered by a length at the finish.

Twilight Son was on top, for now.

In the meantime, Limato had been channelling the old dog that starts to resemble its owner. On pedigree he should have been a miler, but his speed shone through in the care of Candy, renowned these days for his prowess with sprinters. Speedballs like Kyllachy and Airwave brought Candy back into the upper echelons of the training ranks in the early years of the century, while Markab and Music Master had laid the groundwork in recent seasons for another resurgence.

Ground had become an increasingly important concern for connections of Limato, so much so that they skipped Royal Ascot entirely in favour of Newmarket's July meeting and its major prize, the July Cup. He had also been entered in the Group 2 Summer

Mile on the same day and owner Paul Jacobs admitted to having been of a mind to run there instead. "But Henry said, 'you just pay the fees and I'll look after the horse'."

In the race, Limato proved perfectly capable of looking after himself. It is not often that a horse dropping two furlongs in trip is last off the bridle in a Group 1, but that only underlined his superiority. When Harry Bentley pressed the button, his mount went right, going from the far side of the main group virtually to the stands rail, but he was so comfortably on top that his waywardness did not even hamper a rival. As Limato crossed the line to give horse and rider a first Group 1 success, Bentley even had time to punch the air, another rarity in top sprints.

Candy floated a return to a mile in the Sussex Stakes in the immediate aftermath of the July Cup, but when Limato was next seen it was in the Nunthorpe over five furlongs, for which he had to be supplemented. After that display of previously unknown speed in finishing second to Mecca's Angel, he signed off his European season with a dominant success back over seven furlongs in the Prix de la Foret, gaining emphatic compensation for 12 months earlier.

Twilight Son's season ended quite differently. Having been 14th behind Limato in the July Cup, he did not reappear until the Qipco British Champions Sprint in October and was again well beaten, finishing 11th to The Tin Man, whose turn appeared near when he was second to Quiet Reflection in the Sprint Cup at Haydock.

Even if the pecking order in the turn-and-turn-about sprint division was not cut and dried, the human performer of the year can hardly be doubted. With two of the best sprinters around, Candy had that title secured before the nights started drawing in.

▶▶ Master at work: Henry Candy with Twilight Son (left) and Limato

Ed Dunlop visits Ouija Board at Stanley House Stud, Newmarket, in July. Lord Derby's mare, now 15, was a seven-time Group 1 winner for Dunlop and since her retirement in 2006 she has become a prized broodmare, having produced 2014 Derby winner Australia
EDWARD WHITAKER (RACINGPOST.COM/PHOTOS)

FLYING START

Fresh from his illustrious riding career, Joseph O'Brien has been quick to make his mark as a trainer and is aiming high

By Brian Sheerin

JOSEPH O'BRIEN has packed a lot into his young life. In a short career as a jockey, he won two Irish championships and his 500-plus winners featured ten British and Irish Classics, including a pair of Derby triumphs at both Epsom and the Curragh, as well as a Breeders' Cup Turf and a Sheema Classic on Dubai World Cup night. Already, just a few months into his new career, he is a Group 1-winning trainer. And he is still only 23.

That riding career, which was always going to be short-lived because of his tall stature and associated weight issues, was just the prelude. The platform for the real business was laid even before he stopped riding when O'Brien built up a powerful stable of horses at his base in Owning, outside Piltown in County Kilkenny. The team already includes Group 1-winning juvenile Intricately and Ivanovich Gorbatov, who landed the JCB Triumph Hurdle at the Cheltenham Festival.

Of course, as the son of Aidan O'Brien, Joseph has had the best start in life. Owning is where the O'Brien dynasty started. Before Ballydoyle, Joseph's father, mother Annemarie and maternal grandfather Joe Crowley trained on 'The Hill' and won some of the top prizes in jump racing, including big wins at the Cheltenham Festival.

O'Brien is too young to remember the days when Owning Hill was that beehive of activity. He does remember Istabraq, by which time the O'Brien family had moved to Ballydoyle, and he remembers the buzz created by the three-time Champion Hurdle winner.

Fast forward from then to now, and O'Brien is hoping to recreate that buzz with a hurdler who, like Istabraq, began his life on the Flat and carries the famous green and gold hoops of JP McManus.

Notable figures of the past have often been twinned with racehorses who go on to create their own legend in the sporting arena and O'Brien is hoping Ivanovich Gorbatov, who shares his name with the Russian post-impressionist painter, will join their number. The son of Montjeu is being aimed at the Champion Hurdle at Cheltenham in March and, while O'Brien acknowledges the difficulty, he is relishing the challenge.

"This season will be tough taking on the big boys but we're looking forward to it and he's a lot stronger this year. Hopefully he can develop throughout the season and become a Champion Hurdle prospect," O'Brien says.

On his visit to Cheltenham last March, Ivanovich Gorbatov was not officially trained by Joseph Patrick O'Brien. He had missed a trainers' course the previous November when he was away on Breeders' Cup duty in the saddle and the next one was not until May, which meant the horses from Owning Hill had to run in his father's name until then.

In the winner's enclosure after the Triumph, there was no doubt whose winner it was. "I'm delighted to have come here, seen it and been part of it with Joseph," his father said. "He has worked very hard since he was very young. It has been a full-on commitment all the way. I'm so delighted for him, his team and JP." As for Ivanovich Gorbatov's potential, Istabraq's former trainer offered this tantalising comparison: "Joseph won on him a couple of times when he was trained by us and I always thought this was the closest to him [Istabraq] we've had."

Joseph had ridden Shield for his father in the 2013 Champion Bumper but that was a flying visit and, such is the life of a busy Flat jockey, he never got to sample the magic of the Cheltenham Festival to the full extent until he arrived there with Ivanovich Gorbatov. He had relied on the stories told of the great Istabraq, or even horses like Urubande creating history for O'Brien snr, but now he has his own memories.

"Cheltenham was just unbelievable and you couldn't even ➤➤ *Continues page 150*

dream about things like that happening the way it did," he says. "We went to Cheltenham thinking he could run well, but you don't go to Cheltenham expecting to win."

To have a winner in his own name, Joseph had to wait until June 6 after the i's had been dotted and the t's crossed on his application for a training licence. Victory came with his very first official runner when Justice Frederick won the opening seven-furlong maiden at Gowran Park under Joseph's 17-year-old brother, Donnacha. None other than O'Brien snr was on the receiving end, as his 6-5 favourite Leo Minor was beaten a length and a half into second. It would not be the last time he came off second best to his son.

That first day as an official trainer got even better. Within the hour he had his first jumps winner when Mai Fitzs Jack won a maiden hurdle at Listowel and he had another winner on each card later in the afternoon. Four winners from seven runners was not a bad first afternoon's work. Joseph was at Goffs sales but his father, who was at Listowel, said: "It's a very proud day, a massive day for the family. It's an incredible start."

Emphasising that this was always where his son's future lay, O'Brien snr added: "He loves the training side of it. It was tough going for him for a long time with the riding side of things. He loved riding but doing 9st every morning was very hard. He's a big man, he weighs over 11st now and he doesn't look heavy."

Training has proved anything but tough going and O'Brien jnr quickly added a Group 1 Flat success to Ivanovich Gorbatov's Grade 1 over jumps. That came when the family-bred Intricately fended off the challenge of two Ballydoyle fillies to land the prestigious Moyglare Stud Stakes on Irish Champions Weekend, with Donnacha again in the saddle as he got the filly home in front by a short head.

O'Brien snr put into perspective the magnitude of his son's latest achievement in the Curragh winner's enclosure. "To be honest, when both fillies were battling it out towards the line, I was only hoping that our filly [Hydrangea] wouldn't put her head in

front because those Group 1s are just so hard to win. I can't believe that Joseph at 23 is able to train a Group 1 winner. Where Joseph trains is exactly where we trained before and we never won anything like a Group 1. It's great for Donnacha as well and we can't tell you how proud everyone is at home."

At home at Owning Hill and away from all the bright lights and razzmatazz of the big occasion is where the hard work gets done. There are well in excess of 100 horses in O'Brien's stable ranging from precocious two-year-olds to old-fashioned chasers. Donnacha and sisters Ana and Sarah ride a lot of Joseph's runners in their races and mother Annemarie does most of the office work. It is a family operation, much like it was in the early days of Aidan's career.

▶▶ Straight to the top: (clockwise from top) Joseph O'Brien scores a Group 1 success with Intricately in the Moyglare Stud Stakes, leading to congratulations from Frankie Dettori; Ivanovich Gorbatov wins the Triumph Hurdle; (below) Joseph with brother Donnacha after their Moyglare triumph

"I'm very lucky to have a great team of people working with me on The Hill, both in the training yard and on the farm. We all get on very well and everyone contributes a vital role to the whole operation," Joseph says.

Owning Hill has a big history and has well and truly awoken from its slumber. "We left 20 years ago," Aidan recalled this summer. "Just before we went to Ballydoyle we planted the whole place with trees. I wasn't back there until recently and couldn't believe the difference. This is a complete circle."

That hill holds many good memories of the great horses of yesteryear, but it's all about the present for the yard's latest occupant. "I love it [training]. Things have gone well for us and we'll continue to work hard and hopefully we'll continue to improve.

"We won't go setting any big targets, but if we can do right by our horses and win as many races as possible, we'll be doing all right."

GET THE FULL
RACING PICTURE

RACING P✦ST

print | online | social

HIGHS
AND
LOWS

A career of championships,
Classics and controversy
ended in depression as
Kieren Fallon retired at 51

By Keith Melrose

F OR a century or more, the first rule of professional sport was that you do not talk: not about adversity unless there are triumphs over it, nor about the pressures of a career so coveted by the man in the street. And never, ever, about your weaknesses.

Machismo is sport's umbilical cord, joining fights to the death between Roman gladiators with the cries of "Get stuck in!" in modern-day football grounds. It is of great credit to the age that we live in, regularly derided as 'soft', that now some efforts are being made to clamp and cut. A sportsman coming out as gay still makes the headlines, as in the case of Tom Daley, but that is a hugely positive move from its previous slot, shrouded in the innuendo of gossip columns. And depression, that bitter corrosive too often silenced by the old saw that big boys don't cry, has recently become more openly discussed after the high-profile cases of England cricket internationals Marcus Trescothick and Jonathan Trott.

The list now includes Kieren

Fallon, but do not expect him to become a campaigning crusader on the issue. Reticence was a Fallon trademark throughout his decorated career, which included six champion jockey titles in Britain and 22 Classics between there and his native Ireland. His laconic image only makes the very public admission in July to a long-term struggle with depression that had forced him to retire all the more arresting.

When the news broke, it was not Fallon himself who spoke but Dr Adrian McGoldrick, chief medical officer at the Turf Club in Ireland. "Kieren is suffering from severe depression. When he came to me before getting his licence to ride this year it was clear he was suffering from depression and I treated him with anti-depressants. He rang me last week and said his situation had got worse. I met him and on Sunday he told me he didn't feel strong enough to speak to anyone in the media about his situation and asked me to speak on his behalf."

Even from another's lips, "he didn't feel strong enough" strikes as something especially painful and rare for a professional athlete to concede.

The nature of Fallon's retirement stands in marked contrast to those of two similarly revered riders the previous year. Richard Hughes and Sir Anthony McCoy both bowed out literally as champions, truly on their own terms. The last of Fallon's titles came in 2003 and in the 12 months before his retirement was announced his behaviour had become increasingly erratic, with no explanation offered before Dr McGoldrick's statement. After returning from the US in the autumn of 2015, Fallon proved unreliable, even to his agent who would confess to not knowing his whereabouts.

His retirement came suddenly, but few were surprised. Johnny Murtagh, one of Fallon's longest-standing rivals and his successor as number one jockey at Ballydoyle, summed up the feelings of many when he said on the morning of the announcement: "I'm not surprised to hear he has retired

▸▸ *Continues page 154*

because in recent years and months he's not been showing up for meetings and letting people down and that's not the real Kieren Fallon. He loves riding horses, I think he's at his most peaceful when he's on horseback."

One of the most romantic aspects of Fallon's story was how innate his affinity with horses appeared to be. He claimed not to have ridden a horse with a saddle and bridle until he was 18, while his famed propensity to whistle rather than reach for the whip ("nine out of ten horses respond to that; they're trying to get away from the whistle") also speaks of a rider more in tune with his mounts than most.

In that regard, he shares much with Paul Carberry, 2016's other big-name loss to the jockey ranks. Both men possessed the horsemanship and race-riding nous to create what are probably better described as aberrations on the form book rather than shocks. Fallon's most famous included Kris Kin's 2003 Derby ("one of the best rides I've ever seen," said Murtagh) and more recently Night Of Thunder's defeat of Kingman in the 2,000 Guineas of 2014. It was also Fallon who reputedly put no less of a racing mind than Aidan O'Brien on to the merits of Chester's Derby and Oaks trials, recognising the hot-housing properties of the Roodee that could get inexperienced colts and fillies ready for the demands of Epsom.

It is hard to say what type of jockey Fallon would have been had he relied on his talents alone. It was his drive, which shone through time and again in the interviews he gave only reluctantly, that made him a champion. As he chased a seventh jockeys' title in 2011, he told Donald McRae in The Guardian: "I was at Wolverhampton last night, winging it round at twenty past nine, and if they'd let me I'd still be winging round there at midnight. You've got cheap horses running for cheap money but I love it. I don't do it for the money. The money's not worth it. But the buzz of winning makes everything worth it."

It was that same drive that more than once added to the controversy that shadowed Fallon throughout his

career. His first high-profile brush with authority came in September 1994 when he dragged Stuart Webster from his mount at Beverley after the finish. He was banned for six months, a virtually unheard-of punishment at the time, but almost immediately after his return he became embroiled in the Top Cees scandal during which he was accused of 'cheating' before being awarded £70,000 damages in a successful libel suit in 1998.

By then, Fallon, by now champion jockey in Britain and stable jockey to Henry Cecil, had become a firm favourite with punters. For well over a decade, the name of K Fallon beside a

▸▸ Headline maker: (clockwise from top) Fallon heading to victory in the Derby on Kris Kin (yellow cap); facing the media outside the Old Bailey in 2007; pipping Kingman on the line to win the 2,000 Guineas with Night Of Thunder in 2014

horse drew a group of loyal followers, much like those of Dettori, McCoy or Moore. It even survived his sudden and acrimonious split with the equally popular Cecil in 1999.

Fallon was never short of top trainers seeking his services and spent the following years with Sir Michael Stoute and then O'Brien. His time at Ballydoyle was dogged by two drugs bans, both picked up while riding in France, as well as the notorious trial in 2007 at the Old Bailey where he and ten others stood accused of corruption. The trial collapsed after two months when the
▸▸ Continues page 156

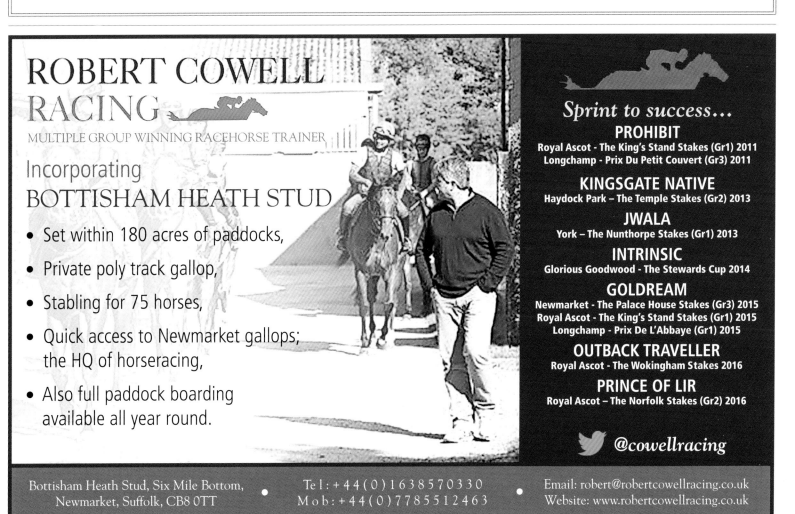

▶▶ Happy days: delight at Longchamp in 2007 after a masterclass to win the Arc with Dylan Thomas; how the Racing Post reported Fallon's Epsom Derby wins on Kris Kin and North Light

judge ruled the defendants had no case to answer.

What had happened less than 24 hours before the trial began underlined that Fallon was as fine a sportsman as racing has been able to count among its ranks. Riding at Longchamp, he was at his coolest and most determined on Dylan Thomas to win the Prix de l'Arc de Triomphe by a head from Youmzain. As performances under adversity go, it would be hard to match.

His drug bans, both for cocaine use, ultimately brought his association with O'Brien to an end and with it Fallon's last truly top-level job, apart from a brief association with Godolphin in 2014. He went nomadic on his return in 2009, with Luca Cumani his most loyal backer, but after his unsuccessful bid for the jockeys' title in 2011 came a gradual downward slide.

Fallon's final season comprised a modest nine wins from 115 rides in Ireland, principally for Michael O'Callaghan, and seven from 47 in Britain. Fittingly, his final winner in Britain came on the day in the calendar with which he will always be most strongly associated – Derby day at Epsom. He steered Blaine to a

MAGICIAN IN THE SADDLE

Full name Kieren Francis Fallon

Born Crusheen, County Clare, February 22, 1965

First winner Picadilly Lord, Navan, June 18, 1984

First winner in Britain Evichstar, Thirsk, April 16, 1988

Derby winners Oath (1999), Kris Kin (2003), North Light (2004)

Other British Classic winners Sleepytime (1997 1,000 Guineas), Reams Of Verse (1997 Oaks), Wince (1999 1,000 Guineas), Ramruma (1999 Oaks), King's Best (2000 2,000 Guineas), Golan (2001 2,000 Guineas), Russian Rhythm (2003 1,000 Guineas), Ouija Board (2004 Oaks), Footstepsinthesand (2005 2,000 Guineas), Virginia Waters (2005 1,000 Guineas), George Washington (2006 2,000 Guineas), Alexandrova (2006 Oaks), Night Of Thunder (2014 2,000 Guineas)

Irish Derby winners Hurricane Run (2005), Dylan Thomas (2006)

Other Irish Classic winners Ramruma (1999 Irish Oaks), Ouija Board (2004 Irish Oaks), Alexandrova (2006 Irish Oaks), Yeats (2007 Irish St Leger)

King George VI and Queen Elizabeth Stakes winner Golan (2002)

Prix de l'Arc de Triomphe winners Hurricane Run (2005), Dylan Thomas (2007)

Top-rated horse (Racing Post Ratings) Hurricane Run (133 in 2005 Prix de l'Arc de Triomphe)

Champion jockey in Britain 6 times (1997, 1998, 1999, 2001, 2002, 2003)

Most wins in a year in Britain 221 (2003)

Total wins in Britain 2,578 (1988-2016)

Compiled by John Randall

four-and-a-half-length success for David Nicholls in the final race on the card, a firm full stop after which he would have no more to say.

No matter the divisiveness of the public persona, few onlookers could wish anything other than a happy retirement to one of the finest jockeys of his generation. We know by now never to assume that the Fallon story is over, but several weeks after his retirement it was reported by Dr McGoldrick that he was doing well, riding out for William Haggas in Newmarket and continuing with his treatment for depression. The evidence casts doubt on whether such an intense and brooding individual is the type to ever seek true peace, but so long as he is healthy and on a horse's back there is every reason to think he is giving himself the best possible chance.

▶▶ Classic star: Fallon celebrates his third Derby victory at Epsom on North Light in 2004

KERRYGOLD

Having taken the reins from father Richard, Kerry Lee enjoyed a first season to remember with a string of big-race successes

By James Burn

MOST jumps trainers would have the Cheltenham Gold Cup or Grand National at the top of their bucket list, but it will take something special for Kerry Lee to beat winning the Coral Welsh Grand National at her first attempt.

The race her family is "kind of famous for" – Lee's father Richard

won it twice – was certainly worth waiting for after it was abandoned last Christmas following heavy rain. It poured and poured when Chepstow's signature contest was staged two weeks later on the soggiest of January days, but nothing could dampen celebrations in the Lee camp after Mountainous ploughed through the mud to record his second win in the cherished staying handicap chase.

"We were fed up when the race was abandoned over Christmas, but we managed to keep him sweet and he really enjoyed the ground," said Lee, a fully paid-up member of the Chepstow fan club. "It's one of our favourite courses – it's one of the few remaining old-fashioned chase tracks and it really takes some jumping. I've been going to Chepstow all my life. I can remember Mum riding around there when I was a child."

The day was even more special as Lee's brother Tom – an important member of the operation based in Byton on the Shropshire-Herefordshire border – was on interviewing duty for Channel 4 Racing.

"It was a massive moment. It's fantastic to win a Welsh National in your first season and to bring a horse back who has already won, and everything went right for us. The rain was torrential on the day and I couldn't have been happier. Someone came up to me and said, 'You're the only person smiling because it's raining'."

The victory kickstarted an excellent run of success in Lee's first campaign that carried her to a near £400,000 prize-money haul, eclipsing her father's best in nearly 30 years as a trainer – and 23 winners at a strike-rate of 21 per cent that was exceeded by only a handful of the other big trainers.

Seven days after the Welsh National, Lee struck with Russe Blanc in Warwick's Classic Chase. "Another brilliant day and another that worked out well as he'd been due to go to Plumpton for the Sussex National, but it was abandoned on the day after they'd run a few races – I don't think I've ever been so cross as Plumpton isn't exactly local to us."

▶ Magic moments: (clockwise from above) Jamie Moore and Mountainous return after winning the Welsh National; Kerry Lee being interviewed by brother Tom on Channel 4 after the race; Top Gamble gallops to victory at Newbury

Lee, who worked on the Channel 4 Racing graphics team while assisting her father before taking over full time, was getting used to being in front of the cameras and found herself in the spotlight again when Top Gamble floored Champion Chase winner Dodging Bullets in what is popularly known as Newbury's Game Spirit Chase.

"Having been on the front of the Racing Post on the day of the Welsh National things become real, but I was conscious to keep my feet on the ground because you've still got a yard full of horses and just because you've had a couple of winners on a Saturday doesn't make everything okay – you've got to keep working hard.

"Top Gamble winning was brilliant because we took on Dodging Bullets and won – people thought I was a bit mad doing that – but I had confidence in the horse and that was the best bit of placing of the season."

Each high-profile victory appeared to propel Lee to bigger and better things. Seven days later,

Bishops Road forged clear to land the Grand National Trial at Haydock. He missed the cut for the real deal at Aintree, but more glory was to come for the first-season trainer.

British trainers have perhaps not always made the most of openings in Ireland, but Lee gave notice she was an emerging force of her trade with a double strike at Fairyhouse's Easter meeting at the end of March.

The first shot was fired by Kylemore Lough, who provided her with her first Grade 1 prize in the Ryanair Gold Cup Novice Chase and not even 48 hours had elapsed when Top Gamble won the Grade 2 Normans Grove Chase, although the elements nearly conspired to wreck Lee's best-laid plans. "When we went to take them on the ferry Storm Katie was emerging and when we got to Holyhead we were turned away and they said no horses would be sailing, so we had to go back to Haydock and try again the next day."

From Chepstow to Fairyhouse,

this was a season to remember for Lee, who took over the training duties at Bell House from her father in the summer of 2015. It was the realisation of a lifelong dream, but Richard Lee is still very much hands on – "I've got the most fantastic assistant" – while mum Carol runs the office and rides out.

"We've taken a more analytical approach to placing the horses, but the gallops are still the same and Mum and Dad are still a huge help – I'd really struggle without them."

Making the most of bargain buys and wheeling and dealing with cheap horses is how Richard Lee came to find most of his success, but the series of winners his daughter enjoyed has allowed her to splash out and JCB Triumph Hurdle hope Mahari became the yard's most expensive signing when he was picked up for €280,000 in the summer.

Hard work and keeping the horses sweet remain the most important aspects of Team Lee, where one great leader has been replaced by an excellent new one.

GROUNDBREAKER

Lizzie Kelly showcased her talents
with two high-profile winners in
the 2015-16 jumps season

By Keith Melrose

IF ACCEPTANCE is what comes when the world has stopped noticing you, Lizzie Kelly may never know the feeling. An engaging presence out of the saddle with a sharp and mischievous turn of phrase, Kelly is unlikely ever to stop drawing attention and, even by the age of 23, has more than done her bit for the cause of female jockeys after breaking new ground in Britain during the 2015-16 jumps season.

While the Group 1 barrier on the Flat had been vaulted by Alex Greaves in 1997 and then smashed apart, at least in Britain, by Hayley Turner 14 years later, it took until the dying days of 2015 for a female rider to win a Grade 1 over jumps. This on the seemingly more egalitarian grounds of jump racing, in which amateurs play a far more prominent role in the top races and some of the best in their ranks are female.

Kelly made history on Tea For Two in the Kauto Star Novices' Chase on Boxing Day 2015 and was instantly, inevitably, lifted up as a pioneer. It is a badge she has worn, if not uneasily, then certainly in her own way. Not for Kelly the if-I-can-inspire-one-other-girl simpering of a Miss World contestant. There is a hard realism to her outlook.

"There are plenty of reasons why trainers don't use girls, and it's never going to change," Kelly said shortly afterwards in an interview with the Daily Telegraph. "Every generation, there are two or three female jockeys who are used, but it doesn't go any further. The subconscious idea of females being the ones who should be at home, looking after the children, is part of our make-up."

If racing is in danger of being too self-congratulatory about its equality of opportunity, Kelly is the antidote.

She said explicitly of her place in the debate: "I don't wake up in the morning and say, 'Today I am going to represent women'. If girls look at me and think 'I can do that', great, but I can't say to trainers, 'You should use girls,'

➤➤ Packing a punch: Lizzie Kelly raises her fist in celebration after becoming the first British female jockey to win a Grade 1 over jumps on Tea For Two at Kempton last Christmas

because the standard of female riders, overall, isn't great."

Kelly's view, paraphrased, is that it is the belief of the individual, rather than the group they fall into, that matters.

"From 12 years old I told myself I was going to be a professional jockey. I can't imagine there are many girls who think that, because they don't think they can do it."

Probably not many women would order Bryan Cooper around either, as Kelly was overheard doing when she wore a helmet camera aboard Tea For Two.

Symbolically, that win in the Kauto Star Novices' Chase, known formerly as the Feltham, remains Kelly's biggest to date but in terms of earnings her win on Agrapart in the Betfair Hurdle in February was twice as valuable as the Grade 1.

How Agrapart came to turn up in the Betfair Hurdle had plenty to do with Kelly's stepfather, trainer Nick Williams.

Williams, who also trains Tea For Two, has earned a reputation for having a mad professor's knack for calculated novelty, so Agrapart's route to Newbury seemed disappointingly mainstream, at least on the face of it.

He progressed well in three starts in everyday novice hurdles, then tried and failed in Grade 1 company before finding handicaps much more to his liking. The truth was a little more nuanced.

"We started thinking about the race after he won at Aintree," Williams explained. "We needed a fourth run for experience and he actually ran well in the Tolworth."

What most notice about the Betfair Hurdle is the prize fund – it remains the richest handicap hurdle in Britain – but Williams unearthed the right race for his mud-loving, prominent-racing novice, the like of whom have farmed the race for much of the past decade.

It does not usually take a ride for the ages to win by 11 lengths, but a fine balance of fire and ice is needed to put a horse in the right position in a race such as the Betfair Hurdle.

Kelly was always prominent but never rushed on Agrapart, even when Starchitect stole what looked like being a decisive two-length advantage before the second-last hurdle. The battle was rejoined, with the race-fit Agrapart just gaining the edge, when Starchitect crashed through the last and was brought virtually to a standstill.

Kelly's confidence marks her out from other conditional riders. To point towards the greater opportunities she inarguably receives by being so closely attached to a top yard would be to miss the point. Prior to the Betfair Hurdle, she was the winner of just 28 contests under National Hunt rules, but afterwards she spoke like someone who had written the race, rather than just won it.

"Everyone's shuffling about and I wanted to be in front of all that, but I was happy to sit behind the leaders. Later on, my plan was to really get them off it so there was no way any speed horses could come back at me."

The distance female riders must still go in racing, or rather how far racing must go to meet them, remains such that Kelly and her generation will be lucky to get within sight of the promised land during their careers.

It is only empirical evidence that will change deep-rooted attitudes and, if last season is anything to go by, Kelly will be providing plenty more of that.

TRIUMPH AND TRAGEDY

Brodie Hampson enjoyed a special moment in her father's colours with an emotional and uplifting victory in the Royal Artillery Gold Cup at Sandown

By Graham Dench

EMOTIONS can often run high in the winner's enclosure but few would have predicted that the most moving scenes of the entire year would follow a race that many would dismiss as a near irrelevance.

Sandown's Royal Artillery Gold Cup has a long and colourful history, but strict qualifications restrict it to chasers rated no higher than 130 and to amateur riders taken from a small pool with very specific connections to the armed forces.

Racing, however, is capable of creating theatre of the highest quality from the least promising elements, and unbridled joy was mixed with sheer tragedy in an unlikely cocktail when Brodie Hampson brought Jennys Surprise from an impossible position to snatch the spoils, proudly wearing the colours of her terminally ill father Mark.

Mark Hampson, a career soldier who served for 22 years in the Royal Artillery, was very much on borrowed time by raceday – February 19 – having been given only 30 days to live almost three months previously. When he needed two blood transfusions the week before it looked long odds against him making it to Sandown, but he had dreamed of seeing his 21-year-old daughter one day ride a winner in his colours and, having survived tours in Northern Ireland, the Gulf and Afghanistan, nothing was going to stop him.

The Gold Cup was Plan B for the Fergal O'Brien-trained Jennys Surprise, who would have run at Bangor the previous week but for its abandonment, but O'Brien had won the race before and his new partner Sally Randell, a former lance bombardier with an outstanding record in Sandown's military races, was Brodie Hampson's boss at the Broad Hinton Stables owned by Andy Turnell.

The mare's owners, the Yes No Wait Sorries, are a generous bunch who were happy to lease Jennys Surprise for the day, and the rest, as they say, is history.

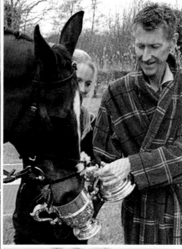

▸▸Fairytale success: (clockwise from left) Brodie Hampson and Jennys Surprise on their way to a dramatic win in the colours of the rider's terminally ill father; Mark Hampson with the Royal Artillery Gold Cup; Jennys Surprise near the back in the early stages; connections with horse and jockey in the Sandown winner's enclosure

It would be impossible to calculate the odds for Mark Hampson making it to Sandown on that February afternoon, although in his own mind there was probably never much doubt about it. It is a matter of record, however, that the win odds for Jennys Surprise after a catalogue of errors touched a high of 970 on Betfair's in-running market when she lost her position down the far side of the track on the second circuit.

Recalling how the race unfolded, Brodie Hampson said: "Paddy Brennan had told me she had schooled superbly, but my God did we miss the first. I went to give her a squeeze and she put down on me. Then we made a big hash of the downhill fence going out into the country for the final time and lost our position.

"She winged the Railway fences – loved them – but it still looked hopeless as the front two had got away and there was nothing underneath me. My only hope was they would somehow come back.

"We were very slow over the Pond fence and had no chance at all – I thought it would take a miracle to get anywhere near – but she has such a heart because most horses that far back would give up.

"She jumped two out very well and I thought 'Jesus, we could get into this' and so I just kept slapping her down the neck. When

we jumped the last, the two in front were walking – literally walking – and then the one on the left hung and I just ran straight. I had to switch my stick, and it wasn't my greatest finish, but we did it."

She added: "It's a dream come true. Dad has been up and down, with good days and bad days, but thank God today was a good day – the best day ever. He always wanted to see me ride in this race in his colours, so to do it and win like that is fantastic."

Sgt Hampson somehow retained his composure while others were in floods of tears and said he was "chuffed to bits" for his daughter, and "so proud of her".

There was more cheer for the family when it was arranged only days later for both Jennys Surprise and the cup she had won to be taken to the Prospect Hospice, near Swindon, but the inevitable had merely been postponed.

Mark Hampson lost his battle against cancer on May 1, aged 45, but Brodie by then had won again in his colours, on Goal in a selling hurdle at Southwell, and also been awarded a Stobart jockey of the month prize for the Sandown ride.

His death hit her hard, of course, not least because he had still been enjoying the occasional 'good' day, but she has moved on in more ways than one and has embarked on a new chapter in her career.

Along with her friend and boss Sally Randell, she has joined the upwardly mobile and forward-looking operation run by the trainer who facilitated that extraordinary occasion. Both have joined Fergal O'Brien's yard, where Jennys Surprise remains a constant reminder of the joy racing can bring.

END OF THE DREAM

Brian Toomey, who made a
remarkable return from his
deathbed to the saddle, was
finally forced to accept his
race-riding career was over

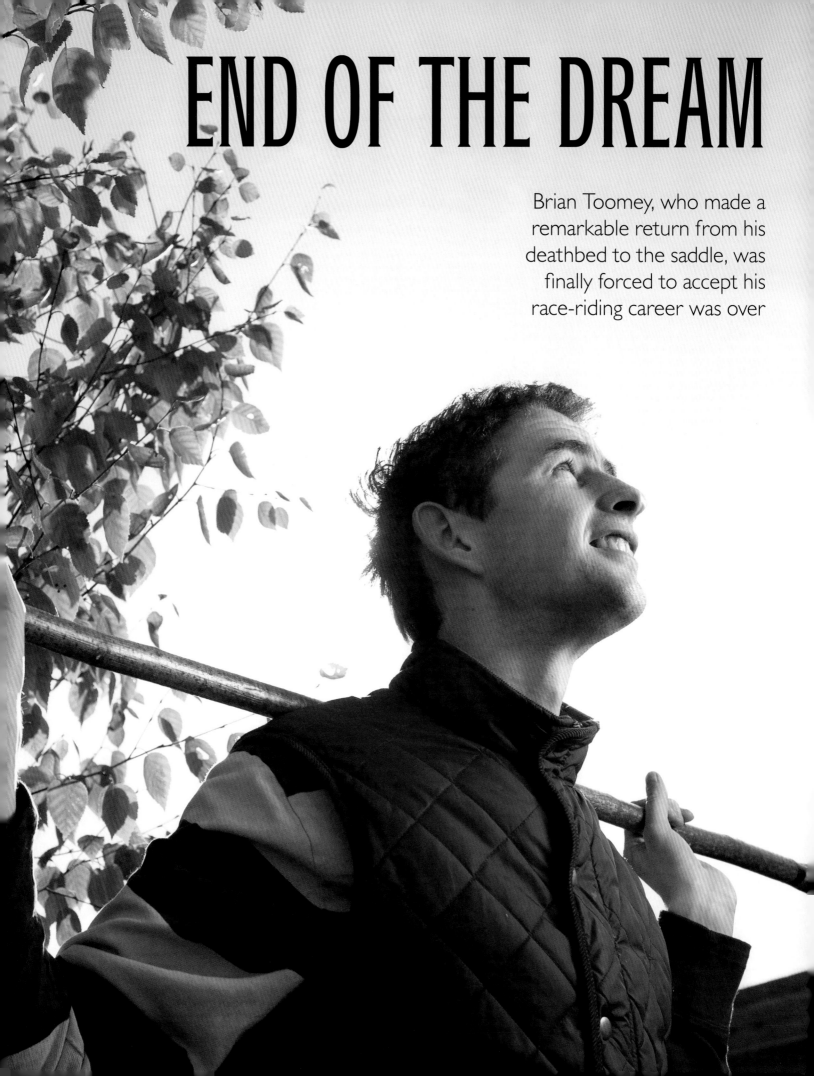

By Stuart Riley

JOCKEYS, like other sportspeople, can experience an acute sense of loss when their career comes to an end, a kind of mourning for the person they used to be. That feeling can take root even after a successful career of sporting fulfilment reaches a natural conclusion on age grounds at 40 or even 50, but to be an ex-jockey at 27 is hard. Just ask Brian Toomey.

In July 2015, Toomey completed perhaps the most astonishing comeback in the history of race-riding but less than a year later his dream was over. The jockey who literally came back from the dead had to accept the inevitable and quit the saddle.

Toomey's return was hailed as a miracle, and in medical and human endeavour terms it was. A fall at Perth in 2013 took him to death's door and he briefly popped inside; he was clinically dead for six seconds. From there he fought for his life – he was given a three per cent chance of survival, he was in an induced coma for 18 days, his family were asked to decide where they stood on organ donation – and then he fought to get his career back.

Finally the BHA granted him a licence again, but then the cold, hard reality of the racing business hit home. In this second coming there were no winners and not that many rides. Announcing his retirement, Toomey said: "I was hoping so much I would get some opportunities but there has only really been disappointment."

A career that brought 49 winners and once promised so much could not have ended more sadly, as Toomey was brought down in a mares' novice hurdle at Stratford in June. His mount, City Dreams, was fatally injured.

Speaking later in the summer, Toomey was still searching for the sense of purpose that a career brings. "I'd love to find a job and be happy and content and settled, and just do well at that," he said. "Hopefully I can be known for doing well at something else."

Toomey's fairytale comeback was a wonderful representation of all that is good in the human condition and yet he cannot help but feel it was one penned by the brothers Grimm when they were in a particularly twisted mood. He is perceptive enough to know he should celebrate his achievement, which made it all the more heartbreaking when he candidly revealed: "In my mind I failed."

All Toomey wanted was to be a jockey again. He turned down the end-of-career insurance money, which under the new guidelines would have seen him receive £60,000 – and at the time of his injury would have paid out even more. "What price dreams?" he said.

Yet it is not the financial loss that eats away at him. "I wasn't disappointed at all, I probably would have blown it on a flash car and flash everything else," he says with humour, before revealing his torment. "I was just disappointed I didn't get going again, I would have loved to have ridden a winner. It would have been big and it could have helped get my career going again."

In total there were 24 rides in his comeback, from which there were two thirds and one fourth. It took some home truths from trainer Enda Bolger, among others, before Toomey finally accepted retirement. Bolger, who lives close to Toomey's family home in County Limerick, said: "I told him he was wasting his time carrying on as a jockey. People were worried about him. Every time he rode his parents' hearts were in their mouths. For the same reasons every trainer would be scared to put him up, just in case something went wrong."

Toomey understood the reluctance of others to put him in harm's way, and the ever-present danger in race-riding was clear on that fateful final ride on the unfortunate City Dreams.

A brief spell as Richard Newland's assistant ended when Toomey realised he was not mentally ready for all the job demanded. "In my mind I was still a jockey," he said. "Come ten in the morning, I was looking at provisional declarations to see if I had a chance of a ride. I was looking at horses for trainers I'd ridden winners for and thinking 'why aren't I riding that?' and I'd

Second coming: (clockwise from left) Brian Toomey works back towards his return to race-riding in 2015; being interviewed by the press after his first ride back at Southwell; being dumped in the water bucket after his final ride before retirement

get down in the dumps about the whole thing. I had a few good chats with Richard. In the end, I said 'I'm not ready for this' and he was very understanding."

Like many people when life meets crisis Toomey went back home. He started riding out every day for Tommy Stack and is still involved in the sport. "I go to the sales and try to pick and buy a few. I'm still in the bloodstock side of things," he said.

"I'm mad keen to do well in racing again. I'd just love to get a good job opportunity, maybe in the sales side of things. I'm keeping my options open but I'm 27. I don't want to keep switching but I do want to find something I love."

His first love was taken away, but it could have been so much worse. As he said himself: "Just to be able to walk and talk again is an achievement."

YOUNG AT HEART

Megalala, the horse who just won't stop, won again at the grand old age of 15

By Nicholas Godfrey

HE IS the horse Old Father Time seemingly cannot catch. Golden oldie Megalala may never have been anything more than a low-level handicapper but the veteran middle-distance performer – long since a racecourse favourite over 12 years' service on the track – earned a lasting place in our affections in the summer when he became the oldest horse to win on the Flat in Britain in the modern era.

Although the achievement was slightly lost amid the hullabaloo of Royal Ascot, minutes after the royal meeting drew to a close on June 18 this remarkable gelding forged a little slice of history under 7lb claimer Mitch Godwin when he won the Heart FM Handicap, a 0-52 Class 6 event over a mile and a quarter on the all-weather at Lingfield Park. Nothing extraordinary in itself, you might think – until Megalala's age is considered.

He was 15, and Racing Post historian John Randall says he is "fairly sure" Megalala is the oldest horse to win on the Flat in Britain since 1945. "The other candidates for that title were all 14," Randall explains, identifying Pheidippides (1969), Le Garcon D'Or (1972), Be Hopeful (1973), Redoubtable (2005) and The Tatling (2011, twice).

Owned by Trevor Wallace, Megalala has won 20 races altogether in a career that started when he was unplaced in a Fontwell bumper in April 2005. For that entire period, he has been trained by John Bridger – himself a

veteran, having held a licence since 1971, the last 36 years based in Liphook on the border between Hampshire and West Sussex. Although Bridger reached the dizzying heights of Group-race success when Hotbee won the Molecomb Stakes in 1985, his best-known horse was that notorious serial loser Amrullah.

Bridger, who bought Megalala in Ireland as a yearling for about £4,000, says his current stable star is showing few signs of age, despite having been racing for 12 seasons. "He doesn't seem any different to train," says Bridger, who turned 75 in October. "We'd never abuse him but he feels no different from five or six years ago – he hasn't wilted and he seems willing."

Evidently Megalala *(below with Bridger)* likes his routine. "He can be a bit mental, lively in the morning," adds Bridger, a former pig farmer whose distinctive Hampshire burr tells of his Cosham roots. "When you get up he's already walking his box, wanting to get out. They all go up to the water trough and have a roll about, then we put him in the paddock – but he can be a bit awkward because then you can't leave him out too long or he wants to come in. I suppose he's just like an athlete: he's always fit but he wants to stay in a five-star hotel.

"He just wants to gallop and when the girls ride him he knows exactly where he's going. We always used to work him on his own because he was so full of himself but now he's a little bit better. But he's a lovely horse – he hasn't got a vice kick-wise or anything and you can put him on the roads and he'll walk all day."

After his Lingfield victory, habitual front-runner Megalala continued to produce his usual game efforts in defeat, especially at his favourite track Brighton, where he has won eight times. "He loves Brighton," Bridger says. "I suppose he knows the place and he always seems to run well there as long as the ground's decent.

"He's a bit of a character – once he's got his revs up, he just keeps going. He's hard to beat if he gets a couple of lengths out of them but unfortunately they follow him a bit too closely now. He's only got one pace and they get on his tail a bit more these days. He likes cut in the ground as well – he can run on faster, but that helps the others to catch him."

As long as Megalala continues in such rude health, he looks set to continue into 2017, when he will try to become the first 16-year-old to win on the Flat for nearly 200 years. "If he's like he is now, then hopefully he'll be back next year," Bridger says. "I don't know what would happen to him if he did come out of training because I'm sure he wouldn't enjoy it."

Neither, for that matter, would his trainer. "They say you're in the waiting room when you're over 70 and my wife keeps saying it's time I packed up but I don't really see it happening. I really don't know what I'd do if I retired – it's my life and I enjoy it. It gives me an incentive. I don't really enjoy holidays or days off, so I'd go nuts. I like doing what I do and what else am I going to do? I'd be like Megalala walking his box! I won't be able to retire until he retires – and he'll be a very hard horse to retire."

IN THE PICTURE

Finish line in sight for Farquhar's epic charity odyssey

A 300-strong field stretched their legs down the Rowley Mile in April when they joined Richard Farquhar for the final leg of Walking The Courses, his epic charity trek that started at Newmarket in March 2015 and ended back there 13 months later.

Farquhar's walk criss-crossed Britain, connecting the country's 60 racecourses, to raise money for Racing Welfare and Pancreatic Cancer UK. By the end of his 2,910-mile journey, he had raised more than £370,000.

The 53-year-old, a racehorse owner with Henry Candy and fund manager in London, was first inspired to make a large-scale charity effort after his father Peter died from pancreatic cancer in 2012, and later when the disease also claimed trainers John Hills and Dessie Hughes.

"It has been absolutely thrilling," said Farquhar after reaching the finishing line at Newmarket (*inset*). "The reality is it has been the most enjoyable, fulfilling, rewarding and uplifting experience of my entire life, by a street. It has been one wonderful week after another, a complete joy from start to finish.

"I've made a colossal number of new friends and renewed friendships with people dotted all over the country. I've visited some racecourses I hadn't been to before and I've been welcomed wonderfully at all of them.

"The only real physical low point was between Ffos Las and Chepstow, when I went lame. By the time I got to Chepstow I was pretty worried but, thankfully, the racecourse doctor gave me a decent shot of cortisone in the foot."

Pancreatic cancer survivor Karen Stead, along with her sister Beverley Williams, was among those who joined Farquhar for the final steps.

"What Richard has done is amazing," Stead said. "I've followed this from the beginning. It has been a big chunk out of his life. I can't imagine how he will be feeling."

An even longer journey in aid of charity came to an end at York in September when Antony Lewis-Crosby completed his mission of visiting not only all of Britain's racecourses but all of Ireland's – and in alphabetical order.

Lewis-Crosby, 69, who lives in London, took seven years to complete the full set and along the way raised more than £60,000 for the Cystic Fibrosis Trust. His son David has the condition and underwent a double lung transplant 12 years ago.

To mark the occasion, he sponsored the final race on the York card – the Racecourse Challenge for Cystic Fibrosis Apprentice Stakes.

Pictures: EDWARD WHITAKER (RACINGPOST.COM/PHOTOS)

'A magnificent man who showed what the unquenchable human spirit can achieve'

JT McNAMARA
1975-2016

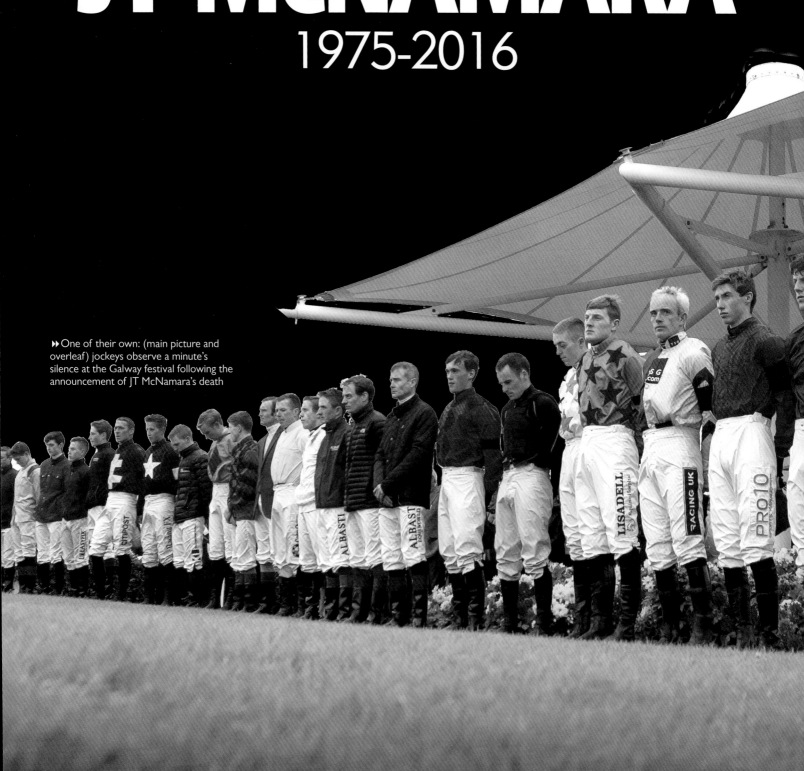

▸▸ One of their own: (main picture and overleaf) jockeys observe a minute's silence at the Galway festival following the announcement of JT McNamara's death

In July the racing world mourned the death of the leading amateur rider who was paralysed after a fall at the 2013 Cheltenham Festival. In these extracts two Racing Post writers pay tribute

By Alastair Down

IN the early hours of a County Limerick summer night, a great struggle fought with inspiring tenacity against the grimmest of odds came to its honourable and inevitable close.

Some three years and four months since his fall at Cheltenham, John Thomas McNamara came to journey's end, having travelled the most harrowing of highways and endured suffering both mental and physical that should lie beyond the capacity of mere mortals.

So it is a time for sadness and it would be a flint heart that did not open to the pain that will be felt by JT's wife Caroline and their three young children, Dylan, Harry and Olivia, for whom the bright sky of having both a mum and dad is now forever clouded.

Not being able to play with his kids was the cross JT found the heaviest to bear. Yet he bore every cross that came his way and usually had something pithy to say about the lot of them.

John Thomas was a jump jockey – an extraordinarily instinctive horseman – and he went out to race with all the carefree courage of his trade. But there is no doubt in my mind that the character, stubborn bravery and point-blank refusal to be defeated he showed every day after his accident far outshone the undoubted qualities he had to show on course.

Jockeys are used to the physical cut-and-thrust of a staying chase – it is second nature to them. But JT fought a battle for more than three years with just his mental virility and unflagging soul as weapons. Nothing moved from the neck down and his horseman's hands lay flat on the arms of his wheelchair. A man familiar with harnessing half a ton of flesh through sheer strength and subtlety had to fight his new war without any weapon but himself.

But in fact JT was never alone. He had one priceless, indomitable, fearless and fabulous asset welded to him by love and sheer determination to succeed in giving her man a life worth the living – his wife Caroline. She had fallen for and married a sportsman, the family home rang with the laughter of kids, but suddenly she found her home had become a hospital, her horizon reduced from the infinite to the infinitesimal as she – with the endless help of her mother Phil – worked their miracles of hope and sustaining love for John Thomas.

That great and incisive saying "kindness in another's trouble, courage in your own" could have been minted for Caroline McNamara. Unstinting, often unsleeping and always unwavering, she simply refused to be bowed. "We are not a teary house," she once said, "though we have had plenty of cause."

And to visit them was to be uplifted not downhearted. John Thomas would be complaining

▸▸ *Continues page 172*

about the fact he should have read the small print when marrying his wife as he hadn't realised how bossy she was, or Caroline would – outrageously – say: "The trouble with you, John, is that you have no patience. The last time you showed any was when you won the four-miler on Rith Dubh."

He should have sued the woman, although to be fair taking your legend of a wife and eternal helper to court might be a little over the top.

What happened to John Thomas is the scenario that gnaws away in the most private and unapproachable part of every jockey's soul. The weighing room has seen its denizens die and their shock and sorrow is always raw at such times of grief. But to be rendered utterly helpless in a chair is some terrifying refinement they fear above all.

John Thomas woke to that living nightmare and, however daunted and desperate he felt, he somehow screwed his courage to the sticking place and faced into that futureless future.

And I would argue that the way he fought the long defeat transcended his incarceration and lifted him to the inspirational. He refused to be ground into nothingness, his fighting spirit never flinched.

Many hands helped – friends, benefactors, and institutions various, all of whom deserve praise. But in the still hours of the night it came down to JT and his close team around him – and this was a man whose 24-hour care was the stuff of living minute to minute.

After he had breathed his last the hospital of home would have begun to wind down. The quiet hum of machinery stilled, the lights on monitors blinking no more.

In the end his chest got him, as it was always known would be the case. But I am not inclined to mark JT's death as a defeat. There is a sense of relief about his release and above all he showed what the unquenchable human spirit can achieve in even the bleakest and direst of straits.

On Friday they will gather for his funeral and John Thomas McNamara will be laid with honour in the ground. A magnificent man in the saddle and also in extremis, may he indeed rest in peace.

'A VERY SPECIAL PERSON'

John Thomas McNamara died at home in Croom, County Limerick, in the presence of his family on July 25. He was 41. The former leading amateur rider had been treated at University Hospital Limerick the previous week for complications stemming from the dreadful injuries incurred when Galaxy Rock fell at the first in the Fulke Walwyn Kim Muir Handicap Chase at the 2013 Cheltenham Festival.

His injuries, regarded as life-threatening at the time, included fractures to the C3 and C4 vertebrae. Following initial treatment in Britain and then at the National Spinal Unit in Dublin's Mater Hospital, he underwent an intensive spell of rehabilitation at the North West Spinal Injuries Centre in Southport.

McNamara became emblematic of the risks attached to jump racing. The respect and affection in which he was held by those who knew him best, in the weighing room, on the point-to-point circuit, and in his local community, permeated to the wider racing world in Ireland, Britain, and beyond.

Leading owner JP McManus, who provided three of McNamara's four Cheltenham Festival winners, echoed the thoughts of all, describing McNamara as "a very special person". He said: "I knew him for many years. The more one got to know him, the more one loved him.

He was very direct and never used two words if one would do.

"We enjoyed many successes together on the track. While he was a very forceful rider, he was also excellent at cajoling a horse to produce his best when that was necessary. His winning ride on Rith Dubh in the National Hunt Chase was a wonderful example and will be remembered as one of the great Cheltenham Festival rides.

"I suppose in many ways his legacy will be that he didn't die in vain. Because of the dreadful injuries he suffered, a lot of good things followed as a result. Other badly injured riders have benefited and will continue to do so in terms of facilities and services, and there is now a much greater awareness among the public of what can happen to riders."

In a career in points between 1994 and 2013 McNamara rode 602 winners and was champion point-to-point rider outright on four occasions, as well as sharing the title in 2002 with Davy Russell.

McNamara belonged to a distinguished Irish tradition, stretching back to the Beasley brothers in the 19th century, as a gifted amateur capable of holding his own against the top professionals, a quietly masterful horseman whose all-round horsemanship gained a wider audience around the cross-country tracks at Punchestown and Cheltenham.

SELDOM HAS A MINUTE'S SILENCE SOUNDED SO DEAFENING
Reaction on the second day of the Galway festival

By David Jennings

IT WAS almost as if the horses knew. They didn't turn a hair. Babies barely budged in their buggies. Bookmakers bowed their heads. Food orders could wait. Drinks were put down. Seldom has a minute's silence sounded so deafening.

When parade-ring compere Denis Kirwan began to tell racegoers about the devastating news we woke up to yesterday morning, we all pricked our ears. John Thomas McNamara was not just a rider. He was not just a horseman. He was a part of this wonderful community of ours and we could not be prouder of him.

Kirwan somehow managed to keep it all together and, after the minute's silence had been observed so respectfully by everyone, he told racegoers to turn to the big screens to watch some of McNamara's finest moments in the saddle. Teaforthree, Rith Dubh, On The Fringe. Smiles started to accompany tears.

This was a day when tears won out over smiles. Backing winners at Galway last night had much less meaning than it usually does. It was almost as though punters felt guilty collecting.

The rain was relentless. When the first shower bounded down on Ballybrit before noon, you sensed it wasn't going to be the last. The weather illustrated how everyone felt better than any of us ever could.

Ruby Walsh somehow managed to snatch victory from the jaws of defeat on Penhill in the opener. So remote looked his chances that he drifted to 999-1 on Betfair and someone managed to get €16 on him. Only very few would have won on him. McNamara was part of that elite group.

Barry Cash landed the beginners' chase on 66-1 outsider Talk The Lingo, edging out Walsh on hot favourite Briar Hill in the most thrilling finish of the night. "It helps when you have John Thomas looking down on you," said Cash before the tears took over.

"He was a gentleman but he was a brilliant jockey too. He was as good as you would see. He was able to win on anything and I think every one of us in the weighing room learned something from him."

Davy Russell learned plenty and he described a normal point-to-point fixture when John Thomas was in his prime. "The last day I saw him ride in a point-to-point was at Ballingarry. He rode three winners and gave the three horses three different rides," Russell said. "He dropped in last on the first of them, he made the running on the second and he sat behind the leaders on the third.

"He knew how to ride a good horse. He knew how to get the best out of the bad ones and he knew exactly what to do with the quirky ones. He could ride fillies too. As regards a jockey, there was none better. For people who did not see him on a daily basis on a point-to-point field, it was remarkable. People used to go to points to watch John Thomas. Not necessarily the horses, but John Thomas."

It was a day for remembering a genius.

These are edited versions of articles that appeared in the Racing Post on July 27

IN THE PICTURE

Hereford jumps back into action after four years in wilderness

Hereford reopened for jump racing in October, almost four years after its controversial closure – along with Folkestone's dual-purpose course – caused widespread dismay.

The two tracks appeared likely to disappear forever when they became the first British turf venues to close since Stockton in 1981 but, while there has been no reprieve for Folkestone, there was a surprise announcement in January that Hereford would hold four fixtures in 2016. Later the track, which first staged racing in 1771, was allocated 11 meetings in the 2017 fixture list.

Arena Leisure Company (Arc), which runs the racecourse, faced a frantic rush to prepare the course for the return of jump racing but was ready in time for the reopening on October 6. The efforts were rewarded by a crowd of 4,501, which was the largest for a midweek meeting at the track in more than a quarter of a century. Attendances were averaging a mere 1,500 up to its closure, which was blamed on the track being economically unviable amid a dispute with the local council over the length of the lease.

Even what had appeared to be the final meeting on December 16, 2012, drew a crowd of just 2,600 to what seemed like a wake. The reopening 1,391 days later had a party atmosphere on a bright autumn afternoon, with a 75 per cent jump on the closing-day attendance.

"I've been waiting with bated breath for this," said racegoer Dave Gillett, who used to be a local boy but had travelled from Oxford. "I remember coming here many years ago with my father and it's great that Arc have got it up and running again. I know I live a few miles away but I'm going to take out annual membership to support the track and the initiative."

The seven-race card was well supported by racing professionals and Nicky Henderson, who sent out Rather Be to win the first race, said: "Most of these things, when they go, they're gone and here's one where they've made a fantastic effort to get it back. To come here and see a crowd like this, it shows what can be achieved."

Herefordshire-born champion jockey Richard Johnson was winnerless on the day but delighted with the return of racing. The track has named the Rusty Bridge restaurant in honour of Johnson's first career winner, which came at Hereford in 1994.

"Hereford was a big loss to the county when it closed down," Johnson said. "It's my local track and it's great that it's back. Hopefully it will go on being well supported."

Pictures: EDWARD WHITAKER (RACINGPOST.COM/PHOTOS)

By Nick Pulford

RAW STRENGTH

America proved a frontier too far for Willie Mullins as a pair of less celebrated Irishmen denied him victory in Tennessee

IRISH connections came out on top in the Grade 1 Iroquois Hurdle in May, setting up the chance of a $500,000 bonus at the 2017 Cheltenham Festival, but it was not the expected victory for the Willie Mullins juggernaut.

The Mullins pair Shaneshill and Nichols Canyon were denied in brave fashion by Rawnaq, who comes from the 15-horse Maryland stable of Cyril Murphy and was given a brilliantly judged front-running ride by Jack Doyle.

Horse, trainer and jockey all hail from Ireland but have found America a land of opportunity. Irish-bred Rawnaq was formerly trained by Robbie Hennessy and Matthew Smith and had 21 races over jumps in Ireland before moving to the US in 2015. He joined Murphy, originally from County Waterford, who was a journeyman jump jockey before he started training with "two or three horses" in 2009.

Around the same time as Rawnaq's move, Doyle decided to try his luck in the States, having ridden almost 200 winners in eight seasons in Britain after moving from Ireland at the age of 18.

The jockey is thriving as a big fish in a small pond, in jump racing terms, and his new-found confidence was evident as he took down the Mullins raiders at Percy Warner Park in Nashville, Tennessee.

Doyle and Rawnaq led all the way in the three-mile Iroquois and had enough left to hold Shaneshill by a neck, with Nichols Canyon three lengths back in third. "We'll put it to them and see what they have," Doyle told Murphy before the race. The Mullins raiders did not have enough.

Mullins was magnanimous in defeat, while pointing out that it might have been one race too many for his runners after a long season. Victory would have given Mullins a shot at the $500,000 Brown Advisory Iroquois Cheltenham Challenge on offer for any horse who wins both the Iroquois and the World Hurdle within the space of 12 months.

That challenge is instead open to Rawnaq and his connections immediately trained their eyes on the prize at the 2017 Cheltenham Festival. "The World Hurdle is a tough race and it's a tough undertaking for us, with the timing, because our last day of racing is the third weekend in November and we don't start again until the weekend after the Cheltenham Festival," Murphy says. "But his owner's keen to go over and Rawnaq is deserving of the opportunity."

Rawnaq has form at Cheltenham, having finished third in the Greatwood Handicap Hurdle in November 2013 and in the Plate at the festival the following season. On both occasions he finished within three lengths of the winner but, with a Racing Post Rating of 147 for his Iroquois triumph, would appear to have no more than a sporting chance in the World Hurdle.

Owner Irv Naylor is nothing if not sporting, however. He was a top amateur rider over jumps in the US and the oldest licensed jockey until a catastrophic fall in the American Grand National in 1999 left him wheelchair-bound. He had planned to ride only once more after that race and then retire.

Now 80, he is the leading owner in US jump racing, with Murphy as his trainer, and has had several good performers in Britain and Ireland, including 2011 Kerry National winner Alfa Beat.

"The owner's very passionate and loves his horses. He's very excited about the World Hurdle, he's totally up for it," says Doyle, who is bullish about Rawnaq's prospects. "I think he can run a huge race. Unless there's a horse like Thistlecrack, he'll have a big chance. Three miles suits him and he's got a bit of class."

Doyle, 27, had a couple of third places at the Cheltenham Festival when he was riding in Britain but his number of rides and winners

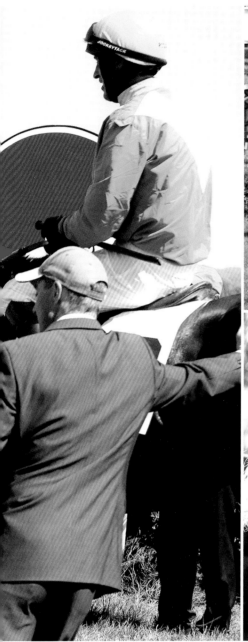

▸▸American dream: (clockwise from main picture) Rawnaq and Jack Doyle in the winner's enclosure with owner Irv Naylor (centre, wheelchair); the pair head to victory; action during the race; spectators near one of the jumps; trainer Cyril Murphy celebrates; Willie Mullins with his jockeys Ruby Walsh and Danny Mullins (right) Pictures: THE IROQUOIS STEEPLECHASE

dipped after Emma Lavelle, his main supporter, appointed Noel Fehily as stable jockey in 2012. He has found better chances coming his way in the US, where he rides mainly for trainer Elizabeth Voss.

"The prize-money is very good, I've won some big races and I'm really enjoying it," he says. "I've ridden six Grade 1 winners in the last two years and I'd be a long time trying to do that in England or Ireland."

Murphy, 44, could relate to that experience. Originally from Tramore, he did not come from a racing background but at 17 he did a course at the British Racing School and then joined Sir Mark

Prescott's stable in Newmarket, where he soon learned he would be too heavy to ride on the Flat.

After four years there, he spent another four with Bill Turner in the West Country and had about 250 rides over jumps, riding 13 winners. He gave up a career in the saddle to join Nicky Henderson's staff – "at the time he had Tiutchev, Stormyfairweather, Marlborough," he recalls – but then decided to try America, where he got the opportunity to ride in races again, including several seasons riding for Tom Voss, Elizabeth's late father.

"From the very beginning training was always something I

wanted to try, and when the riding came to an end I figured I must have learned something along the way," Murphy says. "I got my first licence in 2009 but until I came to work for Mr Naylor I never had more than two or three horses. I had a riding-out job and then I was training my own horses whenever time allowed. But it became a full-time occupation when I came here three years ago."

Murphy, who trains on Naylor's farm 20 miles north-west of Baltimore, highlighted his skill with a Grade 1 victory over Mullins that his counterparts in Britain and Ireland know does not come easy these days. While

accepting that Shaneshill and Nichols Canyon may not have been at their peak, Murphy points out that getting to the Iroquois was not straightforward for Rawnaq either. "It was 12 hours by road, so while they travelled by air, it wasn't like we got in the trailer and went round the corner," he says.

Life has taken Murphy – as well as Doyle – on quite a road trip too and the trainer is excited even to be contemplating the Cheltenham Festival. "It's not the route I'd have imagined taking to Cheltenham – we went away to come back – but it's a great opportunity."

If Rawnaq makes it to the festival, the huge prize on offer will be only part of the attraction.

By Alan Sweetman

UNSUNG HERO

Carlingford Lough has vanquished some of the biggest names in Irish chasing but not always received full credit

THE great Irish staying chasers tend to be measured by achievements in Britain, and more specifically at Cheltenham. Even though Ireland has a long-established programme of Grade 1 races for such horses, the greatest glory is reserved, just as in the far-off days of Cottage Rake and Arkle, for a Cheltenham Gold Cup winner.

Only rarely does an Irish staying chaser make a name for himself without exerting major influence across the water. Merry Gale and Beef Or Salmon are two who spring to mind over the past couple of decades, and last season Carlingford Lough took another step towards similar status by winning the prestigious Punchestown Gold Cup.

The King's Theatre gelding has endeared himself to the Irish racing public with his tenacity in winning

five Grade 1 races since capturing the Galway Plate as a second-season novice in 2013. His popularity has been enhanced by the fact he is trained by one of the most durable characters in Irish racing, John Kiely, a former leading amateur rider acclaimed for his style and strength. County Waterford-based Kiely, training since the mid-1970s in a career distinguished by intensive attention to a small team of horses,

was almost 60 when he had his last mount on the track in 1996 and is still riding out these days as he approaches 80.

True to form, the modest and soft-spoken Kiely, whose quiet demeanour is perfectly in tune with that of Carlingford Lough's owner JP McManus, does not make a big deal about his part in the narrative.

"He's been a very easy horse to train. These last few seasons it's just

been a question of keeping him well and fresh. We were patient with him early in his career. That has helped as the years have gone by. Other than the fact he has never managed to show his best at Cheltenham you could have no complaints. He's given us some great days and is definitely the best I've trained."

April's Punchestown victory was achieved in the absence of Don Cossack, who had relegated

▸▸Giant slayer: Veteran trainer John Kiely (left) after Carlingford Lough's victory under Barry Geraghty in the Punchestown Gold Cup in April, beating Djakadam, Don Poli and Cue Card

Carlingford Lough to fourth in the Cheltenham Gold Cup the previous month, but the form stands up to scrutiny, as he beat the other two horses who were in front of him at Cheltenham, Djakadam and Don Poli, as well as odds-on favourite Cue Card.

It marked a triumphant end to a campaign in which he won the Irish Gold Cup at Leopardstown for the second time with a performance that typified his qualities.

He was ridden from off the pace and seemed to be struggling as the race began to take its final shape out of the back straight. His jockey Mark Walsh confessed afterwards he considered pulling up at that stage, but he persevered.

Carlingford Lough was staying on doggedly when the complexion of the race changed with the unseating of Ruby Walsh from Valseur Lido at the last. At that stage favourite

Road To Riches was toiling and Carlingford Lough drew right away to beat the previous year's Cheltenham Gold Cup third by 12 lengths.

"I knew he was in much better form than at Christmas when he didn't do himself justice in the Lexus," Kiely says. "I told Mark to look after him through the race to make sure he'd finish it.

"He started to run on between the last two fences and everything changed at the last. We were fortunate, I guess, but it was a lovely race to win for a second time."

On the occasion of his first Irish Gold Cup win, in February 2015, Carlingford Lough had taken second billing behind his star jockey Tony McCoy, who had

announced his retirement less than 24 hours earlier. Media attention centred on the Grade 1 victory for the soon-to-be-gone man in the saddle, with the horse who carried him home almost a footnote to the main narrative.

That has been the way for much of Carlingford Lough's career. The Willie Mullins battalions have been the source of most Irish hopes at Cheltenham, along with the odd flashier type from another yard, and Kiely's stable star has never excited the same interest. That helps explain why he was 20-1 at Leopardstown and 12-1 at Punchestown for his two Grade 1 wins last season.

Yet he keeps doing the business and the list of those he has vanquished in the past

two seasons does not make bad reading: Cue Card, Djakadam, Don Poli, On His Own, Lord Windermere, First Lieutenant, Road To Riches, Sir Des Champs . . .

Even if Cheltenham is not his track – and form figures of 694 at the festival suggest it is not – he should not be underestimated. Last season's big wins both earned a career-best 170 mark on Racing Post Ratings and that was bettered by only three chasers in Ireland – Don Cossack, Djakadam and Douvan.

Carlingford Lough has never had top billing and he may not look a star as he toils through some of his races, but he has made his own mark on the Irish chasing scene at the top level. Like his trainer, he is a quiet achiever.

By Nick Pulford

FIFTH place would not have cut much ice with Victoria Pendleton during her medal-strewn cycling career but it was a different story in her second sporting life as an amateur jump jockey. Having been set the challenge of going from novice rider to taking part in the Foxhunter Chase at the Cheltenham Festival in the space of just 13 months, the double Olympic champion achieved that aim – and more.

"It's right up there with anything I've done. It's such a rush, such a thrill. I think it's one of my greatest achievements," Pendleton said after coming home fifth in the Foxhunter on Pacha Du Polder, beaten only two and three-quarter lengths by Nina Carberry aboard On The Fringe.

Not everyone had been happy about Pendleton lining up in the race – known as the amateurs' Gold Cup – but she answered the naysayers with a measured and assured ride. "She has improved enormously and was brilliant today," said Paul Nicholls, trainer of Pacha Du Polder. "She's not won, but she's ridden a winner in everyone's eyes."

This was the most celebrated losing ride of the year and, on the walk back in front of the stands, goodwill towards her poured from the 70,000 crowd. "The reception was almost like I'd won coming back in, which was special," an overwhelmed Pendleton said. "I didn't expect to get that cheer as I came back. It was quite humbling. It was an experience I will never forget. It will rank right up there with being in the Olympic Velodrome."

Another surprise awaited Pendleton when she was welcomed into the winner's enclosure to unsaddle, an honour usually reserved for the first four. This was recognition by Cheltenham of both the media attention in Pendleton and her huge achievement out on the track, in an echo of the day when every one of Michael Dickinson's Famous Five was allowed into the winner's

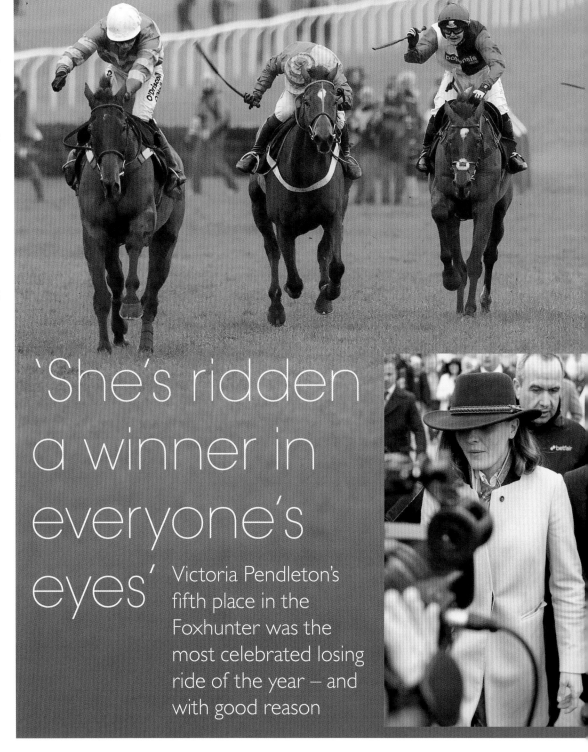

'She's ridden a winner in everyone's eyes'

Victoria Pendleton's fifth place in the Foxhunter was the most celebrated losing ride of the year – and with good reason

enclosure after the 1983 Cheltenham Gold Cup.

Nicholls was minded to refuse, not wanting to steal the limelight from Carberry and the other placed riders, but Robert Waley-Cohen, chairman of Cheltenham racecourse, insisted the galleries would appreciate the chance to see Pendleton. Waley-Cohen had judged the public mood perfectly.

Praise for Pendleton's ride was unstinting, and not simply from the team who had supported her in the 'Switching Saddles' challenge

set up by Betfair. Grand National-winning trainer Oliver Sherwood, who won the Foxhunter twice as a jockey, said: "I'd give her 12 out of ten. She hadn't ridden a year ago and I take my hat off to her."

Pendleton had been tutored and mentored by Oxfordshire trainer Lawney Hill and her husband Alan, who won the 1985 Foxhunter on Elmboy. "Had there been another couple of furlongs, she might have won," said the trainer, whose yard provided Pendleton with around 20

point-to-point rides in preparation for the Foxhunter. "It's a tremendous achievement. It's huge, phenomenal."

Carberry, whose second consecutive win in the race with On The Fringe was overshadowed by the attention on Pendleton, also paid tribute. Having shared the female changing room with Pendleton before the race, as two of the six women among the 24 riders, Carberry said: "It's the first time I've met her and I think she's great. She's got an unbelievable

laudable aim – "I could have fallen off and we would have been in a very different situation," she said afterwards – but she crept ever closer on the final circuit and from tenth place on the home turn, she went to eighth jumping the last and a flying fifth at the line.

Could she have won? Pendleton's first words to Lawney Hill were to apologise and later the rider said: "A better jockey on that horse would have won the race today."

Hill was quick to correct her, saying: "You do yourself an injustice there, Victoria. Paul thinks if we had put one of the lads on there, they would have tried to ride more of a race and therefore would have had less of a chance at the end. Don't do yourself down!"

****

PENDLETON'S quest was often derided as a publicity stunt but, away from the bright glare of Cheltenham, her new-found love for horses endured. Eight days after the festival she was back in the less glamorous world of point-to-pointing at Kimble aboard the Alan Hill-trained According To Sarah, but had to pull up, and she continued riding out four times a week at the Hill yard.

In the summer she had a Flat winner when Royal Etiquette took a charity race over a mile at Newmarket's July course and Pendleton, 36, who now looks after her own two horses at home, was already thinking about the winter. "I'm looking forward to riding in point-to-points next season. I really enjoyed it last season, it was so much fun and I just don't want it to stop."

As her rivals so often found in the velodrome and racing has seen for itself, Pendleton is hard to stop.

attitude to the whole thing and I'm delighted she got round – fifth place is a great achievement. She has the competitive edge and she loves it to bits."

****

THE reaction to Pendleton's riding had been very different just four weeks earlier after she was unceremoniously unseated from Pacha Du Polder at Fakenham in her first hunter chase. Seven-time champion jump jockey John Francome said she was "an accident waiting to happen" and jockey coach Steve Smith Eccles advised waiting another year to ride in the Foxhunter. One Twitter user, far from an isolated example, said: "This farce has got to be stopped! She's useless!!"

The Fakenham fall did not look good, with Pendleton tumbling out of the side door on landing at the seventh fence, and for a while her Cheltenham quest hung in the balance. She made amends on Pacha Du Polder 12 days later with a comfortable victory in a hunter chase at Wincanton but the very next day was unseated again, this time on a bend, at a point-to-point meeting.

Finally, in the week before the festival, Pendleton's participation was confirmed. "By no means was this an easy decision to make. In fact, I've been in complete turmoil over the last few weeks and days," she admitted. On raceday, however, a different Pendleton turned up, much more like her old self from cycling days: focused, determined and competitive.

A clear round would have been a

MULTI-TASKER

James Owen took the trainers' title in Arabian racing, as well as playing a part in the development of some promising Flat prospects

JAMES OWEN had a memorable 2015 both personally and professionally, with marriage to Jenny and the best newcomer award in his first full season of training Arabian horses, and life got even better this year when daughter Millie was born in August and the following month he clinched the Arabian trainers' championship.

In his other guise as a pre-trainer for several top Newmarket stables, Owen also had a hand in the preparation of some highly promising two-year-olds, including Royal Lodge Stakes winner Best Of Days and Washington Singer Stakes scorer Escobar, so all in all these are exciting times for the 36-year-old.

Owen *(left)*, assistant to John Ferguson in his jumps yard for three years until 2014, moved into Green Ridge Stables on Newmarket's Hamilton Road in the autumn of 2015 and was quickly handed one of the top jobs in Arabian racing as a chief trainer for Sheikh Hamdan Al Maktoum. Previously that role had been occupied by Gill Duffield but, with her retirement, training duties were split between Owen and Phil Collington, Duffield's long-time assistant.

The sheikh's trainers vied for the title in 2016, with Owen edging their battle by 14 winners to 11. "It's a bit of friendly competition," says Owen, who took over as champion from Duffield. "I really enjoyed the season. I'd like to thank Sheikh Hamdan and all my owners for their support and I can't wait for next year."

One of the highlights for Owen's 15-horse string was the progress of Awzaan, who won a handicap at Chepstow and was third to the French-trained Sir Bani Yas in the Group 1 HH Sheikh Zayed Bin Sultan Al Nahyan Cup at Sandown in August – the British leg of the Sheikh Mansoor Global Arabian Festival, which is billed as a 'one world, six continents' competition and culminates in a valuable finals day in Abu Dhabi in November.

"Awzaan is our top-rated horse after winning at Chepstow and being placed in a Group 1. He looks a good prospect for next season," says Owen, who is also excited by the potential of the three-year-old Alazeez, a seven-length maiden winner on the final day of the season at Chelmsford.

Owen enjoyed notable success in the British legs of two of the other race series in the Sheikh Mansoor Festival, the Wathba Stud Farm

Cup and the HH Sheikha Fatima Bint Mubarak Apprentice World Championship.

In the apprentice race, at Lingfield on September 10, Owen saddled four of the ten runners and they took first, third, fifth and sixth. The winner was Emiraaty, who scored by a neck under Puerto Rican apprentice Evin Roman. "This was Evin's first time on an Arabian and it was a really good performance," Owen said on the day. "The horse travelled really well and ran all the way to the line for him." The trainer, who rode Arabians in his younger days "when I could do the weight" and also gained a wealth of experience in point-to-points, is a keen supporter of the apprentice series, saying: "Arab racing is good for young jockeys, they get a lot more opportunities and it's a good stepping stone."

That view was echoed at Lingfield by His Excellency Sulaiman Hamid Almazroui, the UAE ambassador to the UK, who praised the festival's role in "promoting lady jockeys, apprentice jockeys and purebred Arabian racing". Lara Sawaya, executive director of the Sheikh Mansoor Festival, was excited by "the promise that the jockeys of the future possess" and in particular by the debut of apprentice jockey Milly Naseb from Jordan, who was invited to the final in November.

Having earned his own place in the final with victory on Emiraaty, Roman said: "This is a great experience for me. I've never been to the UK before and now I'm excited to be going for the final in Abu Dhabi."

The Wathba Stud Farm Cup is held on 21 racedays from Australia to the United States, with four of them taking place at Hereford, and Owen was leading trainer across the British legs with a total of six winners.

Owen, however, was outshone by Collington on Dubai International Arabian Raceday at Newbury in July – always one of the big occasions of the year. Owen drew a blank while Collington sent out two winners for Sheikh Hamdan, including Radames in the Group 1 Jebel Ali Racecourse Za'abeel International Stakes.

In another growth year for Arabian racing in Britain, Steve Gregory also recorded a notable success with his seven-year-old mare Koline in the HH Sheikha Fatima Bint Mubarak Ladies World Championship race at Sandown.

Gregory, 51, a part-time driving instructor who owns and trains Koline in partnership with his wife Helen in New Mills, Derbyshire, along with just two other horses, had been trying for a winner for eight years before the mare's all-the-way success.

"It was an absolutely fantastic day for us, Sandown looked after us so well," Gregory says. "I said to the wife, 'this is the best day of my life, better than the wedding,' and she said, 'I agree'.

We thought she'd run a good race and we would have been happy with a place, but never in our wildest dreams did we expect to win."

▶▶ Success stories: (from left) The James Owen-trained Alazeez wins at Chelmsford on the final day of the season; apprentice winner Evin Roman with Lara Sawaya, executive director of the Sheikh Mansoor Festival; Roman scores on the blinkered Emiraaty for Owen; trainer Steve Gregory with Koline at Sandown after a memorable first
Pictures: MORHAF AL ASSAF & DEBBIE BURT

Gregory's set-up is a far cry from the Owen operation at Green Ridge, best known in recent years as the launch pad for Marco Botti before he moved to his custom-built Prestige Place yard. While the yard has a great Flat-racing pedigree, Owen says he is happy with his combination of Arabian horses, pre-training and a few point-to-pointers.

"It's a business but we have a lot of fun doing it," he says, stressing that Jenny – a vet with the Baker, McVeigh and Clements practice in Newmarket – is a big part of the team.

He adds: "I really enjoy training the Arab horses. You wouldn't want to feed them as much as a thoroughbred and you wouldn't want to work them as much, but they're all so individual. I've learned a lot with them this year and I'll continue to learn because they're so different."

Whether it is with Arabs, jumpers or unbroken Flat two-year-olds, Owen clearly has the knack of learning quickly and achieving first-rate results.

IN THE PICTURE

New era for historic Palace House after grand restoration

The National Heritage Centre for Horseracing and Sporting Art opened in Newmarket in the autumn to great acclaim. Fittingly, the centre was completed in the year Newmarket celebrated 350 years since Charles II's patronage of the sport led to the setting up of the Round Course, the first 'modern' racecourse, part of which is still used today as the July Course.

Spanning a five-acre site in the heart of town, the centre comprises three distinct parts: the National Horseracing Museum, a National Gallery of British Sporting Art and a flagship home for the Retraining of Racehorses (RoR) charity.

The centre stands on the site of the remains of Charles II's palace and racing stables, parts of which date back to 1671. Palace House Stables housed a host of British Classic winners, starting with 1838 1,000 Guineas winner Barcarolle, but had fallen into disrepair after the last trainer, Bruce Hobbs, moved out in 1985. A £15m restoration, over more than three years, created the centre.

Chris Garibaldi, director of the centre, which is hoping to attract 50,000 visitors a year, said: "The National Heritage Centre for Horseracing and Sporting Art is the culmination of a dream that first started 25 years ago. This is a transformative project for Newmarket which finally gives us a cultural heart."

Garibaldi is particularly excited that visitors can see and touch horses in the Rothschild Yard, which has been restored with stabling for up to eight former racehorses. This is the centrepiece of RoR's new home and early residents included Cheltenham Festival winner Our Vic and Grade 1-winning hurdler Walkon.

Di Arbuthnot, chief executive of RoR, said: "Giving the public the opportunity to interact with and see former racehorses adapting to a new life after racing will, I hope, provide one of the highlights for visitors to the National Heritage Centre."

The National Horseracing Museum in the old trainer's house has a wealth of exhibits tracing the history of the sport as well as interactive technology that explores the science and evolution of the thoroughbred.

The Fred Packard Museum and Galleries of British Sporting Art are in the old home of Charles II with loans from the Tate, the V&A Museum and a number of other public and private collections.

The centre is open daily from 10am to 5pm (except Christmas Day) and general admission is £16.50. A family ticket (two adults and up to four children) is £40.00 and concessions are £15.50.

Pictures: **NATIONAL HORSERACING MUSEUM**

▶▶ On show: (clockwise from main picture) an overview of the National Heritage Centre; Frankel's statue in the King's Yard; the Rothschild Yard; Palace House and the Trainer's House; Our Vic with Frankie Dettori and Joe Grimwade, the Retraining of Racehorses yard manager; Walkon with a visitor; The Start, October Meeting, Newmarket, 1957, by Sir Alfred Munnings PRA (1878-1959) (oil on panel; British Sporting Art Trust; image © Estate of Sir Alfred Munnings, Dedham)

THE ANNUAL 20

Our selection of the horses and people – some established, some up-and-coming – who are likely to be making headlines in 2017

CARAVAGGIO

The death of stallion Scat Daddy in 2015 was a severe blow to Coolmore, given his reputation for producing top-class sprinters such as No Nay Never, Acapulco, Lady Aurelia and the Aidan O'Brien-trained Caravaggio *(main picture)*.

The last two in that list set Royal Ascot alight in 2016. Lady Aurelia blew her rivals away in the Queen Mary and Caravaggio did much the same in the Coventry, going clear under Ryan Moore to score by two and a quarter lengths from Mehmas – and that was after racing alone for much of the race in the centre of the track (the next four home all raced on the far side). Given his pedigree, it was encouraging that Caravaggio comfortably lasted out the six-furlong trip on soft ground, raising hopes he would stay further.

Caravaggio – who reportedly set a speed record on the Ballydoyle gallops when hitting 45mph – was equally dominant in the Phoenix

Stakes at the Curragh in August on faster ground, although it wasn't the sternest Group 1 test as he faced just four rivals and was sent off at 1-8.

After that race O'Brien was keen to keep him at sprint distances, saying: "He's so quick and he's the fastest we've ever had. I would imagine that he would be more likely to run in the Middle Park than the Dewhurst." Unfortunately Caravaggio tweaked a muscle in his ribcage prior to the Middle Park and that was the end of his juvenile season.

It will be fascinating to see if O'Brien plots a Classic campaign with him. Caravaggio may see out longer trips because he is so relaxed – he has been given single-figure quotes for the 2,000 Guineas – but if he is indeed as fast as anything O'Brien has had we could be in for a treat in the Commonwealth Cup and July Cup. Let's hope he turns out more like Mozart or Stravinsky than One Cool Cat or Air Force Blue.

HARRY WHITTINGTON

There was triumph and tragedy for up-and-coming jumps trainer Harry Whittington last season. He celebrated a breakthrough first Grade 1 success when Arzal won the Manifesto Novices' Chase at Aintree, only for his stable star to die less than three weeks later when an infection led to complications.

Apart from that setback, there were plenty of reasons for the Oxfordshire-based trainer to be cheerful: his tally of 21 winners was a marked improvement on previous seasons and his strike-rate of 23 per cent was better than any of the top ten trainers ranked by prize-money. Oh, and he

also proposed to his long-time girlfriend, Alice. After getting off the mark in the current season, he said: "We've started buzzing about the new horses. We've got some fantastic new owners too and we're ready to roll again."

The laid-back but talented Affaire D'Honneur, Emerging Force and Bigmartre are potential flagbearers for Whittington, 35, whose wise head was in evidence last season when he wasn't seduced by the lure of the Cheltenham Festival, preferring to wait until Aintree with Arzal.

Young and talented jumps trainers are in abundance these days – Dan Skelton, Harry Fry and Kerry Lee to name but three – and Whittington is another to watch. He has built solid foundations and it may not be long before another Arzal comes his way.

BALLYANDY

One of the most hard-fought successes at the Cheltenham Festival came in the Weatherbys Champion Bumper when the Nigel Twiston-Davies-trained Ballyandy withstood a battery of Willie Mullins challengers to score by a nose. He was the second leg of a Twiston-Davies double following Blaklion's victory in the RSA Chase and both horses came from the same source, Wilson Dennison in Northern Ireland.

Ballyandy has the one attribute vital for any successful jumper – toughness – but plenty of speed too. "I couldn't believe how well he picked up," said jockey Sam Twiston-Davies at Cheltenham. "I knew he had loads of gears but every time I gave him a reminder he went again, and again."

The trainer even went as far as to compare the five-year-old with his

2010 Cheltenham Gold Cup winner. "He's better than Imperial Commander was on the flat, so maybe he'll be better over jumps. We've popped him over jumps at home and he's brilliant. He's a chaser for the future."

Ballyandy can be forgiven a below-par run at the Aintree Grand National meeting in light of the attritional nature of his festival success and he is part of an exciting team for Twiston-Davies, along with Blaklion, Aintree Grade 1 novice hurdle winner Ballyoptic and JLT Novices' Chase runner-up Bristol De Mai.

ALTIOR

Numerically Nicky Henderson is the king of the Cheltenham Festival, having saddled 55 winners at jumping's biggest four days of the year, but his reign at the top is under threat from Willie Mullins, who has 48 and is closing fast on the Lambourn trainer.

Altior could be one who helps Henderson to maintain his lead, at least for another year. Last season's Supreme Novices' Hurdle winner had been as short as 6-1 to win the 2017 Champion Hurdle but the decision was made to resist the temptation to compete against the likes of Annie Power and Faugheen in favour of an immediate switch to fences, with the Racing Post Arkle Chase as his main target.

"He's a six-year-old, rising seven, and if we don't go chasing now I suspect we might never," Henderson explained. "It was also obvious that he'd grown considerably through the summer and, although he was always a big horse, he now looks like a chaser."

One of the characteristics of Altior's Supreme success was his fluent jumping. He attacked his obstacles with relish at speed to record a Racing Post Rating of 163 – higher than those given to Mullins stars Vautour and Douvan for winning the race in the previous two seasons.

It wouldn't be a surprise if Min (trained by Mullins) and Buveur D'Air (Henderson) – second and third in the Supreme – also took high rank in the novice chase division and the Arkle could be a race to savour. Altior starts in pole position, and if he prevails Henderson would become the winningmost trainer of the race (he currently shares that accolade with Tom Dreaper with five wins apiece).

ADAM McNAMARA

Having ridden his first winner in January, Adam McNamara was on the big stage at York only seven months later when he partnered Heartbreak City to victory in the Betfred Ebor.

The 19-year-old apprentice's rapid progress was due in no small part to the late Tom O'Ryan, the Racing Post journalist and jockey coach who died just three days after the Ebor, aged 61. O'Ryan "made me believe", said the County Limerick-born rider. "With Tom speaking to me on a daily basis, I learned to be more patient. It was really only at the Lincoln meeting, when I had a couple of nice rides, that I really started to believe in myself."

With the patience came the winners and McNamara, who describes himself as "driven but laid-back", rode the perfect race on Heartbreak City, settling the six-year-old (who had raced too keenly when well beaten in the Chester Cup), in the rear before coming with a well-timed run up York's long straight to score by four lengths.

Heartbreak City was trained by Tony Martin but the majority of McNamara's winners came from his boss Richard Fahey – no stranger to nurturing a future champion having struck up a great relationship with Paul Hanagan when he was starting out. The young rider joined Fahey after a period with Johnny Murtagh.

McNamara needs to keep an eye on his weight (he has put up overweight more than once) but the apprentice title is sure to be the main priority in 2017 for the ambitious teenager, who believes that "as an apprentice you're wasting your time if you don't want to be a potential champion or land a big job".

DOUVAN

There is no truth behind the rumour that Ryanair supremo Michael O'Leary took his horses away from Willie Mullins because he was denied speedy access to the gallops and had to pay to reserve a seat at the Closutton breakfast table, but whatever the reasons (and it appears it was down to an increase in training fees) it came as a massive bombshell and left Mullins 60 horses light.

If Mullins is to make another serious challenge for the British trainers' championship his existing stars will have to be on their A-game all season. High on the list is Douvan (right) – perhaps the most talented horse Mullins has trained – who needs to make the successful transition to open company if he is to reign supreme again at the Cheltenham Festival like he did in last season's Arkle and in the Supreme Novices' Hurdle the season before that.

Such was the ease with which Douvan attacked his obstacles in the Arkle that winning jockey Ruby Walsh declared post-race that "he makes jumping fences like jumping hurdles", while Mullins was left to wonder whether "we have a Gold Cup horse, or do we want to keep him for the Champion Chase?" The superlatives kept coming at Aintree (where he produced a Racing Post Rating of 176 – the same figure Sprinter Sacre achieved when winning the 2012 Arkle) and Punchestown, where Douvan again effortlessly handed out thrashings to his now demoralised fellow novices, which begs the question: can anything stand in his way in the senior ranks?

Flaws are certainly hard to come by – perhaps a tendency to jump lazily at a slower pace – and it was no wonder Mullins was tempted to forego the 'easier' option of the Champion Chase and instead go for gold. And it will make tasty viewing at the festival if Douvan and a Gigginstown challenger end up going head to head for victory.

AMY MURPHY

When it comes to learning the training ropes, you would struggle to find two better mentors than Luca Cumani and Gai Waterhouse. Amy Murphy was lucky enough to be employed by both of those giants of the game and the experience is sure to stand her in good stead in her fledgling training career.

Murphy hasn't wasted any time in setting up on her own. She was only 24 – making her the youngest trainer in Britain – when saddling her first runner, Pyla, at Thirsk in September and she already has an established owner on her books in her father Paul, a leading breeder

who has had horses with Charlie Longsdon, Robert Walford and Nicky Henderson. Murphy will be training some of her father's homebreds, including Kalane and Mariah's Legend, who have moved from Longsdon to Murphy's 20-box yard on Hamilton Road in Newmarket.

Murphy, who also had a spell

with Tom Dascombe, says: "Training is something I've wanted to do from the outset and it's what my heart has been set on from an early age." She was given a glowing endorsement by Cumani, who said: "It's been a pleasure to have Amy working as my assistant for the past two years. Amy is very dedicated and hardworking and she is well prepared for her new career, as well as any assistant I've ever had – and I have had some good ones."

Perhaps Kalane, a chaser with a Racing Post Rating of 144 who won a Listed race over hurdles, will be the one to put Murphy on the map.

Be wahou, be Barrière

B READY + BREAKFAST

Hôtels Barrière Deauville
Normandy - France

Up to -20%*
OFF YOUR ROOM AND BREAKFAST INCLUDED

Exclusively on www.hotelsbarriere.com or + 33 (0) 2 31 14 39 50

RESORT
BARRIÈRE
DEAUVILLE

CHURCHILL

Winston Churchill features on the new plastic £5 note, which is said to be able to withstand a spin in a washing machine, and the equine Churchill *(right, striped cap)* appears to be equally tough – and certainly worth a good deal more than a fiver.

A typically efficient display to win the Dewhurst Stakes was the culmination of a juvenile campaign that saw Aidan O'Brien's son of Galileo conquer his rivals in four Group races – two of them at the top level. Having kicked off his winning run in the Chesham at Royal Ascot, Churchill gave his two best performances in the National Stakes at the Curragh (thrashing reliable yardstick Mehmas by four and a half lengths, as well as handling the yielding ground) and the Dewhurst. He didn't get a clear run at Newmarket, with Ryan Moore having to switch right over a furlong out, but Churchill responded in professional fashion to score from rank outsider and stablemate Lancaster Bomber.

"He's probably the most imposing two-year-old we've ever trained. He's massive, he's big, powerful and has a great mind," said O'Brien after the Dewhurst.

He went into winter quarters as a short-priced favourite for the 2,000 Guineas, while his relaxed style of running raises hope that he will see out the Derby trip. We'll fight them on the Rowley Mile, we'll fight them at Epsom . . .

O'Brien's recent Dewhurst winners – Beethoven, War Command and Air Force Blue – were disappointments at three and Churchill has to buck that trend (although O'Brien's Rock Of Gibraltar did the Dewhurst-Guineas double in 2001-02). There is also the suspicion that given his size at two he may not have much more growing to do. However, with a Racing Post Rating of 120 in both the Dewhurst and National Stakes, he sets a formidable standard.

TOMMY DOWLING

It is safe to say the current jumps season didn't start the way conditional jockey Tommy Dowling would have wished. His first ride of the campaign was on My Anchor in a handicap hurdle at Fontwell but the 24-year-old only got as far as the first obstacle, where My Anchor fell, causing Dowling to break his shoulder, collarbone and two ribs among a catalogue of injuries.

The jockey had to have two steel rods inserted during back surgery and was expected to be on the sidelines until at least Christmas, so the fact that he resumed his promising career with a winner on Baltic Storm for his boss Charlie Mann at Plumpton in September – less than five months after his fall – speaks volumes about his determination.

Reflecting on his injuries, Dowling, from County Wicklow, said: "Obviously it was disappointing to be out as I was hoping to challenge for the conditionals' title this season, but now I think that may be beyond me. I'll look to ride as many winners as I can."

All he needs now is a bit of luck.

CAPITAINE

One of the features of Paul Nicholls' string this season is the strength in depth of his juvenile and novice hurdling squad, with no fewer than 55 horses set to run in such races, and one of the stars may turn out to be the lightly raced Capitaine, described by the trainer as "the apple of my eye ever since he arrived from France".

Capitaine was made favourite on his racecourse debut in a bumper at Taunton last December and put in an encouraging effort when second to Drumcliff. He stepped up markedly on that performance, and gave an indication of what is potentially to come, at Wincanton four months later when comfortably disposing of his ten rivals to score by 13 lengths from Minella For Me.

From a jumping family (his dam was a Listed chase and hurdle winner), Capitaine could well be Nicholls' representative in the Sky Bet Supreme Novices' Hurdle.

Other talented prospects are sure to emerge from that Nicholls team of 55 – Brahms De Clermont and Movewiththetimes are two more with plenty of potential – and the future looks rosy.

TALAAYEB

It was Markaz, not Massaat, who proved to be the flagbearer for Owen Burrows in his first season as a trainer, landing a couple of Group sprints, but the Lambourn-based former assistant to Sir Michael Stoute would far rather it had been the latter who made headlines. Second place in the 2,000 Guineas promised so much, but then Massaat's season fell into a hole.

Given that Burrows is private trainer to Sheikh Hamdan Al Maktoum, it is surely only a matter of time before he hits the target in a Classic, and in Talaayeb he could have a genuine candidate for the 1,000 Guineas and Oaks.

Talaayeb ran only once as a two-year-old but made a terrific impression in landing a seven-furlong maiden at Newmarket on Cambridgeshire day, earning a quote of 25-1 for the Guineas.

Being by Dansili, she is likely to be most effective on fast ground and she comes from the same family as 2009 1,000 Guineas winner Ghanaati, who also had a light juvenile campaign. She will reportedly reappear in a Classic trial in the spring.

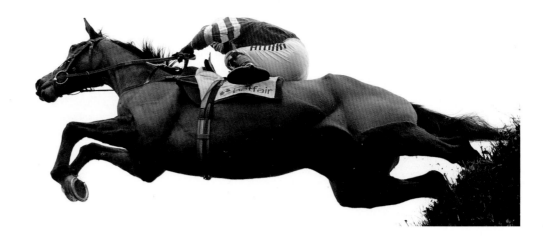

CONEYGREE

In his final PMQs before stepping down as prime minister, David Cameron self-mockingly proclaimed "I was the future once" before exiting the stage, and the same can be said of Coneygree *(right)*, who had the chasing world at his feet after becoming the first novice in more than 40 years to land the Cheltenham Gold Cup with a scintillating front-running success in 2015.

Mark Bradstock's ace started the 2015-16 season in perfect style, being unextended to win a Sandown Listed contest and maintain his perfect record over fences, but he then damaged a hock and was ruled out for the remainder of the campaign.

Having recovered from his leg injury, there is renewed hope that Coneygree could still be the future, with regular rider Nico de Boinville proclaiming in the autumn: "He feels like he did during that fantastic season. We can tell his demeanour by the way he schools and he seems to be schooling very well."

Coneygree will need to be every bit as good as he was when landing the Gold Cup by one and a half lengths from Djakadam, and probably better. Don Cossack – whose Gold Cup-winning Racing Post Rating of 182 was 4lb better than Coneygree's – Vautour, Thistlecrack and Douvan (if Willie Mullins decides to stretch him out) are all exceptional talents. But when you consider what Coneygree did in his novice season and that he has raced only five times over fences, there is the promise of improvement.

Recent Gold Cup winners have failed to reach the same heights after their day of glory, and following his absence Coneygree has it to prove all over again. But he has been expertly handled by Mark and Sara Bradstock and the prospect of him taking them all on from the front at Cheltenham on March 17 is a mouthwatering one.

WUHEIDA

If pedigree is anything to go by, Wuheida was nailed on to win the Prix Marcel Boussac at Chantilly on Arc day, given that juvenile Group 1 success runs in the family. Dad Dubawi (National Stakes) and mum Hibaayeb (Fillies' Mile) were both top-class at two and their daughter duly announced her own talent by winning the mile contest in determined fashion. She could be the one to give Charlie Appleby his first British Classic success and Godolphin their first since Encke's St Leger in 2012.

Wuheida lined up in the Boussac after just one outing, in a small-field Newmarket maiden which she won, but she belied her inexperience in France, battling well for William Buick to beat Promise To Be True by three-quarters of a length.

Visually this was a performance characteristic of a candidate for the Oaks rather than the 1,000 Guineas, but in what looks an open year she went to the head of the betting in both markets.

Dubawi's star efforts at three came over a mile in the Irish 2,000 Guineas and Jacques le Marois, while Hibaayeb had the stamina to land the Ribblesdale, so if Wuheida continues to follow in the footsteps of mum and dad another big win looks assured.

HENRY DE BROMHEAD

The decision by leading owners Ann and Alan Potts to remove their horses from Henry de Bromhead's stable would have come as a bitter blow to the County Waterford trainer, who last season finished third in the Irish standings based on both prize-money and winners and had enjoyed such success with the 'Sizing' horses in the Potts colours, most famously Sizing Europe.

Those departures threatened to make this a testing season for the trainer but as that door closed, another opened with the arrival of a draft from Gigginstown House Stud, including some of the horses taken away from Willie Mullins.

De Bromhead, 44, also took on the training of Gigginstown's Sub Lieutenant from Sandra Hughes and the seven-year-old chaser produced a personal best on Racing Post Ratings on his first start for the yard, jumping like a different horse to the one who hit every other fence in the Irish Grand National.

On the loss of the Potts horses, De Bromhead said: "Things move on and we'll drive on again now." He did just that with Sub Lieutenant and, if he can bring out the best in his other new arrivals, his place near the top of the table should be secure.

SEAN FLANAGAN

Two young Irish jump jockeys have embarked on high-profile new roles this season. Adrian Heskin has moved to Britain to team up with Tom George, while Wexford man Sean Flanagan has taken up the prized position of stable jockey to Noel Meade after Paul Carberry was forced to retire from the saddle at the age of 42.

Meade was, as you would expect, complimentary about the 28-year-old's talents, saying: "Sean is a rider I like and he's done really well since joining me. He has lovely hands on a horse and he's a nice lad I can rely on."

Flanagan has Apache Stronghold, Monksland – who he partnered regularly last season, replacing the sidelined Carberry – and Snow Falcon to look forward to, plus any Gigginstown horses going spare when Bryan Cooper is unavailable.

A professional jockey since 2007, Flanagan has surprisingly yet to ride a winner in Britain, but this is likely to change given the strength of Meade's string. The appointment completes a renaissance for Flanagan, who had a high-profile win with Penny's Bill in the 2009 Pierse Hurdle but then had a spell riding in the US a few years ago after opportunities at home dried up.

Finding winners can be a right scrabble but not if you have the right tools

Members' Club gives you access to exclusive features, including Horse Tracker, Spotlight comments and Pricewise Extra to help you on your way, so why not stay on track with your definitive source of tipping, news, analysis and statistics.

JOIN TO BE A WINNER

RACING POST.com/membersclub

AUX PTITS SOINS

In a battle that didn't end until the final day of the 2015-16 jumps season, Paul Nicholls managed to fend off the fierce Willie Mullins onslaught and retain his trainers' title, but it was surprising that the ex-French Aux Ptits Soins (right, yellow colours) – touted as a potential chasing star at the start of the campaign – was able to contribute just £8,040 to Nicholls' prize-money total of £2.4 million.

For the vast majority of jumpers, fifth place in the Ryanair World Hurdle would represent a significant achievement, but for Aux Ptits Soins it was a disappointing start and end to his season. Hopes had been high after his win in the 2015 Coral Cup on just his third start over hurdles but it took him a whole 12 months to get back on a racecourse after that.

Last season he was blighted by a foot infection and sinus and tooth troubles that required three operations. It must have been so frustrating for Nicholls – and owner John Hales – that plans to send the six-year-old over fences had to be shelved and he was limited to that sole run at Cheltenham.

Reports from Ditcheat this season have been far more optimistic, with Nicholls stating: "He enjoyed a nice summer break and remains an exciting prospect for novice chases."

The festival target is likely to be the JLT or RSA Chase, and now is his chance to make up for lost time.

SENEWALK

Willie Mullins' record with French imports in the Supreme Novices' Hurdle is excellent, with recent winners Vautour and Douvan as well as last year's runner-up Min, and the early moves in the ante-post market for the 2017 festival curtain-raiser suggest he could have another potential star in the shape of the Rich Ricci-owned Senewalk.

The son of Walk In The Park – also sire of Douvan and Min – raced only twice in France, winning a maiden over 1m5½f on his second start when he was ridden with considerable confidence.

Mullins has taken his time with the four-year-old, who did not see a racecourse last season, and there are similarities with Min, who also ran twice in France and was given a long layoff before making has debut for Mullins.

DAVID EGAN

A father and son riding at the same time is a rarity, but that is the case with John and David Egan, and while Egan jnr has a long way to go before he matches his dad's tally of winners, the talent he exhibited in his first season illustrates he has a bright future.

Roger Charlton rarely misses a trick when it comes to getting an edge in handicaps and wisely took advantage of Egan's 7lb claim when employing his services on Cloudberry, with the combination winning at Kempton and Sandown in the autumn.

Egan, 17, whose mother is trainer Sandra Hughes, will continue to hone his style over the winter, but he may not be seen alongside his father on the British all-weather as he is reportedly off to America in order to keep his full claim for the turf. His return is awaited with keen anticipation.

JOSEPHINE GORDON

The odds at the start of the British Flat turf season about Josephine Gordon winning the Stobart-sponsored apprentice title must have been pretty high, but the 23-year-old defied expectations to join previous female winners Hayley Turner – who tied with Saleem Golam for the title in 2005 – and Amy Ryan (2012).

It took determination for Gordon to get where she did – after one particular barren spell in her career she related how "only my family and friends kept me going" – but a change in fortunes arrived after she linked up with Stan Moore.

The big test for Gordon now is to maintain her momentum once she rides out her 3lb claim, which is going to happen sooner rather than later. The target set by her agent Bill Shea is to ride 100 winners in 2017, a total Turner reached but not in the year immediately following her apprentice title win (she managed 100 winners in 2008 and bagged two Group 1s in 2011). The winners dried up for Ryan after losing her claim, so the transition from apprentice to fully fledged pro may not be seamless, but Gordon has a positive attitude. "A lot of people have told me it gets harder after losing my claim," she says, "but I've made a lot of connections in the last 18 months. The main thing is to be the best I can be."

The future also looks bright for two other female jockeys, Hollie Doyle and Georgia Cox, both of whom are four years younger than Gordon. Both broke the 20-winner mark in 2016, with Doyle scoring a high-profile success on Scarlet Dragon at Newmarket's Future Champions Festival.

MATT CHAPMAN

A new year, a new TV racing team. A fresh era in racing broadcasting dawns on New Year's Day when ITV starts its four-year contract by covering Cheltenham, and plenty of attention will be focused not on the horses but on the presenters.

One of ITV's more creative appointments was that of At The Races mainstay Matt Chapman as the chief betting reporter. Chapman, 45, is something of a Marmite character with his trademark cries of 'Yee-haa', but his unorthodox style will add colour to the betting coverage, something that has been distinctly lacking since John McCririck was dropped by Channel 4 in 2012.

How Chapman will go down with a more mainstream audience remains to be seen, but one thing's for sure: he won't be dull to watch. Be prepared for a few 'Yee-haas' along the way.

Racing to a new career at ror.org.uk

rorsourceahorse.org.uk

A new website for selling or loaning a horse directly out of a trainer's yard and for all former racehorses.

Bloodstock Sales

In addition to Horses In Training sales, RoR holds auctions dedicated to horses leaving racing.

Rehoming Direct

RoR has compiled a checklist to safeguard your horse's future when moved directly into the sport horse market.

Retrainers

RoR has a list of retrainers recommended by trainers who can start the retraining process and assess each horse.

Visit
ror.org.uk
for rehoming options and advice

Equine Charities

Retrain former racehorses for a donation, as well as care for vulnerable horses with the help of RoR funding.

RoR is British horseracing's official charity for the welfare of horses retired from racing.

THE BIGGER PICTURE

New Approach, the 2008 Derby winner who now stands at Dalham Hall Stud, is shampooed by head stallion man Ken Crozier (left) before day one of the Darley stallion parade in Newmarket in July, while his handler Darren Palmer gets a bath too

EDWARD WHITAKER (RACINGPOST.COM/PHOTOS)

final furlong

stories of the year – from the serious to the quirky

Kennedy a born leader

By James Burn

ONE of the great narratives of sport is the rise of an exciting youngster with star potential, and in Jack Kennedy the Irish jump racing scene seems to have found its next big thing. Having claimed the conditional jockeys' title in 2015-16, the 17-year-old is expected to challenge for the senior championship sooner rather than later.

Perhaps even this season, when title success would make Kennedy the youngest-ever champion in Ireland and continue a meteoric rise since his first winner on the Flat at Cork in May 2015. The jumps was always going to be his game and, with his efforts concentrated in that direction last season, he took the conditionals' title and plenty of plaudits thanks to his 44 winners.

A fine start to the new campaign put him in

▶▶ Rising star: Jack Kennedy is expected to take high rank among the senior jockeys

position for the senior honour before a fractured leg in September interrupted his progress. If he does take the main title at a young age, he would eclipse some of the best riders of recent times. Sir Anthony McCoy won the first of his 20 championships in Britain at the age of 21, while the Irish title was secured by Ruby Walsh at 19 and by Barry Geraghty at 20.

Going to the top would

be no surprise to those who know Kennedy best. Cheltenham Gold Cup-winning trainer Gordon Elliott, who has been his biggest supporter, said: "What he's doing is amazing. If he stays in one piece you'd imagine he'll be champion some day. He's a rare talent."

Former top rider Conor O'Dwyer, now a trainer, is also full of praise. "I've seen plenty of good young jockeys come and go because they got too much too soon, but that won't happen with Jack," he said. "I cannot think of any other jockey of that age – ever – who does what he does the way he does it. I've never seen anyone so complete at 17."

Cheltenham Festival-winning trainer Enda Bolger agrees. "He seems to be one of those riders that come along only once in a long time," he said.

Kennedy also seems set to be at the top for a long time.

●Big push

CRAIG NICHOL, champion conditional in Britain with 36 winners in 2015-16, is more of a slow-burner than a shooting star but he was rewarded with the title after leaving Lucinda Russell's stable to turn freelance.

"At the start of last season I was just aiming to survive and become my own person, and whether it's freelance or with a big yard all I want to do is keep riding winners," said the driven 22-year-old Scot, whose most important success came on Jonniesofa in the Grade 2 registered as the Prestige Novices' Hurdle at Haydock in February.

Frankie and young fan both enjoy special day

TEN-YEAR-OLD Lillie May experienced "a dream come true" when she got to meet her hero Frankie Dettori at Newmarket on 2,000 Guineas day after a letter she had sent to the jockey sparked a social media campaign to unite the duo.

Lillie May, who goes to St Andrew's Church of England school in Soham, Cambridgeshire, sent a charming note to the jockey requesting a signed picture.

However, the letter was addressed to the site of Dettori's former restaurant Frankie's in Knightsbridge, which is now called Hawksmoor and owned by Will and Kat Beckett.

The Becketts, keen to help Lillie get in touch with Dettori, posted images of the letter to their 50,000 followers on Twitter with the hashtags #FindFrankie and #HelpLillie. It was retweeted on numerous occasions and noticed by Great British Racing, who arranged for Lillie to meet her idol.

As well as meeting Frankie, Lillie was given a behind-the-scenes tour of the Rowley Mile, which included a trip to the weighing room, and was given a signed copy of Dettori's autobiography Frankie, in addition to the desired signed picture.

"I was so excited to meet my hero," Lillie said. "When my school asked us to write to our idols I knew I wanted my letter to be to Frankie. I'm so happy that he sent me a signed picture and to meet him was a dream come true. All my friends at school are very jealous."

Lillie's mother Cathy added: "Lillie is such a big racing fan and she has always loved Frankie. When she sent the letter, I didn't really expect a response and the reaction we've had was overwhelming.

"I cannot thank Frankie enough for his time and kindness, he's made Lillie's day and it's a moment she will never forget."

Dettori, who won the 2,000 Guineas on Galileo Gold later in the day, said: "It's lovely to receive a handwritten letter from any young racing fan and I was only too happy to help and show her what we get up to behind the scenes.

Frankie Dettori
Frankie's
3 Yeomans Row, off
Brompton Road
Knightsbridge,
SW3 2AL

Friday 22nd January

Dear Frankie Dettori,
My name is Lillie, and I'm 10 years old. I am also a pupil of St. Andrews Primary School but I live in Soham. I am a massive fan. When I first met you I was very intrested in horses. Now I have my own horses I'm just like you.

What made it even more special was winning the 2,000 Guineas afterwards – maybe she's my lucky charm!"

▶▶ Dream come true: Lillie May with Frankie Dettori after her letter led to a special visit to Newmarket
Picture: DAN ABRAHAM; Letter: COURTESY OF HAWKSMOOR

●Expensive toilet break

SPENDING a penny cost leading Australian jockey Kerrin McEvoy a lot more than he bargained for when he was caught short just before a race at Randwick, Sydney, in August.

The rider leaped off his mount in the stalls to relieve himself, but his actions were caught on camera and not welcomed by stewards.

Taking into account his good character, they fined McEvoy A$500 (£292/€340) and reasoned he should have been aware of watching eyes.

Explaining his predicament, the Melbourne Cup-winning jockey said: "I was supposed to ride light, but the horse was scratched, so I rehydrated and I needed to go. I wasn't anticipating the cameras."

ANNUAL AWARDS
OUR PICK OF THE BEST OF 2016

Horse of the Year (Flat)
Minding

During a season in which Aidan O'Brien stood over European Flat racing like a colossus, this filly shone out like a beacon with a string of scintillating performances. Classic success at Newmarket came in a canter, her Oaks triumph at Epsom was mesmerising and as the year went on she got even better. There were thumping wins in the Pretty Polly and Nassau Stakes before a gallant third in the Irish Champion Stakes and finally her crowning glory in the Queen Elizabeth II Stakes. A wonderful filly with uncommon toughness as well as rare ability.

Horse of the Year (jumps)
Thistlecrack

Heroes are forged in the white heat of the Cheltenham Festival and if we thought Thistlecrack was good before the World Hurdle, we were certain afterwards. His pre-festival wins were delivered with a rare swagger that hinted at something special, but on the big day the way in which he swept through to lead on the bit with two hurdles to go was scarcely believable. That was enough to earn Thistlecrack our vote in a competitive field and to convince connections that

when you get a horse this good there is only one place to go – the Cheltenham Gold Cup.

Ride of the year (Flat)
George Baker on Harbour Law

One of the best results of the year was delivered with an outstanding ride as Baker pounced at the perfect moment in the St Leger. Steadied at the rear in typical Baker fashion, Harbour Law crept through the field, sidestepping Seamie Heffernan as he was unseated from favourite Idaho before being unleashed with a sustained and devastating late surge to pip Ventura Storm and claim the final Classic.

Ride of the year (jumps)
David Mullins on Rule The World

The 19-year-old produced a ride of great maturity and skill to win the biggest jumps race of all at his first attempt. Tucked in behind the leaders the whole way, Mullins had to hold on tight when Rule The World

made a shocking error at the fourth-last fence, but he quickly regained his mount's momentum and the pair charged to the front after the Elbow to score decisively.

Race of the year (Flat)
Irish Champion Stakes

A star-studded field of 12 included nearly all of Europe's premier middle-distance horses, which reduced Eclipse winner Hawkbill and Prince of Wales's Stakes hero My Dream Boat to 16-1 and 33-1 outsiders respectively. Dual Derby winner Harzand was sent off favourite in front

of star filly Minding but it was the French flyer Almanzor who took the prize from subsequent Arc winner Found. A magnificent race and a magnificent result befitting the top-quality entry.

Race of the year (jumps)
Queen Mother Champion Chase

Sprinter Sacre's season had gone perfectly up to the Cheltenham Festival but could he down the mighty Un De Sceaux? He could and he did in style, passing his big rival before the home turn and charging up the Cheltenham hill into the history books.

Unluckiest horse
Cue Card (left)

Let's start by getting things straight: Cue Card had a most wonderful season in 2015-16, winning the Charlie Hall Chase, Betfair Chase, King George VI Chase and Betfred Bowl. But there will always be a lingering sense of what might have been. With a £1 million

bonus on the line for connections if he could add the Cheltenham Gold Cup to his Betfair Chase and King George wins, the ten-year-old loomed up to challenge Don Cossack and Djakadam at the third-last fence only to tip up and crash to the floor when going so well.

Disappointment of the year
Air Force Blue

Horses make fools of us all but few in recent times have left us feeling as silly as this one did. Red-hot favourite for the 2,000 Guineas after a brilliant juvenile season, he flopped at Newmarket, finishing second last. He then flopped in the Irish 2,000 Guineas (second last again), flopped in the July Cup when dropped to sprinting and finally flopped spectacularly when tailed off in the Group 3 Phoenix Sprint Stakes in August. Retirement followed what was an almighty comedown after all the expectation.

SPECIAL MERIT AWARDS FOR . . . SPRINTER SACRE

Comeback of the year Down and out when pulled up in the 2015 Queen Mother Champion Chase, Sprinter Sacre rose again in a magnificent renaissance. He went through the 2015-16 season unbeaten and his return to the top made the heart sing with happiness.

Best 'I was there' moment Year

after year the Cheltenham Festival produces moments that pass into racing folklore. The roars from the crowd when Sprinter Sacre hit the front and surged away from Un De Sceaux in the Queen Mother Champion Chase were spine-tingling, and so too were the cheers on his triumphal return to the winner's enclosure.

TV moment of the year Using footage from the moving camera on the inside of the course and set to The Impossible Dream by Andy Williams, we watch as Sprinter Sacre stalks, passes and shoots clear in the Champion Chase. A perfect piece of cinematic television by Channel 4 that captured the emotion and excitement of one of the year's best races.

The Jackson Five Tribute Band Award
Aidan O'Brien

The Ballydoyle maestro made the Prix de l'Arc de Triomphe look as easy as 1-2-3 with Found, Highland Reel and Order Of St George.

The Mary Berry Star Pensioner Award
Megalala and John Bridger

There is just no stopping the 75-year-old Hampshire trainer and his stable star, who became the oldest horse to win on the Flat in Britain since 1945.

The Owen Smith Award for doomed challenges against a popular hero
Un De Sceaux

Like the Labour leadership contender against Jeremy Corbyn, Un De Sceaux never stood a chance as Sprinter Sacre surged back to power on a tide of acclamation.

The Blackadder Queenie 'Where's My Pressie?' Award
The Queen

In her 90th year, HRH had to wait until the final day of Royal Ascot but finally got what she wanted when Dartmouth carried the royal colours to victory in the Hardwicke Stakes.

The England Football Team Award for quitting when it starts to get serious
Pelham Crescent

The 13-year-old, having been rescued from neglect and nursed back to health, returned to the track after almost four years off (1,405 days to be precise) and then refused to race at Chepstow. Never mind, he will have a happy retirement now with owner Debbie Hughes.

The Roy Keane Award for wishing you had counted to ten
William Buick and Davy Russell

Both riders found themselves at the wrong end of hefty bans after having heated exchanges with the stewards. Perhaps noted steward charmer Colm O'Donoghue could coach the pair in the ways of coming out on top in the stewards' room.

The Prince Philip 'Did He Really Say That?' Award
Michael Buckley

Having watched Jamie Spencer steer Defrocked to victory at Royal Ascot, owner Michael Buckley was in roaring form in the winner's enclosure. Asked by Emma Spencer, ex-wife of the winning jockey, how extra special it was to win a race with his close friend, Buckley said: "I probably love Jamie as much as you once did!"

The Arnold Schwarzenegger 'I'll Be Back' Award
Hayley Turner

After retiring in 2015, Turner returned to the saddle at the behest of Ascot to be part of The Girls team at the Shergar Cup and duly got on the scoresheet by winning the Shergar Cup Mile.

The Tubthumping 'I Get Knocked Down But I Get Up Again' Award
Paul Nicholls

Willie Mullins threw everything he had at the reigning British champion and more than once appeared set for victory, but Nicholls came back even harder to retain his title.

The Ryanair Award for never forgetting the bottom line
Michael O'Leary

When you're a multi-millionaire who has won the Cheltenham Gold Cup and Grand National in the same year, removing 60 horses when the sport's most successful trainer ups his fees for the first time in a decade is an obvious call. Perhaps Willie Mullins should have a cheap basic fee with add-ons for all the extras such as food, water, bedding and, well, everything.

The Nigel Farage Award for name of the year
Brexit

The Pat Phelan-trained two-year-old ran on referendum day, June 23, but unlike the leave campaigners she was unable to pull off victory, finishing sixth of 11 at Newbury. In fact, she never got closer than five and a half lengths to the winner in any of her four races and was more of a remainer – at the back of the field.

The Albert Einstein Theory of Relativity Award
Godolphin

In September a downsizing of Sheikh Mohammed's global operation was announced. A few weeks later, Godolphin chief executive John Ferguson rocked up to Tattersalls yearling sales and spent nearly 14 million guineas on 26 horses, including three Dubawis for 2.6m gns, 2.1m gns and 1.2m gns. An interesting approach to downsizing.

The Great British Bake Off Award for switching channels
TV racing

Channel 4 gained Bake Off but lost horseracing to ITV and now it's over to the shiny new presenting team of Ed Chamberlin, Francesca Cumani and Matt Chapman to see if they can revive the ratings.

The Leicester City Award for defying the odds
Mrs Danvers

Unloved in the sales ring, where she went through unsold for £1,000, the Jonathan Portman-trained two-year-old went through the season unbeaten in five starts, winning the Super Sprint and Cornwallis Stakes, and earned nearly £200,000 in prize-money. What a star.

>> What's this all about? What's The Scoop takes the final flight at Sandown in good style under Barry Geraghty, but it all goes wrong when he then does a sharp left and heads towards the crowds

Wrong turn by Scoop a costly error

PUNTERS who had backed What's The Scoop for a novice hurdle at Sandown in March could have been forgiven for counting their cash after the son of Presenting jumped the last well clear.

However, the half-brother to enigmatic hurdler Harchibald had not read the script and performed a 90-degree turn to his left, losing all momentum and handing victory to Starving Marvin.

"He wouldn't have a bad thought in his head at home. He's just a big horse and still a baby," said trainer Nicky Henderson, among those to have celebrated prematurely.

More than £29,000 was traded on What's The Scoop winning at 1.01 and Betfair reported only 13 horses since 2011 have had more money placed on them at that price and lost.

Turner back in saddle for special day

HAYLEY TURNER came out of retirement to score a popular victory at the Shergar Cup in August.

Turner, 33, retired from the saddle in 2015 but was enticed back as a replacement for Melbourne Cup-winning rider Michelle Payne and hit the jackpot by winning the Dubai Duty Free Shergar Cup Mile on the Harry Dunlop-trained Early Morning.

Her joy at winning was plain for all to see and, returning draped in a Union flag, she said: "Oh my God! That was amazing. I nearly fell off my horse as I was waving, blowing kisses and punching the air.

"It's so special and I'm thrilled. Coming back for this was the easiest decision ever. This has always been my favourite day of the year and I'm really lucky and privileged to be able

to come back for it."

Asked about a possible full-time return to the saddle, Turner replied: "If every day was like this of course I'd be riding. It's the day-to-day slog that's the thing. It's tough, and I kind of lost the spark for those days."

Turner had another cause for celebration in June when she was awarded an OBE for services to racing in the Queen's Birthday Honours.

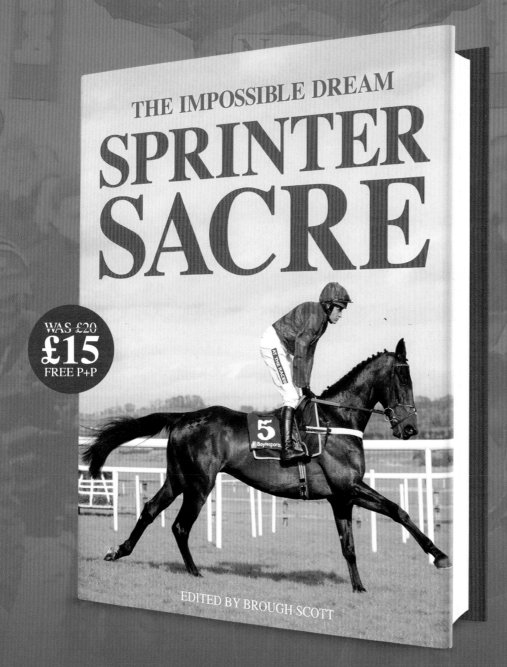

Ambulance brings pain for Meehan

IF jockey Chris Meehan thought things could not get worse after a heavy fall in Italy in July, he was wrong.

In action at Merano racecourse, Meehan *(above)* was kicked by a horse and left with a broken nose and a jaw injury that required 27 stitches, but that was not the end of it as the ambulance sent to assist him ran over and broke his right leg.

"You have to laugh," said the rider, whose father teaches people how to drive ambulances.

The remarkable story reached Racing Post readers in more than 90 countries and Meehan was amazed by the global attention he received.

"I couldn't believe it," he said. "My phone didn't stop. I woke up the next morning when it had been on Facebook and I must have had about 30 friend requests and notifications and messages coming through.

"A lad I knew from Ireland from when I was about 14 lives in New and now and they en sharing it out

●Horses not houses in Newmarket Monopoly

MAYFAIR became Clarehaven Stables and Bow Street changed to Warren Place with the launch of a special Newmarket version of the Monopoly board game.

Priced at £34.99 and available in a limited edition of 1,000, the bespoke edition was created to celebrate the 350th anniversary of racing in Newmarket.

The original property squares were replaced by 22 Newmarket training establishments and other places on the board were taken by institutions such as Newmarket racecourses (instead of Fenchurch Street station) and the British Racing School (replacing the Electric Company).

A great deal of thought went into customising the original board game to fit Newmarket's profile. It took Ami Cosgrave, marketing manager at the National Horseracing Museum, six months to jump through all the hoops – and there were many, given the desire of Hasbro, which owns the brand, to protect the essence of the game.

Each of the 22 trainers whose properties feature on the board gave their consent,

as did those responsible for other Newmarket landmark sites.

"We only told trainers that their stable had been selected; we didn't tell them where they would feature on the board," Cosgrave said. "And once we had the 22 stables, we valued them in relation to where the trainers finished in last year's official trainers' championship. We've had no complaints."

John Gosden's Clarehaven Stables therefore had pride of place as the Mayfair of Newmarket Monopoly. "That was very nice of them, wasn't it?" said Gosden, who played the game with friends on its launch at the July meeting. "We all found it very entertaining."

There were other twists on the original. Instead of green houses and red hotels, players have to buy horses and the more valuable stallions, while the Income Tax square was replaced by Equine Vets Fees.

The project was paid for by the Jockey Club, with all proceeds banked by Palace House, the hub for the National Heritage Centre for Horseracing and Sporting Art, which opened in September.

●Sex change in the nick of time

A SURPRISE was in store when Morning Suit turned up for his debut at Doncaster in April. The Mark Johnston-trained juvenile is a colt but was listed on racecards as a filly following an administrative blunder by Weatherbys.

His undeclared equipment was soon spotted by officials before the race but the son of Street Boss, perhaps aware of the error, tried to prove the point, acting coltish in the preliminaries. Having been given the correct weight-for-sex allowance, he finished fifth.

"As far as we're concerned he has always been a colt," Johnston said. "His passport states he's a colt and all the information sent over to Weatherbys indicates that fact. It was a bizarre error."

Fore! Two sports collide as stray golf ball takes wrong course

JOCKEYS must be prepared for all sorts, but it is hard to imagine Kieren Fox will ever again encounter the scenario that happened to him at Sandown in September.

Riding Luxford for John Best, Fox was unseated when the filly was distracted by a flying golf ball that had ricocheted off the helmet of fellow rider Charlie Bennett.

"She jinked but it all happened so fast I had no idea what had caused it," Fox said.

"When I watched the replays I saw the ball come off Charlie's helmet and straight across in front of my filly's face."

Sandown's five-furlong track runs alongside a golf course and clerk of the course Andrew Cooper said: "Balls are bound to stray and we take all reasonable measures to remove them.

"Thankfully, while we do see one flicked up once in a while, I've never seen it happen with that sort of consequence before."

● Colourful way to help punters

THE colour of the Queen's outfit is a daily betting topic at Royal Ascot, but one Australian bookmaker came unstuck with a similar novelty market when offering odds on what shade of tie veteran political journalist Laurie Oakes would wear on the night of the country's general election.

Knowing there was a market, Oakes wore all six colours during the night, forcing the bookmaker to pay out on each colour. "I thought, why should anyone miss out?" said the punters' pal.

● 'What a stupid (winning) ride'

DESPITE winning on favourite Angel Love at Sweden's Jagersro racecourse in August, jockey Jan-Erik Neuroth was not spared a mid-race tongue-lashing by the commentator.

After Neuroth's audacious move up the farside rail, the caller exclaimed: "He's making the same mistake he made earlier in the day; what a bloody idiot he is."

Even after victory was secured, the commentator wasn't finished. "But what an incredibly stupid ride by Neuroth," came the volley from the booth, which evidently wasn't on the fence.

● Wedded bliss is a dead-heat – or is it?

FOR better, for worse, what's mine is yours, but not necessarily so for married jockeys Dean Yendell and Christine Puls.

They were riding against each other in a race at Mildura racecourse in Australia in April when Yendell forced his mount Worthington up to dead-heat with Welsh Poet, who was ridden by his better half.

It was a perfect result according to Yendell, who said: "My horse dug deep and I thought I'd got her on the line, but I'm just happy to share it."

The feeling was not mutual, however, and Puls responded: "I'm not happy to share it at all. Actually I thought I had it all the way."

● Williams runs late – and then not at all

A NEW watch might be on trainer Stuart Williams' Christmas list after he was forced to withdraw Secret Sonnet from the opening race at Newmarket in April on the grounds of arriving too late to run, despite being stabled only half a mile from the course.

Explaining his tardiness, Williams said: "I was busy with a stalls test and left the passport in the lorry. You're supposed to declare the horse to run no later than 45 minutes before the race starts but we got her there eight minutes late. It's a bit embarrassing when the owners are there but it was my fault and I'll have to pay the £100 fine."

● Mystery takes unexpected twist

AUTHORITIES have to take any bomb scare seriously and when a suspicious humming noise was heard coming from one of the bins in the men's toilets in a gambling hall in Germany the building was evacuated.

However, following a sweep of the area, officers were able to declare the incident a false alarm and put everyone at ease.

The offending object was not a bomb, but a battery-powered sex toy, although it is not known whether the owner claimed their lost property.

● Just Dandy for Santos at 200-1

BACKING Brazil for major football tournaments may not have yielded much success in recent years and certainly not at fancy prices, but supporters of the country's trainer Jose Santos were in the money after Dandy Flame struck at 200-1 at Wolverhampton in July.

The juvenile became the co-second-longest-priced winner in the history of British racing but did not surprise Lambourn-based Santos, who said: "He has always shown plenty of speed at home and I hoped he would win. I had a bit on, but I'm not a big gambler."

A-Z of 2016

The year digested into 26 bite-size chunks

V

F

M

A is for Authorised Betting Partners. The BHA went stick more than carrot with its latest attempt to draw the level of funding from bookmakers it has traditionally received from the levy. Expect this entry still to be eligible for inclusion in next year's Annual.

B is for Brian Toomey. The jockey was given just a three per cent chance of survival after his horror fall at Perth in 2013, only to make a miraculous comeback to the saddle two years later. However, after a struggle to get rides, he retired in June.

C is for Chantilly. The Arc travelled 35 miles or so up the road as Longchamp underwent redevelopment and its new home saw one of the towering achievements in modern training with Aidan O'Brien's 1-2-3. France's ▯▯▯ race will stay there in ▯▯▯ Chantilly will have

to go some to match that sense of occasion.

D is for Don Cossack. For so long an underachiever but always the apple of Gordon Elliott's eye, The Don confirmed his place as the best chaser around with a consummate display in the Cheltenham Gold Cup.

E is for eighteen and out. Dermot Weld's domination of the Galway festival came to an end, for now at least, when Willie Mullins became the first besides Weld to win the award for leading trainer at the meeting since 1997.

F is for floodlights. Newcastle's Tapeta surface opened for business in May after much controversy. The change had just about been accepted in time for the first use of the floodlights

along the straight mile in September.

G is for Grand National double. In an emotional spring for Mouse Morris, he dedicated Rogue Angel's Irish National win to son Christopher, who died of carbon monoxide poisoning in Argentina, and then 12 days later won the Grand National with injury-prone Rule The World.

H is for Hampson family. The victory of Brodie aboard her father Mark's Jennys Surprise in the Royal Artillery Gold Cup in February was one of the most emotional stories of the year. Mark had been given 30 days to live in December 2015 but survived until May, long enough to see his daughter win in his colours for the first time.

I is for ITV. News of terrestrial racing coverage switching from Channel 4 to ITV broke on January 1 and echoed throughout the year. Anyone who wants to see racing preserved as a mass-audience sport must wish the new broadcaster every success.

J is for JT McNamara. The former top amateur, paralysed from the neck down by a fall at the 2013 Cheltenham Festival, died in July at the age of 41.

K is for knighthood. First he was Tony, or AP, now we salute Sir Anthony McCoy, who was knighted in the New Year's Honours list.

L is for late arrival. Few stories underline the strength in depth of the Willie Mullins/Rich Ricci axis better than the Champion Hurdle, in which defending champion Faugheen was ruled out, only to be replaced by Annie Power, who proved similarly dominant.

M is for MMM. Richard Johnson, for so long in McCoy's shadow, secured his 3,000th jumps winner in Britain and Ireland on his way to a first jockeys' title. Frankie Dettori, seldom out of the limelight in his 30 years in Britain, reached the same total on the Flat in his adopted country.

N is for North Americans. For once, it was not just Wesley Ward who barged in on the pageantry of Royal Ascot. His Lady Aurelia took the breath away in the Queen Mary, while the Queen Anne was taken by Tepin for Mark Casse, who made his name at Woodbine in Toronto.

O is for old dog, new tricks. Dermot Weld gained a long-overdue first success in the Derby with Harzand in June. The colt then went on to become the first horse outside of Ballydoyle to do the Epsom-Irish Derby double since Sinndar in 2000.

P is for phoenix from the flames. If you did not call for Sprinter Sacre's retirement at any point, your name is probably Nicky Henderson, Caroline Mould or Nico de Boinville. Trainer, owner and jockey had the last laugh in the Queen Mother Champion Chase, but we all joined in gladly.

Q is for the Queen. Every milestone for Her Majesty demands a Royal Ascot winner, it seems, and in the year of her 90th birthday Dartmouth delivered a royal triumph in the Hardwicke Stakes.

R is for rookie success. Kerry Lee only took over from father Richard at the start of the 2015-16 season but gained six Graded-race wins in the first few months of the new year, including the Welsh National and Ryanair Gold Cup.

S is for switching saddles. Not only the codename for Victoria Pendleton's ultimately successful venture into hunter chases but also a moment to praise former jump jockeys Jim Crowley and Dougie Costello, who both made big splashes on the Flat in 2016.

T is for Thistlecrack. Whatever he does over fences, Colin Tizzard's stable star has earned a place in history for his exploits over hurdles in 2015-16. In style and substance his dominance of the staying hurdle division matched even Big Buck's.

U is for union. The merger between Paddy Power and Betfair in February created a betting colossus from two of the industry's major insurgents. Two long-standing big beasts, Ladbrokes and Coral, soon lined up their own merger.

V is for Vicente. In the Scottish National, he landed the decisive blow in the toe-to-toe fight for the British trainers' title, in which defending champion Paul Nicholls out-jabbed the harder-punching Willie Mullins.

W is for wish them well. Two punters' favourites in the riding ranks, Paul Carberry and Kieren Fallon, were forced to retire due to accumulated damage to the body and mind respectively.

X is for xenophilia. Few trainers, especially over jumps, have been willing to try as many new jurisdictions as Willie Mullins, who as well as just about winning the trainers' title in a foreign country also looked towards France, Italy, the US and Australia.

Y is for youngsters. The progeny of a stallion has rarely been scrutinised as much as Frankel's first crop. He made a perfect start with Cunco and kept on in a similar vein, earning more bang-per-buck than any other first-season sire.

Z is for zooming in. More than once, but most famously with poor old Seamour in the Northumberland Plate, TV cameras were prematurely switched to focus on leaders. The visual equivalent of a 1.01 gubbing.

FLASHBACK

1986 Dancing Brave wins the Prix de l'Arc de Triomphe

By Steve Dennis

IT WAS the year of Dancing Brave. From April to November 1986 he commanded our attention, dominated our conversation, raced himself into memory banks that even now provide a substantial rate of interest.

At this remove of 30 years it's still scarcely credible how much Dancing Brave crammed into a campaign that will chiefly be remembered for one shattering moment of disaster and one uplifting moment of triumph. He won the 2,000 Guineas, Eclipse Stakes and King George VI and Queen Elizabeth Diamond Stakes, but it is not these glories we recall.

Disaster came first. The unbeaten son of Lyphard, trained by Guy Harwood in deepest Sussex, was expected to win the Derby easily, but ... as undone by a patient ride from ... e Starkey and a slackening pace ... al juncture. He lost position,

dropped to the rear and had an impossible amount of ground to make up. Despite charging down the straight like a sprinter under a frantic Starkey, he failed by half a length to catch Shahrastani.

The debrief still continues, liberally peppered with 'if only'. Starkey should have done this, shouldn't have done that. The episode broke the spirit of the veteran, and despite being in the saddle when Dancing Brave won the Eclipse, he was then replaced by Pat Eddery, who rode the colt to revenge victory over Shahrastani at Ascot.

All roads led to Longchamp and a Prix de l'Arc de Triomphe for the ages even before the stalls opened. Some say it was the best field ever assembled for the race, others reckon it merely second-best. Of the 15 runners, 11 were Group 1 winners; the Hardwicke Stakes winner was a mere pacemaker. Only a great champion could win such a race. Dancing Brave was such a horse.

▶▶ Making of a legend: Dancing Brave and Pat Eddery (pink cap) swoop on the outside to record an impressive Arc victory

Picture: GERRY CRANHAM (RACINGPOST.COM/PHOTOS)

Yet it was not only the winning, but the way he won. As the field fanned out into the straight the finest horses in Europe threw down the gauntlet one by one in a mighty show of strength. Eddery left his move to the last, and in so doing created a legend that will never fade.

A bare furlong and a half out, Eddery drew Dancing Brave to the outside and bade him stretch, and such was the colt's stunning acceleration that he passed all his brilliant rivals in the space of a furlong and won easing up by a length and a half. People remember where they were when they saw it, such is the enduring power of Dancing Brave's Arc win.

After that, of course, he was trounced at Santa Anita in the Breeders' Cup. It didn't really matter then, it doesn't really matter now. Dancing Brave was not perfect, but 30 years ago, at Longchamp, he let us see what perfection looked like.